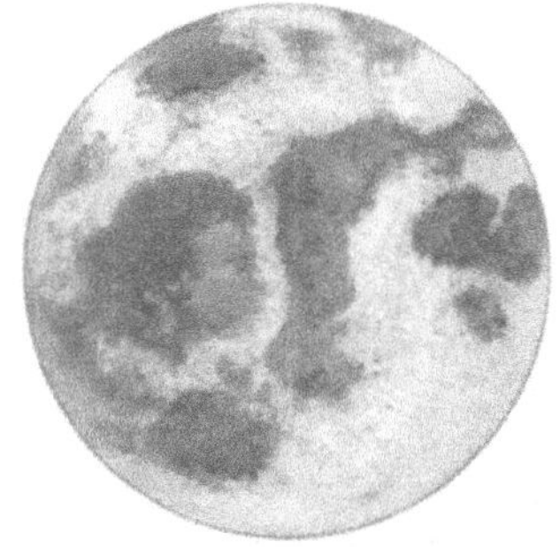

Reflections in a Paper Moon
Book Two Zodiac Map

L. A. Espriux

$\mathcal{B}$ook Two titled Zodiac Map is a continuation of early memoirs shared by the author beginning after return from the jungles of Vietnam a decorated Marine Corps Sergeant actively engaged in war operations in South East Asia during the early 1970s. Dedicated to the service, a potentially successful military career seems imminent. However, these days of the dragon intersected by fulcrum of an unexpected spiritual event, becoming substance of greater challenge changed from darkness to light. Here passage of a *Zodiac Map* drawn in heaven witnessed through *Reflections in a Paper Moon*.

Reflections in a Paper Moon Book Two Zodiac Map

Printed in the United States of America
ISBN: Softcover: 979-8-98677838-7-1
            eBook: 9798330478118
            Hardcover:
Republished by L. A. Espriux
Publication Date 09/20/2024

Special dedication to Rudy, Penny, Cendi

Acknowledgement to the Artist of this Book

Part Five Illustration **Passage of Angels** by *Cendi Baugus*
Part Six Illustration **Saving Rocky** by *Cendi Baugus*
Part Seven Illustration **Illuminations at Perigee** by *Cendi Baugus*
Part Eight Illustration **Venus Ascending** by *Cendi Baugus*
Part Nine Illustration **Zodiac Map** by *Judi;*
Moon by: *Cendi Baugus*
Back Cover Illustration by *Cendi Baugus*

CONTENTS

Part Five

Passage of Angels

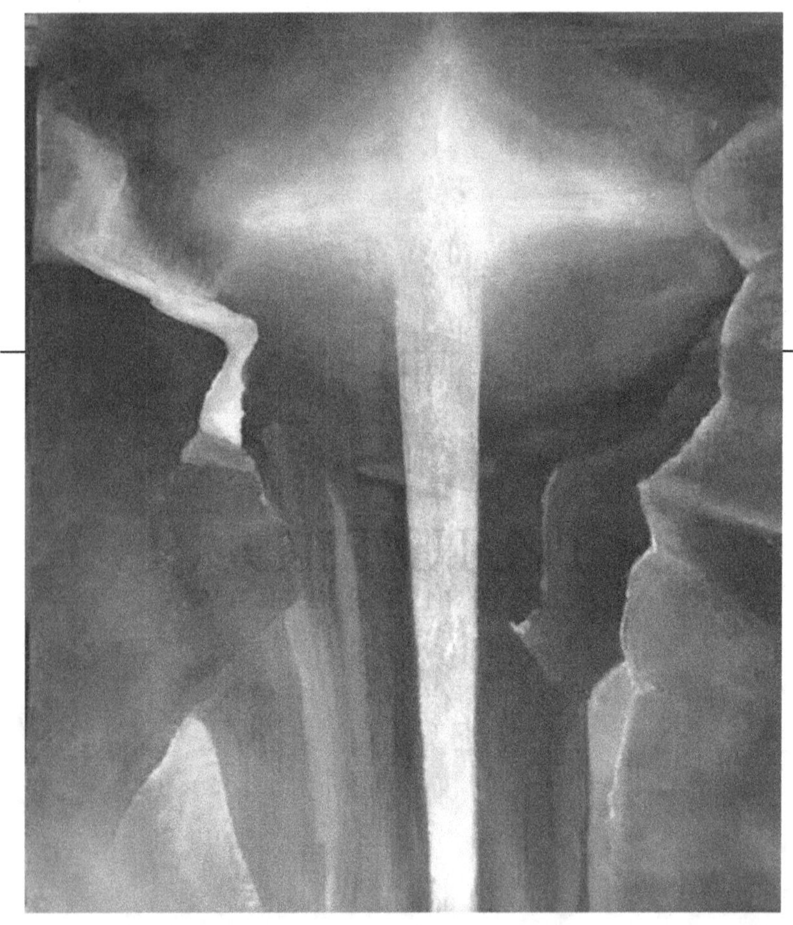

Lazarus

What of Lazarus
When the darkness rolls away
And he rises again weak and mortal as any man
With hands and feet bound since a millennium
His eyes blind behind a veil of soft linen
Carefully wrapped to last forever
Cries of his sisters distant mourning an eternity ago

What of Lazarus before
A finite spark ignited among the elements
Awakening him from oblivion
His bones cold as silent stone
His former body melted into clay
Sealed carefully inside a cave
Sealed against curiosity and the living
Against wailing and laughter
And forgotten cares of generations

What of Lazarus then
As suddenly stars born in a void
Light escaping hot whirling galaxies
Flung into infinity and beyond infinity
Beyond truth and beyond existence
No more Lazarus or knowledge of what was
All flesh his flesh
His blood mixed with eternity
All the universe a lost firefly fading into the distance

Seen through the mind of God
What of Lazarus in time divide
His name resurrected from beyond the abyss
Lazarus Come Forth
Constellations moving slower and slower
Element and spirit reshaping his mind anew
Time reinvented just for him
His soul restored but for a moment
To weeping and to laughter
And to hours and days and dying

And what of Lazarus now
Once born and laid to his grave
Covered with silence and prayers
Did once he remember
Was he reborn wiser
No more afraid

$\mathcal{I}$ gaze often up into the night sky in search of a dragon night when once I knew purpose of meaning. I see my own reflection in the face of all those old soldiers I have passed along the way. We are all as weapons secured in fortress of an armory waiting for deployment, waiting for a dedicated hand to squeeze the trigger, waiting for another engagement. Now I know truest meaning of the term *Men of War*.

Stateside military duty is like any other job, with the exception that a shadow of readiness permeates every waking and sleeping moment with the uncertainty of sudden Evac-Orders. It is a position without roots, an occupation not recommended for family men, and men of sedentary disposition. I am once again growing bored of routine and wanting change. The Vietnam conflict now winding to an end; nor is there prospect of any other engagements for which to volunteer. Now I understand why men become mercenaries and the compelling forces that drive them into foreign legionary conflicts. I begin reading issues of Soldier of Fortune, as I consider my future options. I am now physical measure of forged steel, purified on the anvil, and tested by fire, ready, angry and itching for battle; a potential danger to civil society, no longer civilized.

Since the time of Sun-Tzu and *The Art of War*, since the success of Roman strategy and conquest, since the necessity of resolute resistance to invading tyrannies, the frontline soldier has always walked point. Trained for one purpose only: to face the enemy of one's fear; and to become greater than the shadow of that fear. A soldier without a war is as a blade without hand of conviction, a dangerous surplus with unpredictable potential of consequence. I have come to the realization that even military protocol a lie; the only truth being combat zone deployment. I now miss the raw exuberance of my days in Vietnam; long for the unmasked reality living on the edge. I miss being made alive by fear: to be part of a purpose, to be heart of the dragon!

Sadly, I realize that the only fulfillment in a soldier's existence is to stand alone in the closing jaws of death and life-- to face the enemy head on, rather foreign or domestic! At least in battle there exist truths without the mask of hypocrisy. I feel altogether dead to sentiments of hate and of love. Dead to the shared genesis of my world and dreams shared by others. Without realizing it, I have become a lone wolf even more dangerous.

Well-meaning church groups or individuals, whose mission to convert lost soldiers from riot and wantonness, often assault me when least expected. Usually, those sent to sow light work in the daytime; but in times of calling enter into dens of darkness. I run into one such witness soon after my brief encounter with the singing angel. I do not remember her, exactly; nor the promise made to attend her church. Nevertheless, her eyes continue to haunt subconsciously, a glimpse of something beyond physical explanation. This other emissary of the Holy Spirit manifests as an old man slumped on a barstool beside me.

"You look as empty as that glass you just finished. How about I buy you another drink?"

I greedily accept the offer. After all, free whisky is free whisky. I raise a toast to this stranger's generosity and gulp down the cheap elixir. In the dim light of this dark lair his eyes burning embers piercing into my soul.

"Still wanting more, don't you," he says, taking a sip of his beer. "Feels like a big hole at the bottom of that glass, and no matter how much you drink never enough. I used to feel that way myself before Christ found me."

I now regret accepting that drink, and want to say to this fellow:

"Who are you to preach to me, considering that we are both in the samebar watering from the same trough?"

Yet, somehow, I know he is not like me, and that he has a peace I do not understand. Therefore, I only shrug my shoulders and rise to leave, wishing in the moment to escape into the impossible depths of the hole he describes, to get as far away from this stranger as possible.

"Here, take this." He hands me a cartoon pamphlet titled *'This Was Your Life'*. "God is knocking on the door of your heart, do not ignore it."

Once in the safety of my car, I feel more at ease. My first impulse is to throw away the pamphlet, but become curious by its black and white comic strip style. As I begin to read it through, the meaning terrifies me. The message simple: about a man that chooses to live after his own definition of righteousness, only to perish as all flesh, only to be resurrected in a day of judgment. He is condemned to everlasting hell because of everyidle word and deed. If this man, who is as the cream harvest of everyone I have ever known and respected, finds himself condemned beforethe judgment seat, then how might I even begin to reason the way toGod— *if God even exists!*

Nevertheless, this cartoon message disturbs me more deeply than ever I have been disturbed before. That night I have a particularly horrific dream. I am sliding down a flaming waterfall into a lake of fire surrounded by howling demons. I awake, sweat clustered on my brow, and remain sleepless, until gray morning shadows creep into the nebula of my thoughts, advocating tangible proof of imminent mortality. Of the many spirits encountered, this inner conflict most disturbing of all, witness of self-condemnation manifested by a groaning within and a haunting without.

It is just another hangover Sunday morning, as I try to remember how I arrived back on base since departing Friday night. Evidence of fresh cuts on my knuckles testifies that I have survived a fight or two, only there is no clear memory of the event. I reach on the top shelf of my locker and a crinkled piece of paper falls to the floor. At first the name and address unfamiliar; then I remember the lovely singing blonde angel and an invitation to attend her church. Once again, it is one of those beautiful mornings unique to Southern California and a long drive will help clear my head.

I arrive just past 1100 hours at the street address located in a suburb of east Long Beach expecting to find a familiar religious edifice. I drive twice around the block searching for the missing address. There is nothing here, except an expanse of lawn that sweeps through a corridor guarded by two monarch Weeping Willows. As I prepare to leave, a rush of heavenly melody carried upon a breeze, entwines with large spreading upper branches of a natural canopy clearly audible. It is the distinctive music of *The Choinia Christian Rock Band.*

Like a moldering palace abandoned in the fictional kingdom of Middle Earth, structure of a school auditorium resurrects out of shadow. The walls cracked and stain by time through years of neglect, today it is the house of a church congregation. In the main atrium are men, women, and children singing with their hands raised-up in supplication-- weeping, laughing, and seemingly intoxicated. Upon entering this chamber, I feel the jolt of a physical presence, an abiding energy of inexplicable source. A tall young man comes and places his arm on my shoulder.

"Welcome brother," he says tenderly. "You are welcome here."

"Get your arm off of me," I demand reflexively and pull away.

"I am just sharing God's love," he replies peacefully and moves off.

The morning service already at an end, I stand solitary near the back and watch as many go down to the foot of an erect wooden pulpit weeping and praying. Others drift toward the exit doors laughing and talking, seemingly drunk with joy. I feel shaken by an inexplicable emotion—no, not emotion! It is something else, something alien and purethat disturbs my soul even more.

"If you are real, then prove it!" I demand to an invisible presence; then leap up and head toward the exit.

Here I am once again intercepted by the angel, her eyes as clear passages through heaven's gate.

"I saw you come in," she says tenderly, reaches out and touches my hand.

"I arrived late. A longer drive than expected, plus I was looking for a real church." I manage a weak excuse.

"Oh, but this is a real church. 'Where there are two or more gathered in my name, says the Lord, I am in the midst'. All that really matters is that you came."

We talk until her parents arrive, two pleasant people, reminding me of Grant Woods American gothic painting of a farmer holding a pitchfork standing beside his rosy cheeked wife. To my surprise, they invite me to their home for coffee.

Dick McDonald and his wife, Henrietta, together for fifty-two years, have sired into the word two children. Karen McDonald is the true apple of their eye, and the last in the nest. Their eldest son, married since a month, now lives in Kansas with his new wife. After a light snack and quaint conversation, I guiltily accept their invitation to accompany Karen to a nearby stable for an afternoon horse ride. I suspect all along she is a virgin, and has not been broken by a man. Also I have never been with a real virgin before.

The horses, already saddled by the time we arrive, wait patiently tied to a gate. My mount, an older Pinto, hangs its head as we approach, while Karen's younger Bay begins neighing with affectionate recognition. Karen gives both animals a cube of sugar and begins calming the Bay with long stokes along its face.

"You do know how to ride?" She inquires stepping into the stirrup; and then swings naturally up across the back of her mount.

"Of course," I lie.

In truth, I have been on a horse only once before while still a child on my grandfather's farm. The Sorel so tired and broken from pulling plows and wagons, it barely flinches when Grandfather Hamby places me on its back. I have also watched numerous Saturday morning westerns, remembering something John Wayne said in one of his movies about showing the horse who is boss.

Following Karen's example, I swing up on the saddle feeling the confidence of a master. The Pinto turns its head back, looks straight at me with those large globular eyes, as if to say 'you've never been on a real horse in your life, and we both know it'.

Instantly, the animal bolts into an open field with me hanging onto the reins petrified. I remain in the saddle only by sheer strength and stubborn will. The pinto charges straight toward a bobbed wire fence, stops at the last minute, flinging me bodily against the rusted barrier. Karen arrives within moments, her Bay smirking down at me with arrogant pleasure.

"Are you hurt?"

"No," I smile up at her, not fully taking into account my battered pride. "That's a strong-spirited horse. I'm used to riding them more tamed."

"Perhaps it would be nicer if we just walked for a while. I think that the horses would appreciate the rest." Karen suggests in an attempt to rescue my remaining dignity.

I accept this offer with little resistance. The Pinto stares victoriously into my eyes, daringly waving its flaxen tail. We walk through a rolling pasture hedged by sentries of trees with budding leaves. Splotches of white and yellow flowers shoot above fields of pale grass reviving from winter and gradually changing darker green. Flocks of birds swoop down and devour clouds of insects rising just above the ground, all signs of an early California spring approaching. Winter still grips the North American continent everywhere except here, a place out of season.

All I can really think about is intoxicating presence of this beautiful girl becoming a woman. I cannot help but imagine pleasure of making love to an undefiled angel. There is something excitingly dark about lustful thoughts in the presence of innocence, like the hunger of a wolf disguised within, waiting for the right moment to pounce.

Karen seems oblivious to the dark potential in my mind, an innocent lamb allowing herself led to slaughter, as we penetrate ever deeper into the cache of a secluded valley.

"Look at the blue in the sky," she says nonchalantly. "Have you ever witnessed anything so wondrous? My God and your God created this for us."

I look at the sky, and it suddenly changes to most profound blue, deep, eternal, a vastness dwarfing the magnitude of every realm of imagination.

"Look how green the grass. It spreads over the whole earth as pleasant pastures to provide hope and nourishment to all. My God and your God created this for us"

I gaze across the fields and they change emerald green filling me with a peace not known since many years.

"Look at the flowers so richly adorned. They lack nothing in season, but are the majestic evidence of provision. My God and your God created this for us."

I see the flowers in wondrous detail for the first time. Not just the vibrancy of their colors, but in the artistry of fabrication incomprehensible through mortal design. Karen opens my mind– no more than the mind! She makes my soul aware of intricacy in creation! I witness birds chattering in the boughs of sovereign tress, elegantly dressed flowers dancing in their shade, and insects that proficiently ride invisible currents of air.

This moment she inspires to my awareness things so obvious that they have grown imperceptible in my rush to become a man. She sheds light, where only darkness resides now. She usurps anger in favor of peace. And although I do not know it in the moment, something inside has begun to awaken; an innocence of being, once I knew, and lost along the way. My passions of lust are slain to the core.

I feel somehow different upon returning to the stables. No longer do I perceive this pretty girl an object to satisfy carnal desire, but a guide of purest light overwhelming the logical definition of a worldly mind.

Supper is prepared and on the table by the time we return to the home of Dick and Henrietta. After insistence that I join them, we bow our heads and give thanks before eating. This tradition Rudy used to perform during the early years, while there still remained a little faith in our family unity. What happened, I really am not sure, only that at some point we stop the empty ritual of memorized thankfulness. Maybe he just decided it no longer fit his agnostic way of thinking. At least he was not a hypocrite.

I can tell that for Dick and Henrietta, and especially for their daughter, this act fully devotional. Afterwards, we all retire to the den to talk. Dick begins to rehearse his miraculous survival while serving in the Navy during the Second World War. His position was Mid-Shipman aboard the Portland-class cruiser USS Indianapolis, the last major U.S. Naval ship sunk by the Japanese. At around midnight on July 30, 1944, after the delivery of critical parts for the first atomic bomb to an airbase at Tristan Island, the vessel is torpedoed by an enemy submarine in the Philippine Sea. Although many survive the sinking, nearly all the crew lost to dehydration, exposure to the elements, and shark attacks. Dick's eyes become hard, darkened by the memory of those terrifying hours in the water.

"I felt a nudge against my boot," he says, his gaze seeing events twenty-seven years in the past. "All night long screams, sounds of water splashing… and the moaning. Suddenly the man next to me stiffens, and looks up into the predawn sky; his mouth opens slowly without uttering a sound. Then he flips over like a make believe doll. Nothing left from the waist down, only blood and tattered strings of flesh and bowels. I knew then that none of us would survive. Those of us the sharks didn't take floated for days, some dying from fever, others just dying. I wished to pray, only to realize I didn't know how." Then tears fill Dick's eyes. "Praise the Lord! He had mercy on my soul. If I had died then, I would have died in my sins and never known the mercy in Christ. All those men lost… and only by grace I survived."

Henrietta reaches over and pats Dick's hand consolingly. I see in her expression that she has heard this account often. I can also tell it genuinely touches her deeply, a symbiotic emotional bond existing between them as experienced by loving couples of many years of marriage. There is a long silence bred of respect and in honor to those less fortunate. We talk about many other things as well: about my future plans to remain in the Marine Corps, about my own family back in South Carolina, about the upcoming Presidential election. And of course we talk about Nam.

However, we do not talk about religion, which relieves me some. I expected an evening of Bible-thumping, considering the situation of this encounter and the obvious devotion of this family. Except for an occasional outburst from Dick about *"going home in the rapture"*, the conversation remains on earth and in the moment.

It is already half past ten; the McDonalds tired and ready for bed. Henrietta kindly urges me to remain for the night, their son's room available since his recent marriage. Usually, I might not have accepted such a personal invitation, and from people I hardly know. Because the following Monday Washington's Birthday, along with enticement of a church-member potluck dinner the next evening, I choose to stay over. Deep down I know it is also because of a feeling of profound peace, a peace I have not felt since a long time. In some abstract way this family feels like my own, who accept me into their hearts and home without motive.

The next morning, we eat a late breakfast and play cards around the kitchen table until nearly noon. After a sparse lunch, I sit alone in the backyard watching billowing white clouds race through the blue zenith of sky and think about a book read as a child chronicling the life of Joan of Arc. This moment I even consider that there might possibly be more to heaven and earth than I think to see. Yet, I remind myself that so many things have changed since then, so much of innocence forgotten through bitterness. Here I remainrest of the afternoon just being in the moment: a moment when I am part of the sky, the grass, things seen and unseen, timeless... and most importantly just in the now without future or past.

"You understand." Karen says joining me.

"I understand something." I reply. "Only I don't know what."

"Understanding is the beginning of wisdom. There is nothing done in secret, if only you open your eyes to see, your ears to hear, and your heart to the true measure of what really is."

What is truth, I think to myself. Is it possible that life could be so simple, as seen through the eyes of this innocent young woman— and can I ever truly again see through eyes so innocent?

At 1700 hours, I accompany the McDonaldsto the sponsored potluck dinner hosted at the home of someone in their church congregation living in south Long Beach. The plan is that after this event I will take the nearby Interstate 5 back to my base. After enjoying a hearty spread of homemade dishes, I engage in a conversation with two young men around my age about the Vietnam War. An escalating sentiment has begun to infect America with propaganda that the more than ten year conflict in South East Asia a vehicle of corporate greed only, becoming a subject of polarized debate, with some going so far as to suggest those that participated in it willing pawns lacking conscience.

The conversation turns around recent news event about a military officer blowing his brains out in front of his wife and children after returning from Nam. This is proof in their minds that evil exist; proof that many returned demon possessed. I cannot argue against the darkness of that place. Now every place seems the same to me. Seems America has altogether forgotten about the threat of Communism, about the wars of extermination conducted by dictator regimes slaughtering millions. Perhaps the Vietnam War not pure, or so clearly defined, as many wars preceding it; nor can it be as simply labeled through presentation of objective reason. Yes, I believe in evil; but also believe that only evil of greater force able to stop its spread. I was there!   A part of me stillthere-- and will always be there! Then one of them says something that ignites the fuse of my anger; something I have heard more than oncesince returning.

"We shouldn't have been there in the first place. All wars come down to money. And money is the root of all evil."

"What do you know about Nam?" I demand angrily, leaping up and pounding my fist on the coffee table. "You civilians don't know shit about war!"

I see the familiar terror in their eyes. We are perhaps the same generation, but not of the same experience. I know this moment I do not belong among these sheep-- and must get out of here now before I do something regrettable!

Without further debate, I begin saying my goodbyes, methodically hedging toward the door. Karen approaches; enquires if I will come back. I say of course I will, which means I never   will. Upon reaching the door, a tall man with grey hair intercepts me. He looks steadfastly into my eyes.

"Son, have you ever accepted Christ as your savior?"

Altogether stunned by the blunt directness of his question, I back away, and proudly extend my chest.

"I know you people believe something… maybe something that I don't know." I hesitate. "I have a lot of failings, but like my father I am not a hypocrite.   I honestly don't know who this Christ is, or even if there is a God. I wish I could believe in a salvation, but I don't. Even if I did, I don't deserve it!"

He then places his hand firmly on my shoulder.

"No one deserves salvation, son." He states compassionately. "No man is justified by his own actions, but by the grace of God. You are here in this moment because the Holy Spirit has led you here. But it is up to you to decide. I was once as you, only God saved me in season by the blood of Jesus Christ. He can save you, too, if only you let him into your heart."

This man then begins to share with me his experience as a B-17 Bomber Pilot during the last days of World War II. He flew several retaliation raids over Dresden; their mission to break the German resistance. His plane shot down, he manages a crash landing in the city outskirts. Carrying the wounded co-pilot on his back, this man finds himself in the midst of smoldering ruins in an apocalyptic nightmare. Body parts like dismembered dolls strewn everywhere: arms, legs, and heads of men, women, and children littering the cratered streets of a once peaceful metropolis.

"A city no different than Los Angeles, or New York, a habitation of people and dreams smashed to rubble in an instant." He remembers, seeing still the devastation burned forever into his mind. "I realized then the true destructive force of a bomb— bombs I had dropped! The blood of innocence stained on my hands that no amount of washing able to cleanse. I returned stateside after the war, became a successful businessman. I told myself that I had been the instrument of a necessary destruction to stop an even greater threat. But there was no reasoning with the demons of my nightmares and no joy to fill the depth of my sorrow. Then one morning six years ago, I received an invitation from a fellow executive to attend a Christian Businessmen's Breakfast. That morning I accepted Christ as my savior by power of the Holy Spirit, the burden of nearly a quarter century instantly lifted away. After this, I turned from the destiny of this world and enrolled into Bible College, determined to dedicate my life to preach the word." His eyes pierce deeply into my soul. "I know the Lord has called you to this place, and even now knocks on the door of your heart. This is the most important moment in your life. If you will pray with me and the Lord reveals eternal salvation to your soul, then consider the gain. However, nothing gained is nothing lost. Long Beach is a large city, California a state even larger, and the world beyond this place larger still. Chance is you will never see us again; nor we you. This is an appointed time and place, but the choice yours to make."

I am aware of a tremendous battle taking place. A battle fought since earliest memory, a war of raging forces, with my eternal soul weighed in the balance. I stand at the threshold of some grand unknown expanse, a bedlam of voices each pleading a different cause. Yet, I know beyond the knowledge of my reason this man right. I have arrived at this crucible in destiny-- my destiny! A place manifested through each step unaware, and now the moment of final decision.

"If your God will prove to me that only he is God beyond all doubt, then I will follow this God the rest of my days."

These words as sincere as any I have ever uttered.

"Let us pray together."

I sit in a chair. He places his hands on crown of my head, my eyes closed, my hands palm-down on my thighs. I feel in this moment peace, my entire body relaxed. Then my pride defiantly begins to usurp itself again. I am a Marine Corps Sergeant! Who is this man? Who are these people? I determine abruptly to leave this place— why should I care what a bunch of goody civilians think about me! Then something peculiar—something inexplicable and frightening— something beyond the veil of my understanding begins to happen.

I can feel my hands on my thighs, acutely aware of this man's hands on my head, aware of others in the background mumbling something in the spirit, aware of present being. I do not feel drugged, nor do I feel restrained. Yet, I am unable to open my eyes, nor exercise simple motor control of will to move my hands. It is as though my body that of someone else, someone once me, but not me. Through final awareness of my conscious, I grasp at a logical explanation. What really do I know about these people? What do I know about these people? What really do they believe? I think about an incident that recently happened on a busy street in Los Angeles, when a group of Satanist swarmed and disembodied a motorist stopped at a traffic light and disembowel the unfortunate driver. Suddenly, I am gripped by uncontrollable terror. Then my mind sinks into landscape of a night eternal.

I am in a familiar place, a place I have always been and will forever remain. Here a confined chamber, vast as the physical universe, void of stars, or any light element. Only a sense of being prevails. Awareness that I am here without comprehension of anything before or anything after-- a manifestation of presence eternally now, without the medium of time or reference constructed of reason. Parasitical creatures attach to me, sucking the energy of my soul; a symbiosis relationship, emptying my substance into void of illusion. There is no sense of cognition here, no past, no future, only the hunger of insatiable need.

A blade of purest light ignites suddenly the blackness, a piercing fiery pinnacle intersecting every atom of every molecule in constructed state. Etched through the center of this blazing apex is the visage of a man lifted above all principalities, a corporeal body stretching into infinity and with eyes the magnitude of many suns. This the man I witnessed mortally crucified upon the face of a cliff. A distant reflection of a benign presence sent to save my mortal soul from depths of guilt and personal despair. This image now changed brightness of the universe: a light sent into darkness blinding every spirit. A pause of timeless silence and then a voice that clearly proclaims:

"Put your eyes upon me."

Fearful and ashamed, I begin to turn away from the intense judgment of this apparition. In the surrounding dark are hosts of other beings; those many parasitical creatures apprehensive of their turn to feed. Although disgusting, these ravenous spirits not terrifying, but rather promise an opiate of satisfaction. Their habitation a place separated to an advent of eventual end. Their temporal promise a lie perpetuated from the womb and entwined in deception to distract through complacency of physical senses.

I am also aware of something else in this moment. Here is the time and place I must decide, a position prepared, eternally fixed in confusion of a cosmic conundrum. This abiding apparition of light manifested since the beginning to purge the chaff of elemental creation, an assurance provisionally fulfilled before the micro event of inception. Yes, I know this is Messiah, the infused hope to all creation at a prescribed resurrection. Only I am bound by invisible arms of fearful pride and doubt.

Ashamed and condemned by this presence of absolute authority, I begin to avert my gaze. Through sudden comprehension I know this to be the dividing sword of inevitability, forever separating light from darkness: the darkness as familiarity of the womb; this other a quantum altogether alien to my present state. Instantly, I am inspired with clear vision of a decision that must be made. I stand at fulcrum of a definitive crucible. The choice I make now the directive of immortal consequence-- a singularity inspired in shadow of everlasting death or glorified into everlasting life! I turn, look into the searing passage of those fervent eyes, and hear a voice cry out—

"Yes Lord!"

Shard of this flaming spirit shoots up into the blackness, curls down, and stabs through me as the point of a kindled javelin. My immortal soul baptized in this spark of unquenchable fire-- *I die.*

From distant perspective, I see the vacated shell of an earthly body floating above embers of a remote dying universe, light and shadow congealing slowly into a finite center. The pure essence of my revived worm drawn irresistibly back into the presence of this restored being, filling again an elemental vessel like warm milk, first ebbing into the soles of the feet, through the trunk of a physical body, and overflowing the crown of a consciousness regenerated.

It then spreads upward into a joy unspeakable, becoming an eternal praise joined by angels to the God of creation and to the glory of salvation prepared since this world's foundation! *I am born again.*

Once again aware of existence; except I am no longer the person I was-- no longer fixed in the clockwork matrix of time and space. I am now lying prostrate on the floor, surrounded by my new brothers and sisters. I leap up, tears flowing from my eyes, and begin praising the Lord of heaven and earth, whose name I know for the first time. Now released from grip of those many unclean spirits, I know now without any doubt that there is a God in heaven; and that this God has sent his only begotten son to save my soul! Not my soul only, but the souls of all humankind! Yes— I know Jesus for the first time in my life. Who this Jesus was in mortal time—and what this Jesus means today!

I sing and worship late into the night, unaware of measured

reference, oblivious to politeness of social etiquette. Sometime around midnight, I am lovingly ushered to the door and handed a pocket-sized New Testament Bible. I do not remember much of the conversation, only something about everyone having to work the next day and that I am welcomed back to their church the following Sunday.

"Jesus is the good Sheppard of our souls. He alone knows his own sheep." Karen whispers sweetly at the door.

Then the door closes and I stand solitaire in night air, surrounded by a multitude of stars filling majestically the designed lattice of an ebony universe.

The drive back to base remains vague in my mind, not like any excursion made before or since. I am not even sure if I the one navigating. All I remember is seeing legions of angels mounted together for an approaching apocalyptic battle. Some part of me stands with them there; some part of me here. It seems but a narrow chasm fixed, as I desperately wish to leap across the temporal divide and join the ranks of this exalted celestial army. However, a proclamation declares no—my place in present time to remain here in the now. Reluctantly, I accept to occupy as a continuing emissary: the present living testament of the wonderful things I have seen and heard. Many things not yet, but are surely to come.

I wish to recount here another experience I will have fixed many years into the future. At this point in my life, I am again engaged in spiritual battle, only realize almost too late that the powers of darkness always present. This particular day I am on a thirty-six-foot-high building and inadvertently touch a 12000-volt medium electricity line. Upon contact I see a massive tongue of fire lash-out toward me. All changes black, and again I think I am on a battlefield in Nam. I begin running to avoid ricochets. Then I am in a void, falling into pit of everlasting darkness.

Everything changes slow motion. I see off on distant horizon a jet plane descending through cloud; flutter of hanging clothes in a mid-summer breeze. A sense of peace, as though I am floating, descending slowly. Upon hitting the earth, I altogether I leave the physical body again, accelerated through time and space to an eventual destination prepared to all in course. I see from this perspective, Earth and grandness of the universe once I knew, now only a fading twinkle in dilation of expanded time.

"I have died today— and didn't know I would die! I shout in sudden apprehension.

Then a voice speaks clearly from surrounding void:

"No— not now!"

Like a kaleidoscope in reverse, I return to presence of corporeal time. This death and resurrection designed through reason known only through preparation of the Holy Spirit. A correction made; a battle fought and won by hand of God's Messiah. It is as though the reverse of a full circle completion from that day to this day. And abiding purpose of why I write this testimony now.

This night, upon returning to my Sergeant quarters, I lay down in grave of my bed exhausted and wonder before my eyes close if all this real. I question if I will awake the next morning and the revelation gone, as so many other enhancements achieved using drugs and alcohol, through chants and meditations, and principalities of demons I have known and that have known me so well? I wish to sleep and never awaken again, rather than awake to emptiness indwelling the shell of my existence before this night. I pray with all my heart that Christ will never abandon me. On this note, I descend into slumber, into a peace surpassing all worldly understanding.

Morning light caresses me awake-- my joy still with me! It is not a dream after all! Nor is it some elaborate illusion. I am a new creature, magnified by grace through every fiber of my being, fully persuaded by arevelation not manifested through worldly experience. Yes, this is true salvation: a gift no man, or principality, or mortal presence able to take away!   I dress quickly and rush boldly out to meet the familiar company of my men, determined to share with them this wonderful good news of life's truest meaning.

"This day I want you to consider this hour we walk together upon the earth," I begin with burning enthusiasm. "Consider the grass that grows humble beneath your feet, the mighty trees providing shade in season, and touch of a gentle breeze soothing to all creatures great and small. These many gifts so easily taken for granted in the living moment. I come to you now as one newly born to speak plainly that we have a heavenly father, who loves us and has not forgotten his creation. Consider this day beginning testament of salvation to your mortal souls provided by God in accordance with a love immeasurable. Because of this love, God has sent Jesus Christ, the first begotten for the salvation of all that accept gift of this sacrifice. Jesus, a man made elemental in time, whose death and resurrection our death and resurrection, now transcending time, no longer mortal, no longer subject to convention of this fixed illusion made of many lies. This is a wonderful thing accomplished in season to restore that which was lost from beginning. I am today evidence of this salvation and tell you plainly that I stand before you a work of grace and a bearer of good news. One, who was dead; and now I am alive. Consider grandness of this event as you walk to your perspective duties. Today, while it still can be called today, is first day of new heaven and earth, when even the angels shout Hallelujah! For this day the Lord of salvation is risen from the grave as a living new testament in one you have known from before!"

In retrospect, it was not me that testified to these men, but the Holy Spirit. This is truest meaning of what I said then, if not the exact words. Perhaps these men under my charge thought me altogether mad or that I had dipped too deeply into the wrong pot. I have been made mad before by will of extraordinary force; and am witness to many principalities of the mind designed through fleshly entry. Only this day my delirium not a psychosis induced by influence of a drug, seduction of any cult, nor is it through pride of any earthly spirit. I am testifying by power of the Holy Spirit, no longer controlled by will of the person once I was, freer than ever have been.

Since this day I have been perceived by many as madness of a wondering muse. To some I speak words of sincerest compassion; to others voice of judgment with powerful conviction. But on this particular day I proclaim a testament of purest joy, reviling the person of sin that once I was, allowing love unfeigned to flow through my mortal presence. I will certainly have many future battles between that Marine Corps Sergeant, forged in anger and blood, now a creature reborn by grace to the end of reconciliation. This is the beginning of my New Testament, proclaiming miracle of the first resurrection.

$\mathcal{I}$t is not possible to hide light under a bushel. By the end of that first day, not one encountered escape without hearing the good news of salvation. However, for at least two men, this news less than good; potentially even dangerous to their mafia interest, and I become perceived as a threat to the future of their corrupt secret enterprise. Gunny and the Lieutenant consider my salvation a personal betrayal, both only concerned by the demands of their baser natures. This mainly because I make it clear that I will no longer participate in any more pilfering, but also affirming that they might continue in accordance with their own consciences without fear of reprisal, since I did not consider it my place to judge or condemn. They only eye me coldly, and then at each other. I should have suspected then that these hounds not the trusting types, capable of a conspiracy that nearly cost my career, and would have changed the course of my entire life were it not for divine intervention.

I am startled awake early one morning a few days later burdened with restless conviction to return everything I have taken since beginning of this new assignment. Arising immediately, I drive to the warehouse and place every single item back into inventory and then open the ledgers to adjust the books accordingly. However, to my surprise there is no discrepancy. Someone has already corrected the inventory. Still I am oblivious to the setup.

Upon arriving to work a few hours later, two MPs, accompanied by a gold leaf Major, intercept me with the Lieutenant and Gunny tailing behind. They demand that I open the trunk of my car. Of course, they find nothing. The Lieutenant rudely brushes aside one of the MPs and begins pulling back the carpeted panels, only to find the Bowie Knife I have brought back from Nam stashed inside the spare wheel-well.

"What is this Sergeant?" He demands, unsheathing the blackened blade.

"That is personal property, Sir." I reply calmly.

"Lieutenant this is clearly not Marine Corps issue," reports the Major sharply.

"We know he took something— ask Gunny here— because the books don't add up." "Yelp-- we're missing a riflescope from a lot we got in just last week, and one of the compasses." The Gunny pants, his hat pulled over the slit of his eyes, only the long snout of his nose protruding below the brim.

The MPs next search the interior of the car, even removing the door side-panels. After a thorough inspection of the engine compartment, they enter the warehouse, the Lieutenant leading the way like a nervous hyena. Once inside, he confidently produces the inventory books, turning to the pages showing the number of the new riflescopes and compasses.

"According to these entries you should have a total of thirty-eight riflescopes, and forty-two compasses." The Major says, examining the figures.

"That's what the book says," affirms Lieutenant Jackson.

The two MPs laboriously count each riflescope one by one, and then recount them again totaling thirty-eight. The same done for the compasses, and once again, the inventory exact. Turning abruptly toward my two accusers, the Major hisses a sigh of disdain.

"Lieutenant, I find no discrepancy in your inventory, nor any further reason to detain this man." Then glancing back at me, "excuse us Sergeant. You are dismissed from duty for the day. I don't take lightly false accusationsagainst an innocent man. I promise it won't happen again."

It is obvious that he dislikes Gunny and the Lieutenant even more than I do in the present. I spend the rest of the day under a tree reading the pages of the pocket New Testament given me. As I read, I understand. I know this Jesus; comprehend the meaning of his words and the later teachings of his apostles. It is not an indoctrination of learning; rather, confirmation of what I already know by revelation, the Holy Spirit bearing witness with my spirit of things not based on reason or perceived experience alone.

I receive new reassignment to the Armory. I think the Major had something to do with this after the attempt to frame me. He knows bad eggs when he sees them. It is my understanding that eventually Gunny and the Lieutenant, caught and charged with a list of crimes, including Grand Larson, both spending time in the Brigg and dishonorably discharged. They definitely pulled the wrong tail when they got the Major, a seasoned military Colombo, involved in their web of blackmail felony.

At first, I do not particularly like my new position, considering it a demotion in responsibility. However, I soon realize that a less demanding duty does not exist anywhere in the Corps. It is like being an executive with my own private office and the occasional form to sign, witnessed by two Lance Corporals, who actually perform all the weapons maintenance and assignments. Therefore, I have a great deal of time to read, to think, and to meditate on my new born spirituality.

Each Sunday I return to the schoolhouse church, discovering a meaning in fellowship and true worship through the energizing of the Holy Spirit. This may sound like a lot of religious mumbo jumbo, but I assure you it is not. I have stepped through a door and enjoined to a condition transcending eons of human history. It is a spiritually inspired congregation in the beginning, filled with holy submission and led by angelic instruction. A door camouflaged by common façade, seemingly the same as all religious doctrines with hidden agenda, iconic, lacking substance. An opiate created by monarchy to placate the masses.

Once, I too believed this to be the substance of all belief. Now I understand the power when hearts and minds accord praise to the one God. At the core of this praise is testament of an eternal resurrection, with present time and space being a conventional passage only. This man, Jesus, born flesh and blood to live and to die a death that all men die. But this Son of God resurrected from the grave a glorified being, immortal; an archetype of a new kind of man reconfigured to inhabit a creation not constrained to thermodynamic inevitability. This hidden mystery so apparent, often confused through instruction, and clouded by false promises of wealth and victorious acquisition.

There are no divisions in the spirit even though there are Baptist, Catholics, Jehovah Witnesses, Jews, Buddhist, Muslims, and Animist: multitudes from different cultures and differencing interpretations of worship. Division of all inspired through comprehension of mortal understanding, as when the Scribes and Pharisees desperately tried to make Jesus conform to limits of their understanding. My comprehension is that all avenues of faith potential gateways made one spirit by the inception of God's Messiah. This singular manifestation in time divided by time accomplishing what sterile religion interpretations unable to secure through crusades of empire building based on politics of condemnation and self-righteousness. This Messiah sent to reconstitute the fallen state of a universe destined to eventual destruction. Mortal existence is analogist to a seed planted in earth, which must rot away through interaction of elemental design, stimulating germination of an invisible code stored within the physical matrix. Or it is like the caterpillar feeding upon a leaf in season, to one day fall asleep inside a cocoon, only to reawaken with wings. In other words, death is a perception, not a condition.

This truth I hear whispered to my spirit through presence of mortal being of a greater promise immortal. The Jesus Christ I now know, good Sheppard of my soul standing at the gate of infinity. I thank my God that I heard dispatch of his messengers in the season sent. I do not know what my life might have been were it not for this intersection, or if I had chosen to remain in the womb of that darkness. Only I know that person would have lived a life of many other choices very different.

The McDonalds become as a second family to me. In the beginning, I visit their home nearly every Sunday after church service. I meet two young men, who have an obvious crush on Karen, both friends since childhood, and members of the Choinia Band. Brandon, a tall handsome clean-cut cowboy, and the elder of the pair, shares Karen's interest in horses. He would have been my first choice, considering their physical compatibility. Shawn, on the other hand, is a revived flower child. He has a tendency to stagger when he walks, aftermath of childhood polio, and his speech slurs a little when he becomes overly excited. But he also has a singing voice comparable to that of an angel. However, both these men share two common things: both love the Lord, and both in love with Karen McDonald. I think they imagine me new competition, never missing opportunity to impress the woman of their dream.

I consider Karen a beloved sister, for whom I have to this day an enormous respect. I am certain we would have made a wholesome team, only both sent on other missions of destiny; yet our mortal paths spiritually forever linked. The truth is that at the time I consider Karen too young, a lovely girl pure in her dreams and affections. I like both of these boys and hope that one of them might make my friend a good companion. In the end, Karen will choose neither of these young suitors, and eventually move away to Kansas with her parents in search of other souls to save.

I begin playing chess again. I play better than I ever played before, ruthlessly defeating every challenger. In fact, I become obsessed with the strategy of the game, seeing in my mind the many possible combinations of movements of each piece. I begin seeing the board in my dreams, my two Knights forming a strong offensive with my Queen positioned for the death strike. Henrietta quietly observes my obsession and says nothing. Then one sunny Saturday afternoon as we all sit in the backyard huddled around the patio table, she whispers something in my ear just as I am about to execute the third devastation against Brandon's persistent challenge.

"Is winning more important than brotherly love?"

These words sting me deeply. Through calm clarity, Henrietta observes the spirit that grips my pride. I beat Brandon anyway, the victory less sweet. Then it is Shawn's turn. Whereas Brandon a stimulating opponent, Shawn is altogether inept, lacking the strategy or the comprehension of how to use his pieces. By his fourth move, I see clearly the path to crushing victory. Then on the sixth move, I glance into Henrietta's eyes and know what I must do. I recklessly expose my Queen— not because I want to lose— but because I do not wish to win. Even then, it takes Shawn nearly a half dozen moves to declare checkmate. I wish to make something clear. I never consciously forfeited the game; rather, a spiritual battle raged within, the chessboard and pieces only avatars of greater forces at work.

"I win!" Shawn shouts cornering my King with his Rook and Castle.

Brandon shortens the execution by predicting the fatal conclusion two moves earlier. Of course, I was doomed since the seventh move, just becoming a question of how many moves. Brandon insists on a rematch, realizing an opportunity to regain some of his lost stature in the apple of his eye.

"No," I plainly conclude. "The Lord has shown me that this game is a poison to my soul. I will not play Chess again so long as it occupies the throne of my pride."

I now see what Henrietta sees. Clearly discerning the spirit of pride I have known, and knows me so well. I will realize over time that there are many such enclaves requiring constant diligence. However, in this moment, at least, the Lord has given me a spirit of discernment and power of restraint.

Brandon and Shawn only look at me perplexed. Nevertheless, as faithful brothers, they accept my decision by faith and without judgment. I think Brandon struggles most since his archrival now holds the undisputed title of chess master. Therefore, he dares not risk a direct challenge. As for me, Chess no longer just a game of challenge, but represents a passage of dark consequence requiring powerful deliverance from a pride of execution. Not that I will always win by losing, but this day I did overcome.

The next morning before church service Dick McDonald invites me to attend a men's breakfast composed of mostly businessmen and church officials. In retrospect, I think they saw potential in me joining their ranks. By now, I have begun considering the possibility of enrolling into the ministry and seek spiritual confirmation for this most important decision in my life. The idea of spreading the gospel of salvation now the only duty I consider truly worthwhile. I still have not given up the idea of remaining in the Corps, but the prospect of serving the Lord in some other missionary capacity more appealing. Also, I have a burning desire to know. Before the Holy Spirit I knew nothing. Now I know without any doubt that the beginning of all understanding is the birth, death, and resurrection of Jesus Christ. How is it that the pillars of worldly conversation oblivious to this fact, so easily dismissing this most important verifiable event as a doctrinal collection of religious instruction? Why is it labeled under theological debate, and not included in the table of historical records? If I received nothing else from Rudy's agnostic views, it is that all facts must be examined with scrutiny. Now I know this fact indisputable. A fact concealed within layers of many other facts. Nevertheless, I know it is tangibly real and not an abstraction of doctrinal belief only. For this reason I also bear a conflicting interest to pursue a course of secular research to better understand the foundation of this world's knowledge in order to unravel the lie of academia. Not for my sake, but for Rudy, and all like him divided by scientific speculation, choosing to examine only a small portion of available information because of empirical restraints. I know without any doubt that seeds of all meaning are here, if only the roots might be exposed. This part I will keep secret to myself.

At the end of our breakfast, we all standup and pray together, asking the Lord to bless and direct our lives. These men then crowd around me, laying-on their hands.

"Dear merciful Lord we ask that you deliver this individual from a sensual spirit," boldly proclaims one of the men.

At the time, I honestly did not understand the reference of his meaning, or take it as a judgment, but rather an observation. I thereby submit in the spirit, asking to be purged of any remaining uncleanness. These men begin praying fervently in the spirit. Then my peace returns again. Not because a spirit has vacated, but that something remains because it is God's will. The only justification I can provide is that a thorn left in my flesh to serve a purpose. This element of temporal position remaining by design to serve as a tool of temperance through many fiery trials destined for a future battles still to come. Sadly, I never receive another invitation to attend the men's breakfast after this.

My last days in the Marine Corps are vague. I remember undergoing treatment for a multitude of maladies. Plantar warts have bored into the soles of my feet and heels. A parasite infects my acne, causing grotesque boils on my cheeks, later resulting in horrible scars. The most serious condition is advanced tooth decay requiring many days of drilling. I should have paid more attention to Jean's rousing lectures on oral hygiene. Those last few weeks I spend almost every day at the base clinic undergoing acid treatment on soles of my feet, syringed needles painfully pierced into pulsing acne sores, and long hours in a dentist chair. In the Corps, you are either short or career. But regardless of one's status or rank, those returning from a combat zone receive priority treatment, ushered to front of the line. There were so many others not so fortunate. Those that came back severely injured: loss of limbs, organ damage, and even paralysis. And some wounds less evident. Images they cannot forget and things that continuously haunt their minds with unforgettable memories and unforgivable deeds, a darkness gnawing in their conscience for a lifetime. I will later learn that VA Hospitals less diligent, too much bureaucratic, and often lacking compassion. Yes, I am one of the lucky ones. Only I little comprehend at the time just how fortunate. How blessed I am to find salvation in season and passage of escape from a world of secular reality.

One morning a notice appears on the bulletin board that reads:

"UCLA Extension is receiving applicants to its Spring Quarter Session for discharged personnel wishing an evaluation study program for future integration into the higher education system."

At first glance this posting appears an immediate confirmation to my prayers. I check with Adjutant of Administration to find out if I qualify.

"Well, Sergeant, you have a GED, which is a respected High School equivalent. The only problem I see is that the course begins April 5, and your release date is not until the twenty-first. Let me see what I can do for an early release."

Within twenty-four hours, I have my final answer. The Marine Corps is letting me out 29 days early. On March 7, five days after my twentieth birthday, I am officially released from active duty, a little less than three years to the day I started my enlistment. I will always remember those last hours day with some confusion. Along with a group of nine other men, I wait in my dress greens outside a staging barracks pending receipt of final orders. I lie under a tree watching the speckle of the afternoon sun peak through the leaves, acutely aware of every minute. It is as I felt leaving my family for the first time. I am proud of my rank, proud of my accomplishments, experiencing a profound affection for the Marine Corps and all it has given me. I deeply respect the ideals it stands for and its readiness to defend in time of war. Here I have learned true meaning of honor, strength, and faithfulness to others. But mostly I have learned dedication to a cause, sad to leave this strong brotherhood. Nevertheless, an even stronger calling now calls me: a voice spoken above sound of all dominions and principalities impossible to ignore.

A young Second Lieutenant arrives clumsily carrying a familiar stack of vanilla envelopes. He calls each of our names, passing out our final orders. This accomplished, he snaps to attention and salutes.

"Good luck, gentlemen," he says ceremoniously. "You have served your country well. Serve your society even better."

At 1200 hours, I pass through the main gate of Camp Pendleton to never again return. I am a civilian now, alone in society; yet not alone. This represents my first step of faith back into the greater world. I feel like the patriarch Abraham departing from the city of Ur into uncharted wilderness, called to a promised land. There are presently still those I must testify to. They will remember me as the person I once was, now changed, and will surely receive gladly my good news of salvation.

$\mathcal{I}$ still have three weeks before the Spring Session begins.

As a departing gift, the Corps grants me a round-trip ticket to Greenville South Carolina on military standby. It takes me more than eighteen hours to get there. From Los Angeles to Dallas, Dallas to Atlanta, and then a rickety old two-prop with an obvious crack in the metal fuselage just below my seat that visibly separates as the engines throttle for take-off.

I find this last one-hundred-and-thirty-mile leg of the trip curiously exhilarating, as I consider possibility that this old crate might split apart and I will join my lord in eternity. However, we make it safely, landing at the Greenville Airport just as the sun crests the lush southern horizon. The majestic Appalachian foothills off in the distance slope smoothly into a familiar milky basin stirring up many childhood memories. I am home, and happy to be home, happier than I have known since a very long time. Changed in a way that Rudy and Jean find threatening, a feeling of strangeness prevails between us. Instead of embracing this better-changed me, they feel threatened, thinking that the *'Good News'* of salvation I share with them fanatical, my testimony perceived as unwelcomed preaching meant to condemn their values. Both think that I have joined a cult, unable to see the greater significance.

"The words of the spirit are not fine prints in a contract drawn up by advocates created with loopholes for private interpretation to condemn men," I lovingly defend. "These are words of spirit and life, declaring in clear speech testimony of the risen Messiah sent by God into the world of men. I am but a messenger sent; and living example in your generation of God's grace. I am saved not by subtlety of doctrine, nor by acts of good works according to the standards of this world. I testify sincerely of those things I have seen and know, fully persuaded it is God's desire that none should perish in sin. This love I share with you now. You know me from before; know my imperfection. I come to you on a mission of grace to testify of grace and of love greater than any I have known."

I truly think in the moment they might understand my meaning, and be changed miracle of change evident in me through supernatural force. I want them to see and to hear-- need them to hear! Not for me-- but to the benefit of their own souls. Surely they can see that I am no longer the violent person of those earlier years. My only desire is to share the full measure of the Holy Spirit with the ones dearest to my heart.

They make it clear they want no part of this miracle. Maybe I have changed in their eyes: only now their perception that I have become a religious fanatic. This makes them even more uncomfortable. I am no longer comprehensible to their ways of thinking. Each day grows more strained than the one before, until finally Rudy and I have our traditional confrontation.

"This is my house," Rudy growls confrontational after returning from his Barber, glaring at me like a mean freshly razed Bull Terrier. "I don't want to hear any more of this God shit— is that clear?"

I can smell the Vodka on his breath. Since early childhood I retain the image of this man arriving home drunk, head shaved, and ready for battle. He is now dangerous and unpredictable. I am less frightened, as part of me wants to accept his challenge, only constrained by a greater authority.

"It is your house," I reply submissively. "In times past I disgraced your home because of anger and confusion. Now I come to you in peace and love. If you consider yourself unworthy to hear these words of truth, then I kick-off the dust from my feet. This time it is not me who offend. You are offended by calling of the Holy Spirit."

I thought he was going to hit me. He growls inhumanly, turns, and stomps away. I sadly bow my head, go inside, and begin packing my bags. Even Jean remains strangely quiet. Instead of her usual protest when I prepare to leave, she just sits complacent in the sacred solitude of her special room and stares out the window.

It continues to remain mystery why this message of my spiritual revival the straw that finallybreaks the camel's back. Why their reaction so defensive. I often think that maybe part of the ambivalence toward me generated because of my acceptance into a major university, even though it only an entry level program. Nevertheless, I would be the first in my family to even dream of the possibility of a higher education. Rudy, a brilliant man, but lacking opportunity, always made it clear he resents "jack leg college people, who didn't know the difference between a hammer anda paintbrush."

Maybe he took the things I share with him on this visit as a personal challenge to his intelligence, a feeling of jealousy that I mightexperience the things he should have had, but deprived like so many of his generation. If only he might have heard with his heart and seen through eyes not blinded by worldly frustration. But most he has made agnosticism his religion, fearful that anything not based on rationalism and empirical proof a threat to his intelligence. I am now everything this man of worldly belief finds threatening.

There will come a time in his life, when Rudy will be faced by an imperative for which science and reason will hold no answer. On that day I will testify again, and he will hear. But in this present, he can only see the prodigal son of all he disdains in life. Of the many ways I have disappointed my stepfather in the past-- times of confusion and violence-- this testimony of Jesus Christ being my personal Messiah equivalent to driving a holly stake into his heart.

My mother does something special for me my last day, something I continue to treasure to this day. First she takes me to her bank and cashes four hundred dollars of Federal Savings Bonds I have accumulated since the last three years. We then go to K-Mart, where she purchases a new Presto Stainless Steel Pressure Cooker.

"Sunny this is something you will be able to use for a long time," she says prophetically, and then cries as always she does before I leave.

After only a few days, I am back on a plane heading west feeling truly rejected in a way that grieves me deeply. It is not just a rejection of me, but of the most important message I have ever delivered.

I accept I am only a messenger, and the message rejected. Through me a testament presented of something more enduring than angry disputing or prideful swagger, greater than riches-- more profound than life itself! I had been sent humble, bearing the simple testament of how God saved me by strong revelation-- an event as great as genesis. Yet in this season my beloved family unable to understand.

Nevertheless, I will continue to pray for them, as I do for all, without judgment, believing always that the moving of the Holy Spirit a manifestation without the need of seeing with the eyes, or understanding with the mind. This is a faithful thing-- the angels in heaven engaged in continual warfare against strong principalities, the final battle already won.

I continue to love my family, as I love all whose paths I cross, making no difference in the flesh. At this junction in history, I was sent to them as an emissary to proclaim the good news of salvation at a prescribed hour.   As so often Christ knocked on the door of my heart when I did not hear, I will not tire to testify in name of my Lord and savior. And this all I need to know.

My first challenge upon returning to California is to find a place to live near the University Extension. The Los Angeles core is a tangle of streets and freeway overpasses with surviving pockets of culture camouflaged in a maze of superstructure. To find an affordable accommodation near the downtown core is a daunting task. Especially in the early seventies, when finding any place in Los Angeles an epic challenge. I know nothing about the area, except the location of UCLA Extension on San Pedro Street near the Hollywood and the Harbor Freeway Interchange. This morning I get on my knees and ask the Lord to guide me to a dwelling suitable for my needs.

Parking my car near the University Extension on Third and San Pedro, I begin walking in a southwest direction. I could have gone north, or east, but feel compelled to hold the chosen course. I arrive at a small park with a variety of trees and several benches occupied by old men and women. At one end of this sanctuary rests the edifice of a Catholic church fashioned after the architecture popular to the Mexican territories before this south western region ceded to U. S. control by the Treaty of Guadalupe Hidalgo. This also brings end to the Mexican-American War. It is peaceful here, a place out of time, a small eddy of solitude surrounded by the torrential rushing of cars and implacable hordes of pedestrians. Beneath shade of a California Ash grove is a tranquility insulated from city heartbeat creating pulse of this mega city, like all cities racing blindly into an uncertain future. As an explorer discovering a new world my eyes fasten on a sagging building at the dead-end of a small adjacent street named Scarff Avenue. This sarcophagus was no doubt once a splendid hotel before the economic crash of the 1930s, ornately trimmed with French balconies, Colonia styled windows, and enclosed by a warped wrought iron fence with an Art Deco front gate sagging on rusted hinges. As providence would have it, a discreet For Rent sign hangs in the window at the entrance indicating a vacancy.

"Thirty-five dollars a week, furnished, and all utilities paid," growls the building super, a battered old crow of a man, which landed here some time ago never to fly again.

"I'll take it."

I know the Lord has led me to this place. It is perfect to my needs; within walking distance to my classes, a single room completely furnished, including a small kitchenette with a stove and refrigerator more than a decade old, yet still functional. A tiny window without curtains faces east overlooking the peaceful Eden of the park. I move in immediately, kneel down on the rich Persian carpeted floor and bless my new dwelling.

The first day of classes is as much intimidating as exciting. I never performed well in an academic environment, and fear I might fail now. Nevertheless, if the Marine Corps has impressed me with nothing else, it is unfaltering determination to try. If I fail, I will fail trying: greater than my fear is a desire to know, and a willingness to understand. I need to buy two large book bags the first day of class, because there are so many. Books on speech and communication, Greek and Latin etymology dictionaries, books on social science, math and literature, and some books with subjects I have never even heard of. Upon arriving home, I place the battery neatly on the floor beside my bed. It promises to be a marathon lasting twelve weeks.

That spring, I also fall in love with Debbie Sickinger. Debbie is a shy mousy girl with long flaxen hair, eyes that glitter with the Holy Spirit, and perfect in every way. She is in the last undergraduate year at UCLA, and when possible attends Sunday service with a group of several other students, all born again Christians. Fortunately, gas cheap then, so I drive to the UCLA campus in West Los Angeles every Friday night for Bible study and fellowship prayer. Now looking back, this transit represents a wonderfully pure period of my life. I am like a newly emerging flower hungry for the spiritual water of life and fellowship. These become my new family; a communion not based on fraternity or deeds, but forged in the one loving spirit of Jesus Christ.

Unfortunately, I become super infatuated with Debbie, even to the point of believing that God means for us to be together. I am Adam; she my Eve. However, Debbie has already formed a relationship with an intelligent young man named Daniel, who is also a paraplegic stricken with advanced Lou Gerick's disease. He projects a calm benevolent exterior… too calm... almost calculating. I sense that Daniel perceives I am a threat. My eventual sin is that I fail to consider him at all. In my youthful arrogance, I think it unfair to have to compete with someone handicapped. Why could he not be a worthy opponent, whole like any other man? It seems somehow not fair that I also feel pity for Daniel.

This causes me enormous guilt because of my innate feelings of desire for the woman that attends to his needs with such affection. I can sense that Debbie shares a mutual attraction for me, but governed by loyalty and compassion to a friend of longstanding. Because of my immaturity, I allow jealousy to soil my conscience. Even though I do not consciously wish to violate the friendship shared by these two, I desire to connect with Debbie on a level more than friendship. The truth is I am sickened by the weakness of my jealousy. I want to be noble, to have the strength of character to walk away, but inside I struggle with a contemptible nature. A mutual acquaintance in the prayer group discerns my struggle, and in an unpresuming way provides me with the spiritual guidance most needed in the moment.

We jokingly often refer to this fellow as happy tall Jiff, after the character on the label of a peanut butter brand, which he consumes regularly. His real name Jim, a mild-mannered Clark Kent type with thick black-rimmed glasses, looking in every detail like a Business School Graduate. He is the roommate and loyal companion to Daniel, projects a quiet demur and rarely says much. One evening after a pray meeting, Jim speaks pointedly to me, the Spirit having shown him the personal struggle of my conflict.

"God knows the heart of a man. The inner man shapes the outward appearance, and that spiritually perceived."

"Right now my heart feels confused." I confess. "I feel like clay without any real shape. One part of me wants to surrender, another part wants to take. One part weak, the other part strong-- only I don't know which strong and which is weak."

"In reality you are a Splough.""A what--"

"A *Splough*-- in fact we are all *Sploughs* prepared for a purpose." Jim smiles, reminding me in that moment of Disney's cartoon character, Jiminy Cricket, profoundly wise. He clears his throat, and begins telling me a story.

"Once, there was a kingdom ruled by a King that has everything this world can offer and all that his mind can imagine to gain." Jim speaks seriously. "But in time this King grows bored with all his possessions realizing that nothing he has provides him pleasure, his soul empty and still wanting more. He sends out a proclamation that anyone who can bring him something unique, he will give the quarter of his kingdom. There arrives to his principality a Tinker, who humbly bows before the monarch, and solemnly promises:

'Sire, I will make for his majesty a thing so unique that never was, nor ever can be again.'

The King is beside himself with joy and anticipation. As requested, the Tinker is provided a chamber with a balcony in an upper tower overlooking a moat that surrounds the castle walls. The Tinker locks himself within and begins hammering incessantly the metal of his trade. This persistent hammering goes on for days and nights. The King so excited that he neither eats nor sleeps. He paces anxiously in front of the locked door, wishing for even a peek at the wondrous device promised by this metal smith. Then, one day the door opens, and out steps the Tinker. In one hand is something spherical, covered beneath sheet of a black cloth.

'Sire, your Splough is complete,' he says bowing.

'Wonderful –wonderful— let me see it— quickly— quickly!'

The Tinker lifts the handkerchief. Resting in the palm of his hand is a metallic ball completely disfigured with dents and depressions made by instruments of his delicate hammering. In fact, there is not a single place, which does not bear a precision nick, or some intentionally crafted mar. It is like nothing the King possesses, like nothing he has ever seen, or even imagined could be.

'Quickly— show me how it works!' The King demands impatiently. 'I must know the uniqueness of this thing! Indeed, I have never seen anything like it, but what does it do?'

'As your Majesty desires,' replies the Tinker.

He steps to the edge of the balcony, extends his arm, and releases the metal ball. The King watches in horror as it falls down… down… and down. Upon striking the water in the moat below it makes a most distinctive sound-- *Splough*!

'I give the King something that never was, and will never be again; a thing as unique as a droplet of water in winter storm— as impeccable as life itself!'

After a moment of reflection, the King nods his satisfaction. He gladly pays the Tinker the promised reward, continues to rule his kingdom with greater contentment, now knowing that at the bottom of a surrounding moat exists a promise inimitable to all creation."

Jim pauses to clear his throat. I see in his eyes a genuine carrying; not just for me, but for Daniel and for Debbie as well.

"So you are saying that I am a Splough?" I ask trying to better understand meaning to the story, which I know told for my benefit.

"We are all Sploughs-- me, you, Daniel, Debbie— each created uniquely and with a severalty of differing gifts. God is the Tinker of our souls. Let your life be shaped by his spirit through faithful acceptance, and be not conformed to the course of fleshly lust, which has an end."

I understand what Jim has so beautifully said to me, knowing that in these words comes instruction of the Holy Spirit. I like this tale about the *Splough*, and determine then to turn away from the nature of my jealousy. I will continue to long after Debbie, but quietly, and from a distance. I know Daniel has not long to live, and decide to allow him his heart's desire. After all, Daniel is my brother in the Lord. How can I in good conscience conspire to betray him? Jim is right. We are all *Sploughs* shaped in timeby the hand of the Holy Spirit: Daniel, Debbie, me, all instruments made for a purpose as yet not revealed. At least in this moment, I have peace of acceptance; my loneliness now less lonely.

*A*ltogether I immerse myself in weeks of challenging study, my mind expanding in many different directions at the same time. Knowledge of the world is a transforming experience, especially to one who knows nothing as once thought. Particularly fascinating is the etymology of words and constructive language of speech, further accentuating discovery of the Holy Bible. Every syllable, every inflection fit marvelously together, creating a clear map of past, present, and future. It is as a singularity ignited in time and space, expanding into exciting potential. I desire nothing of the world, yet hunger for the meaning embedded within the pillars of worldly knowledge. This hunger remains insatiable still today-- my soul even more hungry to know. Not for the pleasure of personal fulfillment, but as a voice of reason in context of many other voices with agenda deceptive in interpretation.

The months I live on Scarff Avenue are as mythical as any fairytale. The old stone church at the end of the park is a castle of light in my mind with doors open wide late into the night, an invitation to all, rich or poor, to those religious and to those without faith. Not being Catholic, or even religious, I think of this structure as a beacon reminding the world of the Lord's physical presence upon this earth. I have seen many such structures abandoned of anything living, empty tombs that only appear, dead within. In contrast, this monarch building feels somehow alive, a wonderful presence facing the window of my one room apartment opposite the park providing comfort during long study periods.

At night I often take walks through a maze of avenues laced through this more ancient district of East Los Angeles, exploring the strange sarcophagi of granite stone buildings made by human hands, many boarded up and vacant, haunting epitaphs of generations gone by. One such building is the old Christian Science Library on Grand Avenue, with walls that bleed black between the masonry. This place gives me a particular chill one night when I press my face against one of the soot-covered windows to get a better look inside. I later learn that the founder of this deceptively labeled religion, a respected woman named Mary Baker Eddy, who died horribly proclaiming nightly assaults by demons. All I can confirm is that on this particular night I glimpse in my spirit a malevolent presence glaring back at me, and decide never to venture here again.

One evening, I quite by accident stumble upon a Kathryn Kuhlman revival meeting held at the Shrine Auditorium on nearby Jefferson Boulevard. This is the first and only time I hear about this lady or her ministry. As I pass the elaborate Spanish-styled building, I feel a jolt of the Holy Spirit, as strong as my first encounter. I detour inside without hesitation and am ushered to a seat in one of the upper bleachers on the third balcony. The evangelist appears a small white ash in the distance: an energetic being exuding dynamic force-- something extraordinary happening here tonight.

The Shrine Auditorium is as an ornate palace survived from an age of antiquity, richly trimmed in gold and fiery ruby, acoustically designed to sponsor any event. With over six thousand seats, it has been the host platform of the Academy Awards, the Emmys, the Grammys, and much more. There is not a national award from the past not sponsored here at least once, as well as being the home of the USC Trojan Basketball team. It embodies a feeling of nostalgia, permeated with an odor of oldness.

At this time perhaps a little less magnificent, and is pending a needed future renovation that will happen in years to come. Historical records say the original structure, built in 1906, burned to the ground after eighteen years, only to be resurrected in 1926. According to estimate, over 118 miles of nails were used if laid end to end. Cantilevered balconies rest upon classical supporting pillars, and in the main center hangs an enormous chandelier ignited by over 500 bulbs shining through colored glass, and according to official documents weighs in excess of four tons. The Shrine is a remarkable testament to earthly achievement, a temple ingeniously conceived, fabricated through human imagination, representing the patient craftsmanship of many human hands.

This particular night it is a revitalized soul, inspired by the Spirit of spirits. Yes, the Shrine Auditorium lives this night transformed into a holy church! No longer worldly, no longer fixed in mortal time and space, it is as New Jerusalem magnified in this fleeting hour, becoming a place of eternal passage. As this woman of God calls upon the Holy Spirit for healing, I witness a wave of pure energy pass over and through the congregation of souls. Upon touching me, I am suddenly light as air, swept up into another heaven, and begin weeping with joy.

This night I witness droves of people from every conceivable demographic leave their seats and crowd around the stage claiming healing from various physical and spiritual maladies. I cannot describe with any logical certainty the extraordinary events witnessed, only that I know it not the fabrication of a hoax; nor can I verify the certainty of the events through natural reason, or even why I am led here. It embodies a mystery of grounded potential contrary to present day pragmatism. Men, women, old and young, all staggering about weeping and praising God, all filled with the Holy Spirit, as filled me, and as filled the Lord's Apostles on the day of Pentecost recorded in the Book of Acts, Chapter 2, verse 1-4 of my recently acquired King James Version Bible.

"And when the day of Pentecost was fully come, they were all with one accord in one place. And suddenly there came a sound from heaven as of a rushing mighty wind, and it filled all the house where they were sitting. And there appeared unto them cloven tongues like as of fire, and it sat upon each of them. And they were all filled with the Holy Ghost, and began to speak with other tongues, as the Spirit gave them utterance."

My rented room shares a common toilet and shower stall located in the hallway; and at the end of this hall a door leading to another apartment adjacent to my dwelling. Each night at around half past ten, a lumbering presence stomps bearishly up the stairs to the second floor and down the narrow corridor, fumbling forever with annoyance of rattling keys, before finally gaining entrance. I imagine a drunkard, a lost soul, like so many in this building, trapped in a cycle of alcohol and poverty, oblivious to the concept of coexistence with others. One evening, just after dozing into exhausted sleep this ogre arrives, bubbling clumsily along the narrow passage. Spontaneously leaping up, I fling open the door and intrepidly face this intruder once and for all.

"There are people in this building trying to sleep!" I scold sharply in my Marine Corps Sergeant voice.

The man is literally a giant. He reminds me of the newsprint cartoon character 'Little Abner', standing more than six feet tall, muscular, clean cut, and holding a black Bible in his right hand.

"I'm sorry little brother," his voice deep and rumbling. "I surely didn't mean to disturb anyone."

I inquire sheepishly regarding a worn black Bible tucked under his arm, and hesitantly accept his extended hand.

"My name's Ron. I guess we be neighbors."

"Are you a Christian?" I ask regarding the Bible

"Praise God— and born again! Why don't you come in and have a tea."

I accept with delight. It turns out that Ron also received blessing of the Holy Spirit just in the past few months. His nightly arrivals a return from pray meetings. It is another miracle of God bringing the two of us together in much needed fellowship. Ron, a man in his early thirties, recently separated from a wife of many years named Willowbeth; and also the absent father of two children. His occupation is truck driver for Farmer Brother's Coffee Plant located in Torrance California, which often sends him on long hauls across the southwest. He is waiting for God to reunite him with his estranged family, believing his present isolation to bea time of penance. Before his conversion, Ron admits to being abusive to his wife, allowing alcohol to destroy ten years of marriage. Since receiving Christ as his Savior, Ron has altogether given up drinking and cigarettes, faithful that God capable of healing the wounds of a dysfunctional past. He also has given up drinking coffee, preferring tea. I think this ironic since he works for Framer Brothers, a world nationally renowned coffee plant.

Sadly, Ron and Willowbeth will not reunite. His separated spouse has determined never again to suffer abuse at the hands of this man, defiantly swearing she would rather die. Personally, I believe Ron a changed person, but also understand Willowbeth's reluctance to try. They had met each other out of high school in Oklahoma and relocated to Southern California in search ofa better life. I think what confuses Willowbeth most is how much Ron has changed. On some basic level she is accustomed to the kind of man   Ron was when they married and questions in herself: *who is this peaceful spirit-filled changeling in his place?*

Willowbeth wants no part of his Holy Spirit doctrine, preferring the detestable person of a manly presence like her father. Of course, she also hates her father too, which confirms to Willowbeth all men the same-- all misogynous woman beaters. She will have many relationships after their divorce, all with the same thing in common: all like Ron before his conversion.

Ron and I become good friends, a friendship that will span decades. I especially remember the time he shares with me the moment his soul filled with the Holy Spirit. He describes it as a racing train passing through him. I can see it as though in a vision, a ghostly locomotive ripping through the tattered walls of our temporal dwelling and lifting Ron into eternity.

Several years later, Ron will have an accident that nearly proves fatal. He has driven his truck in and out of the plant for over fifteen years, crossing the same set of railroad tracks just outside the main gate. For some unknown reason, he does not see the flashing warning lights or the approaching locomotive. The huge metal monster, weighing in excess of 3000 tons, makes impact just behind the driver's cab, splitting open the loaded trailer, dragging the screeching semi several hundred feet down the track. Ron will describe the event in terrifying detail from his hospital bed the day I visit.

"The interior begins collapsing around me crushed by an evil hand," Ron recalls with tears in his eyes, relating the terrifying event. "The windshield burst, popping out of the frame. I can feel God's angels all around me; and for just a moment I am somewhere else. It seems everything happening in slow motion. I remember reaching up and pulling myself through the opening with one arm as the metal cage crumples behind me. Then I am on the tracks rolling in front of the twisted wreck. How I managed not to be pulled under with the debris, I don't know. Then all got still; and I manage somehow to crawl off the littered metal and gravel tracks to a place with green grass. I know I should have died that day, but God let me live."

Ron suffers relatively minor injuries and eventually returns to his job. However, this terrific accident will be several years down the road. For the moment, we are both as babes cherishing the milk of God's word and prayer. This is the second miracle on Scarff Street, but will not be the last. I will never again have a friend of greater consequence and meaning than shared with Ron. We become as brothers, share as brothers, loyal and faithful through many adventures together; and there are few peopleI respect more.

The time passes quickly, each day as a blur of constant study, eating out of cans, and the occasional few minutes of prayer with my seldom home neighbor. In June Debbie goes back to San Jose to live with her parents during summer break. She gives me her home address and phone number, which I suppose she lives to regret.

The first week in July the anticlimactic day of graduation arrives. No ceremony, no special honors, just a barrage of test and acknowledgment that those of us that pass eligible to be granted a certificate rating and exclusive application into rated institutions of higher learning based on proficiency of our final scores. The ratings are A: University B: State College C: Junior College. To my delight I receive an A rating. By now, I have devoted many hours to decide where I wish to attend for my future studies. I first apply to Clemson University only a few miles from where Rudy and Jean live, to The University of South Carolina in Colombia, and finally to UCLA. This choice is just because Debbie still a final year undergraduate there. To my surprise, UCLA is the only one that responds back with an acceptance. I still have two and a half months before the commencement of Fall Quarter, so I pack-up my few belongings, say goodbye to the pleasant giant, and drive 400 miles north to San Jose.

I do not know what I thought I might find there. Perhaps I hope Debbie andI can discover one another differently, without distractions or feelings of guilt. Deep down my hope is that we might engage in a way that I hopemight be God's ultimate plan for our lives together. However, it will not work out this way, becoming a choice of action that will instruct my heart with a rod of reality. Through this experience, I will learn differencebetween the will of the flesh and the will of God.

San Jose is a lovely little city less than an hour drive from San Francisco, an area surrounded by semi-arid desert mountains mostly uninhabited. Mount Hamilton, home of the famous Lick Observatory, is the highest of these, rising to an altitude of 4200 feet above sea level approximately 20 miles from city limits. In course of time, this sleepy hollow existence will explode into an economic chimera, becoming the capital of a new chip technology industry known as the Silicon Valley. But at this junction it is just a pleasant town with many suburbs.

First on the agenda is to find a place to live. I respond to an ad in the local paper regarding a room for rent at twenty-five dollars a week, a single level residential home located in a quiet neighborhood owned by a fellowwith a heavy German accent.

"Ya' I am Hans", says a slightly built man in his early forties. "No girls and no parties, and you buy your own food."

A week paid in advance and the advertised room becomes mine. I soon discover that Hans is going through a difficult devoice, renting out furnished rooms in his three bedroom house to keep up with the mortgage payments. He usually sleeps on a cot in the dining area or stays over night at the home of a female acquaintance. Now, at least, I have a base of operation. Next I must find a job. After pounding the pavement for a week without success, I expand my search into nearby San Francisco.

At the end of another exhausting day, I find myself in *Ghirardelli*

Square, home of world-famous chocolates and a Mecca for tourist. Here I meet a young Irish street-vendor roughly my own age selling Yoyos that light up when spun. The principal behind these ingeniously crafted devices are two simple battery powered electrical contacts, positive and negative, that touch through centrifugal action of the spinning Yoyo. I immediately see the potential and offer to engage in his enterprise for a commission. I take one end of the square and the Irishman the other. In less than three hours, I sell forty-two Yoyos at a personal profit of fifty-cents each. Ironically, my largest transaction is to a Japanese businessman, who purchases ten Yoyos to send home to family and friends.

"Japanese are always my best customers," the Irishman laughs, counting his money and giving me back twenty-one dollars. "If only they knew that I get these things from a Japanese importer. It takes an Irishman in America to know how to market to the Orient."

We go to an Irish pub in *Ashbury Heights* and order fish and chips. I abstain from having a beer, taking a soda instead. After eating, my companion suggests that we cop some LSD. I decline the invitation, sharing with him the testimony of my deliverance through Christ. I quickly perceive that he is disturbed by this unexpected testimony. Quietly excusing himself, he goes to the bathroom. I will never see the Irish businessman again. Convinced that my companion has stiffed me, I ask the waitress for my portion of the tab.

"Your friend paid for you both and left several minutes ago," the older woman smiles; she looks like a Koala Bear with yellow ribbons and red beads tied in her flaxen hair. "He said to give you this and to tell you thanks."

She hands me a package containing one electric Yoyo, a novelty I will cherish for a long time. The *Haight* is a district in San Francisco centrally beginning at the corner of *Haight* and *Ashbury* streets, a haven for every kind of drug and Hippie popularized during the early sixties with hordes of peace children migrating to the district from all over the country-- maybe even the world. Then the Summer of Love becomes the defining moment of the Hippie counterculture introducing the concept of communal living, equal sharing, and free love. It must have been beautiful in the beginning. A socialist subculture designed after the similitude of Christian fellowship, as presented in the book of Acts of the New Testament Bible. Except for the drugs, it might have worked. The aftermath of human vice and laziness altogether corrupts the spiritual idealism of Timothy Leary. Instead of a unified brotherhood, the district divides into principalities of competing drug dealers, self-enlightened gurus, and many addicts. By the seventies, the once beautiful flower children changed to fallen angels of despair, crumpled petals huddled on city sidewalks: unclean, diseased, and living from one chemical hit to another. It sickens me to see the carnage of human waste. Young men, their eyes soulless and burned out; and once lovely girls with nothing left to give. Was a time I would have given anything to be part of this grand illusion, but now my eyes open. The truth, although deceptively camouflaged with psychedelic promise, now so terribly clear. By now satanic worship, witchcraft, and all manner of evil communication infest this experiment community utopia, now a fertile ground to every foul spirit. Almost I expect to find Joseph and Mary among them; but also hope they are not here.

"This is Peter," Hans makes introduction the next morning before I depart on another day of serious job searching. "And the man seated across from him is Fred. They live in the other two rooms."

The first gentleman seated to his right, a heavyset ruddy complexioned blond man dressed in a pastel shirt, matching pants, and white wicker shoes, only nods his head nonchalantly and continues to eat. I will later learn that Peter is a promoter for golf and other sporting events. However, my gut feeling says Peter a slick Con Man always looking for free lunch. This man of obvious taste drives a tan convertible *Carmengia,* spending most of his time traveling around the Bay area looking for events to sponsor. When he is home, Peter stays mostly in his room avoiding contact with others. I suspicion at the time that he might be gay, considering the way he dresses and the way his manicured fingers wave the air when he gets excited. Nevertheless, Peter remains a person of arms-length respect in my mind. In retrospect, I suppose this man of more refined temper might have considered me a little threatening, since I still often project the often gruff demur of a Marine Corps Sergeant.

"I've heard about you from Hans," Fred volunteers. "I work down at the corner gas station."

This man is simple by comparison. I like Fred right away, mainly because of his calm and unpretentious nature. I will later have more than a few conversations with him alone and learn that his wife took their only child, leaving the state with another man. In time, however, it also becomes apparent that Fred has a serious drinking problem. Regardless of what he says, I soon realize Fred content with pumping gas for low wages and then drinking himself quietly to sleep behind a closed door.

After these brief introductions and something to eat, I set-out on another day of job quest, determined to find stable employment. More importantly I will discover an excuse for the real reason I have come to SanJose. Because I have Debbie's address, it will be just a matter of time before I unearth her. How surprised she will be when one day I show up at her front door unannounced.

Through the help wanted ads, I find a position at a Sears and Roebuck Company outside San Francisco, as a member of the night maintenance crew consisting of myself and two other men. The pay and the hours good, locked into the department store each night after closing, remaining prisoners until it opens again the next morning. Our assigned tasks to wax and buff the floors, dust all the displays, and ensure proper placement of the merchandise. Usually, we finish in less than five hours of an eight-hour shift.

My two co-workers, being veterans, know the positions of all the store cameras and make it clear that our primary responsibility after completion of our itinerary is to remain out of sight. This suits me just fine. So after each marathon session, we each find a comfortable mattress in the bed section and sleep until halfan hour before the doors unlocked. Looking back on it now, this is the best civilian job I will ever have. Were it not for my burning desire to acquire a higher education, I very well might have been tempted to remainon this laid-back graveyard shift until retirement. However, I am compelled to know more about measure of existence, than to just exist on a shoestring of easy street. Not that I judge those that do, only it not my calling.

Debbie occupies much of my mind and my heart. Now that I am more settled, it is time to drop in on her. The magnitude of this error I cannot even begin to relate properly. To this day, I do not know what scenario I imagined. I suppose it might have been better had I called by telephone first. A woman answers the door resembling Debbie, except many years older. Like Debbie, she looks beaten down, oppressed in a way that makes me feel sorry for her.

"I'm a friend of Debbie from the prayer meeting," I say through the locked screen door.

Her expression changes terse. She turns and calls for someone named Sam. Moments later a burly man appears holding a lead pipe in one hand.

"What do you want?" He demands crossly.

"As I said to your wife, Sir, Debbie and I attend the same campus prayermeetings. I just dropped by to say hello."

"We are Catholic— our daughter is Catholic! We don't want any part of 'holy rollers'," he growls, slamming the door.

I stand there for several minutes shocked and angry. Upon leaving, I see someone peering out of an upstairs window like a trapped bird in a cage. I am certain it is Debbie, but when I wave the specter disappears. Obviously, this first encounter is a disaster. I ask myself what went wrong. Is it the way I dress, my manner of speech, or maybe because I am so obviously ex-military? I later share my perplexity with Hans and his girlfriend during a Sunday brunch.

Hans and I become more acquainted since a violent incident between him and Fred. Hans, a small delicate man, has a shy nature when it comes to conflict. One Sunday morning, Fred, hung-over more than usual, becomes belligerent and starts threatening Hans. I quickly intervene, stepping between the two men. Avoiding a swing of his fist, I grab Fred by the throat, swing the man to the ground, and pen him there.

"You will be still," I command in a loud voice.

After struggling for several moments, the man relaxes, and begs me to release him. I comply, backing cautiously away. Han's gentle nature forgives Fred immediately his indiscretion; adding sternly that if he ever does something like this again, then he will need to find another place to live. After this incident, I take on the role of unofficial bodyguard to my new landlord.

Hans, a religious person, who attends a German church regularly with his girlfriend Pat, asks if I would like to accompany them for morning service. I miss group communion and gladly accept the invitation. The German Church of God, established since 1960, is located on Newport Avenue near Pat's home. To my disappointment, the sermon all in German, a service much drier than my expectation, and altogether lacks vitality of the Holy Spirit. Nevertheless, it is a faithful gathering, so I submit to the moment by faith. The preacher, an animated man with stocky features, often waves his arms wildly like Germany's Consular during World War II. At other times, his demur changes stoic, then emotional, near to crying. At first, I am altogether bewildered, finding the man's voice harsh and angry sounding. Hans, on the other hand, stands translated, as he raises his hands in supplication. I decide to follow his lead and allow myself lifted by the spirit of this place, without judgment or restrictions of the mind. By end of the service, I am certain I understand a little German, receiving the full blessing of God's word with understanding.

Pat also does not speak a word of German, but attends in loyal fellowship with Hans, whom she noticeably wishes to marry. Pat is a voluptuous woman; her round face framed by horned eyeglasses with sparkles. She wears too much makeup and has an obviously carnal nature. Nevertheless, she is nurturing and funny, which makes-up for her several faults. After the church service, we go to her home and share a delightful brunch consisting of smoked salmon with cream cheese on bagels. As so many things in my younger days, this is my first introduction to bagels, lox, and cream cheese. This new adventure of different cuisine remains memorable, and I feel truly blessed to partake of this wonderful delicacy with my new friends.

"My grandmother served this every Sunday." Pat remembers, delicately raising the compliment to her lips, and then adds apologetically: "She was married to a Jew— but of course, I'm not Jewish! My grandparents proclaim lox, cream cheese, and bagels the cuisine of god. I never knew my grandfather very well, because he died when I was young. But he gave to our family an appreciation of life's finer things."

Hans only smiles boyishly, looking at his girlfriend with affection as he consumes his prepared bagel in two hungry bites. After the first taste, I need no further coaxing and follow suit. Fresh bagels and lox are indisputably a delicious combination. Yet, for some reason it will never taste as good as on this day.

After lunch, we watch a special Masterpiece Theater presentation of Goethe's famous play Faust, adapted by the playwright Christopher Marlow. The story is the allegorical tale of a learned doctor, who makes a pact with the devil to live forever in the quest for earthly knowledge and what it ultimately means to exist. The only stipulation is that Faust must make a pact to forfeit his soul when finally he dies. Being a pragmatic man, he sees no virtue of logic in keeping something that has no existential value. A demon named Mephistopheles becomes his constant companion through the centuries of human history fulfilling Faust's every curious and often despicable fantasy, all the while waiting for the moment to snatch his soul to hell. I find the German classic compelling, dark and disturbing. I pity Faust by the end and wish that he might find a clause of escape from the terrible binding contract. To this day, I still remember one line Faust cries out to heaven, as Mephistopheles steps from the shadows to claim his due.

"The blood of Christ flows like a river through the universe, but not a drop to save the soul of poor Faust!"

That night I dream Faust finds mercy, his eternal soul saved by that drop of grace in the blood of Jesus Christ, the Lord Savior of all humankind. I ask myself is my thirst for knowledge different from his? I already know all that I need to know. Why should I choose pursuit of a secular education awarded by an institution established in a principality of rebellious hubris already destined to fall? In my mind, I know Faust only a fictitious character in a story. Nevertheless, my spirit wrestles with something more real, something not altogether of this present earth. Through mortal reason I wish that even the demon Mephistopheles might find a way of repentance; or is choice directionally fixed to heaven eternal?

The following week, I accompany Hans to a Flea Market. I never knew such a thing existed, at first apprehensive as to its legality. Hans assures me that it is all perfectly within the law, and even points out two motor cycle cops stopped briefly to browse. As appealing as some of these deals are, I will be leaving soon for Los Angeles and with little room to spare in my Fairlane. But there are few human events of more interest than a California Flea Market.

Within the first hour, I buy several items I do not need, and do not even remember now if I took them with me. We are on our way to the exit when I see a faded green fifteen-speed bicycle hanging from the open door of a Volkswagen Van suspended from a tarpon porch. A scarecrow with a scruffy grey beard dozes under the shelter in a garden lounge chair.

Through the back open hatch, I see an unmade bed and dirty laundry strewn through the interior. This battered old vehicle is not just a resident of business, but also mobile living quarters.

"Want to buy something?" The man hisses, leaping instinctively to his feet.

"How much for that old bike," I inquire trying to sound nonchalant.

He shrewdly begins scratching his matted beard and his mated grey eyebrows knit thoughtfully together.

"I'll let her go for twenty-five dollars."

I remove the object of interest from its perch for inspection being surprised at how light it is.

"Fifteen," I say. "It seems to need a lot of work."

"Twenty— not a penny less," he haggles.

Hans takes me aside and whispers that this is an Italian racing bike made by Bianchi with aluminum tubing and that twenty dollars a steal. I know nothing about bikes, much less about precision racing bikes. The fact that it is a man's bicycle little deters my plans for it. Finally, the bartering ends, and I agree to pay eighteen dollars.

I spend two days cleaning it up: oil and grease, removing, and retightening nuts, bolts, and cables. By the time I finish, it is lovely beyond my expectation, sleek and shiny, so light that I can lift it with two fingers. I make a test ride up to the Observatory near the peak of Mount Hamilton, a round trip of over twenty miles. It is like riding air, the gearing precise, designed for speed and responsive handling. I fall instantly in love with this virtuosity of engineering achievement. I should have kept it for myself, yet I have already made a selfless vow, determined to impress the woman of my future aspirations.

Debbie's father is mowing the front lawn when I arrive. He stops his circuit and watches me curiously as I lift the bicycle out of the trunk.

"This is for Debbie," I submit humbly.

The man looks over the peace offering and grunts approvingly.

"It's a man's bicycle," he observes, grunting in a way that I interpret as approval.

"Yes sir, but it is so light that I don't think Debbie will mind."

"Wait here, I'll go get Debbie."

He lifts the expensive bike over his shoulder and heads toward the open garage door. This will be the last time I will ever see the Bianchi. Moments later, Debbie appears, wearing her traditional jeans and a halter that only emphasizes the slump of her shoulders. All I can see in the moment is a nubile young woman with whom I wish to spend the rest of my life.

"Why did you come here?" She demands crossly.

"I found a job in San Francisco, and thought that maybe we could see each other."

"My parents don't want me to date anyone not Catholic— and whatever you do don't mention that you are a Vietnam veteran. You have to understand the way they are."

"But I just want us to be friends. I really like you."

Debbie looks worriedly toward the open garage door. Clearly she is dubious of this idea.

"Why don't you join us for Mass this Sunday morning at our church and see how things work out," she sighs, handing me a folded piece of paper with a scribbled address.

It is not all I hoped for, but at least it is something. I shake her extended hand politely and leave. The next Sunday I arrive at the Holy Family Church on a quaint street called Pearl. Relocated during the construction of the 101 Freeway, it is the first cathedral, and oldest Dioceses in San Jose. I am little versed in traditional Catholicism, assuming that the worship in Christ the same in all of Christendom, except for maybe the Germans. I soon realize these Catholics particularly obsessed with the day of lamentation, signifying the crucifixion, mystery importance of the Eucharist, and worship of Mary, the earthly mother of

Jesus. The main service is in Latin, except for the occasional *"Hail Mary"* repeated in unison by the congregation. Besides not understanding anything, something just feels wrong. Instead of praising the living Christ, they seem unable to get past the death of Jesus' earthly sojourn, as though Christ, the Messiah not risen, but still dying on the cross. In many ways, it is like attending a funeral, seeing the shell of the body, with the absence of a soul: a form of religious participation without the substance of joyful resurrection. It bewilders me how Debbie continues to allow herself to participate in this dead ritual after knowing the living movement of the Holy Spirit. At the end of Communion, I locate Debbie and her parents as they make their way toward the parking.

"Did you enjoy Mass," inquires Debbie's father.

"The Lord I know is not dead, but alive." I reply without hypocrisy, a grimace distorting Debbie's pretty face, as does the face of her two parents lording at her side.

"So you disagree with our way of worship," Her father Sam states, assuming an aggressive stance.

"All that I know is that God does not live in a building, nor found through ritual or worship of idols. Sir, I perceive that you know the religion of your youth as taught, but not the Holy Spirit of the living God."

Sam staggers back, the meaning of my words cutting deep into his soul. But these words not mine, but of the spirit. Tact has never been my better quality, and perhaps this time I should have kept my thoughts to myself. But how can I in good conscience allow this man to remain unchallenged in blind piety? Of course, my outburst means that my chances of seeing Debbie again while here next to nil. I glimpse on the face of Debbie and her mother a certain pleasure, a glimmer of something I can only interpret as satisfaction. I will later learn from Debbie that she and her mother have been trying for many months to encourage Sam to attend another church where the spirit alive. After this unpleasant encounter, he will eventually do so and be born again.

"Come— we're leaving!" Sam commands stomping-off toward his parked car.

Debbie tells her mother to go, and that she will follow. The woman smiles back at me, a smile of respect.

"Thank you," Debbie says squeezing my hand warmly. "Father's a stubborn man, but deep down good, and is searching. I'm flying back to Los Angeles in two weeks so I will see you there at the prayer meeting."

I am too stunned to say anything. Everything about this moment and the events leading up to it seems so surreal, as though from pages of a badly written script in a comedy sitcom. Debbie turns to leave, and then gravely adds something that disturbs my conscience even more.

"I have received word that our brother, Daniel, is very ill. I believe the Lord will soon take him. Remember him in your prayers."

I will not see Debbie again for many weeks. I later learn Daniel died that same day of complications from pneumonia. I find myself glad in part that he has finally escaped the bonds of his earthly restrictions; but more saddened by the truth that I once perceived in this beautiful young man a competitor of my lust. I failed him as a brother; failed to love him, as surely he loved me.

That night before retiring I see in the bathroom mirror Sam's arrogant nature reflected in my own soul. Now I understand the real reason I disliked this man from the beginning. He is me, an individual still clinging to false pride. I realize I am not the person I think myself to be. Not enlightened, not a pillar of salvation to the weak; but as an errant child with much to learn. Only I have no idea just how young and immature I really am. Perhaps Daniel knew– so obvious to Debbie and Jim– to all my brothers and sisters then. My weakness of flesh apparent to all, except to me, with still many more fiery trials to endure.

Part Six

Saving Rocky

Mortal Eclipse

Eyes of my father after the eclipse
Deep and penetrating
Born of illusion and disappointment
Light made wings to carry him
Beyond time and shadow before Moses
An infant in slender princess arms
Read in the clock of distant constellations

The circumference of a new moon
Etches delicately among the stars
Wind tip-toeing ever so softly
In nights filled with passion
With dream and with hope |
All things lost and none survive
My father buried in darkness
Sealed to the day of promise

He rises noble
From dust of forgotten centuries
Beyond a river rolled into night
All stand naked before the King of Kings
Scepter of purest gold in his hand
As a lion hunched in royal glory
Given a book opened to the last page
A gaze distant and translucent
Once reflected in zenith of mortal time

$\mathcal{T}$ime grows every day short. In less than three weeks, the first Fall Quarter at UCLA will begin. I give notice to Sears that I am leaving, say goodbye to co-workers and new friends, and begin organizing my few possessions. First on the agenda is to renew my vehicle registration. All California DMVs are interconnected; therefore, it does not matter if I make the annual renewal in Los Angeles or San Francisco County.

One afternoon before work, I locate the nearest office, pay thirteen dollars, and receive a new certificate. As I prepare to exit the office, I notice a rotary index containing all of the registered vehicles. The father I never knew shares my family name, with last known whereabouts somewhere in California. By impulse, I decide to scroll through the records listed by alphabetical name little expecting any results. To my surprise, I find one with my last name, an entry dating back to 1958. It is a mistake to remain in the records for so long, an oversight through years of sorting, somehow missed by each attending clerk. I remain transfixed for several minutes completely awestruck.

Then someone behind me asks if I am finished. Quickly write down the address and stuff it into my shirt pocket. That evening I compose a letter of introduction, requesting contact at the phone number of my present residence. Nearly a week passes. Thursday morning Hans knocks on my door, informing me there is a woman with a foreign accent on the phone asking for me.

At first I think it might be my mother, since a southern accent might sound foreign to my German friend.

"Es esto Sunny?" A frail shaky Spanish voice asks.

"Yes," I reply slowly, since no one but my family still calls me, Sunny; yet sound of this voice altogether alien.

"This your Grandmother," she affirms in broken English.

"My Grandmother--" I am even more confused.

"Uno momento--"

"I'm your father," a male voice blurts at the other end of the line.

I think the excitement of this unexpected possibility infects us both. I will later learn, my father has married and divorced seven times and has sired four children. I am from his first matrimonial union with my mother and siring me as his only male heir-- *or so I believe in the moment.* His other three children- all from different marriages-- are girls. However, decades later, will come revelation of a fifth offspring that no one knew about named Robert.

Robert did not learn until adulthood that his father my father, believing himself the son of another man he never had anything in common with. Ten years younger, he looks me up, and we hit it off as only brothers made of the same fiber can.

However, in this present, I believe my new-found father as curious to know what a man-child of himself might be like, as I am driven to know the progenitor of my genesis. We arrange a rendezvous for that Saturday. He lives somewhere in Malibu and makes plans to drive up the coast alone, with scheduled arrival sometime in the early afternoon.

How does one prepare for a date with one's father? A man I have never seen, except in a faded photo, and know nothing about? I own only one change of clothes considered dress. A pair of new brushed-denim, a plaid shirt, neck open, and rolled at the sleeves. Add to this seventies look a slick pair of artificial leather Italian boots recently purchased from Sears with a sporty side zipper, I am as dressed as ever I will be. This has morphed into my style, a combination of observation and media influence, personal taste, and self-perception. I am sitting in an armchair facing the door, alone, no one else at home. I must have dozed off, because suddenly there is sharp tapping on the front screen door causing me to leap up startled. It is an uncanny moment. Through the mesh of the screen stands a man about my height and build, a matching haircut, neither short, nor long, and dressed as though we have coordinated in advanced what we will wear for this occasion. Of course, he is more sheik and in fashion, with designer jeans, a black silk shirt, Porsche sunglasses, and smooth handmade imported boots. Nevertheless, the style unmistakable, an observance neither of us miss.

We sit and talk for a few minutes. He tells me that he has changed his named to Rocky Belmonte since several years for reasons he prefers not to elaborate, which makes it even more astonishing that I found him at all. Rocky is particularly proud of his new Silver Porsche 914 sport car, which he clarifies as belonging only to him, his wife owning a Bronco. This sounds like vain material bragging to me, but I ignore the inference, not wishing to offend my newfound paternity. He suggests we go out for dinner to a seafood restaurant he knows in San Francisco named *Scoma's Fisherman's Wharf*. I am not very big on seafood at this time of my life, especially since the Lobster incident in Vietnam. Nevertheless, my motto has always been that beggars cannot be choosers. Besides, the food is of less importance, than this opportunity to spend time with my lost father.

Rocky parks his car off Bay Street, and we hop onto the Powell and Hyde trolley to Hyde Pier. From here we walk to Pier 45. The tourist map I acquired on the way only creates more confusion. It shows Pier 45, a massive loading dock for cargo ships, Pier 43 ½, and Pier 41, but omits the listing of Pier 47. Rocky, however, knows where he is going. He has a way about him that I respect in men, no nonsense, no beating around the bush. He does and speaks what he thinks in the moment. This is the way of his generation and of mine-- the way of all ex-military men. In time I will discover that Rocky has his faults, but procrastination not one of them. Also, that I am more like him than I care to admit.

We eventually arrive at an arched wooden sign that reads Fisherman's Wharf. Rocky claims to know one of the two brothers that own the place, a man named Joe, promising I will not be disappointed. The restaurant is small compared to most in this area, discretely located behind a fish processing station. There are several long wooden tables covered by sheet metal, as a gang of seasoned men inside prepare fresh orders mostly for takeout. Rocky asks our waiter if Joe in, and if so to tell him that the Rocco wants to see him. Moments later, a tall weathered man skates from the kitchen sporting a grin of familiar recognition.

"Long time no see," the man says, embracing my father. "I didn't know you had a brother Rocco!"

"This is my son just out of the Marines."

"The Marines— your son— there's a lot I don't know about you my friend. Here's my card, Rocco, call me sometime when I'm not so busy."

Joe then looks in my direction and winks.

"Try the crab cakes. My own mother's recipe made from the finest Dungeness Crabs caught fresh daily. I knew the moment I saw you that you and Rocky related. A son fresh out of the Marines-- who would think you have a son Rocco? You old son of a gun— all these years and you never told anyone."

I can see a glimmer of satisfaction in my father's face. For so many years, I wished that Rudy might look at me this way, to say even once that he is truly proud of me. It makes me feel good to be in the presence of this man-- my father found at last. I find the Scoma's famous crab cakes delicious, and discover I like saltwater fish after all. Rocky orders for him a king lobster, which I still find repugnant. However, in time I will learn again to cherish even this ocean delight. We talk little that day, our communication being less verbal, and more in looks and subtle actions. In a way, we are like two awkward lovers on a first date, only we share a bond greater, a bond of blood and DNA profoundly immutable. Through our table window, we have an unobstructed view of Alcatraz Prison closed since the early 1960s, an austere rock with a walled citadel and a windowed watchtower like an airport control tower.

"When I was a kid, I saw the Bird Man of Alcatraz starring Burt Lancaster," I reminisce with fascination.

I want to say that it was one of Rudy's favorite films, but decide this reference to my stepfather might spoil the moment. Nevertheless, I pleasantly remember that one night clearly in my mind, our family huddled around the TV shelling and eating peanuts. It is one of those rare moments when Rudy truly content, identifying with the character of Robert Stroud, a hardened man humanized by his compassion for a crippled bird. In this story Stroud pursues knowledge of avian behavior spurred by a frustrated desire for freedom, becoming a self-taught scholar cataloging many species of birds. Because of this film, I better understand Rudy's feeling of being in a cage with no future of escape.

Rocky does not say anything, but continues to eat his meal without even a glance at the notorious prison. This barren rock jutting in the middle of the bay less than a mile and a half from the mainland represents the incarceration of many men with notorious reputations, such as Al Capon, Doc Barker, and Floyd Hamilton, brother to Raymond Hamilton, a member of the ruthless Bonnie and Clyde gang. Because of sharks, the cold bay waters, and treacherous currents, no one on the official record ever escaped during it twenty-nine years as a human kennel. Although many tried, most end in fatality. I see something in Rocky's eyes, something angry and disturbing, which makes me wonder if he has more than casual knowledge of this dreadful prison institution.

After eating, we walk along the sidewalks and through hidden lanes of San Francisco, a city undergoing transformation, reborn in the night, becoming another metropolis, shedding into a beast of dazzling light. Beacons on the Bay Bridge point direction across the harbor to Oakland; the Golden Gate as a celestial pathway to Sausalito. In the opposite direction rises Coit Tower, standing erect among a twinkling array that surrounds Nob Hill, and then flows down into China Town. Perched demonically in the distance is heart of the financial district. Here also crouches the newly constructed Transamerica Pyramid dominating the skyline like a one-eyed Gargoyle and reminder to a fleeting world of the true source of power here. And as bright as these illuminations are, darkness prevails in this Babylonian city moving invisibly.

Rocky and I stop at a nightclub and have a drink. He quickly realizes that I will not be a drinking buddy, nor will I participate in the kind of pursuit he might have liked. Past midnight, he drops me home with the promise that we will see each other again soon once I get settled in Los Angeles.

"Here's my home phone and address. If my wife Inez answers just say, you are my son."

I watch as the sleek sport car flashes down the street, the distinctive German designed engine whining into the night long after the lights have vanished. It is so like the pages of a fairy tale that I look up into the night sky and wonder if this day part of some extraordinary dream.

$\mathcal{D}$ay before my scheduled departure, Hans arrives with a proposition. He remembers from previous conversations that my stepfather a professional painter, and mistakenly believes I inherit at least some of these skills. Also aware my first Quarter at UCLA begins in two weeks, Hans desires to give me the opportunity to make a few extra dollars.

"I will pay you $75.00 to paint my kitchen," he proposes, producing two cans of cheap Acrylic white paint. "Do you think two gallons enough?"

"Yes," I reply, heartily accepting the contract.

The truth of the matter is that I never did any actual contract painting in my life. One summer Rudy got me a job as a sander on one of his company projects. The closest I ever got to painting is the occasional trim touch-up. Then I fell ten feet off of a scalpel on the third day. Even though unhurt, he decides I am too clumsy to work near construction, sending me home never to return. Nevertheless, for as long as I can remember I watched Rudy complete masterpieces with flawless attention to every detail. Once again I overestimate my ability and like all laymen--I think how hard could it be?

I spend the rest of Saturday afternoon packing my car and begin the task of preparing the kitchen by moving everything out of the way immediately after supper. The original color, a dark dirty yellow, is a 1950s style, dripping with years of grease and requiring a laborious wash with STP. It is past nine o'clock by the time I begin applying the first coat. I have not taken in account the cabinet interiors or window trim. What I thought would require only a few hours, becomes an all-night affair. Just before sunrise, I tiredly dab the last drop of paint on the final rib of a windowpane. Mission accomplished, I proudly step back and survey the gleaming white finish. Then tiredly collapse into bed.

At half past ten, I stagger out of my room and find Hans sitting on a barstool surveying the finished kitchen in stunning apprehension. This is when I see the truth. In the light of day, the white has changed to a pale uneven yellow with hardened droplets hanging from the ceiling and dripping vertically along the walls. Every pane of glass smeared with brush marks between the ribs of each panel, and with droplets pooling along the bottom sill.

"I guess the paint was not a very good quality," I remark incredulously.

Hans turns, looks at me, and begins laughing hysterically.

"The paint," he remarks in his heavy German accent, tears in his eyes, "yes— it is the paint!"

Hans cooks us both breakfast, as I attempt with little success to clean the hardened Acrylic from my skin and hair. In final frustration, I resolve to cut clumps from my head; and even then, it will be weeks before removing it all.

"I don't understand," I apologize; "last night it looked fine."

"I guess if I keep the curtains drawn, it won't be so bad." Hans sighs optimistically, and then heaves again into hysterical laughter. "I don't think you should follow in your father's footsteps. Not all are born to the same purpose."

Realizing I must be in Los Angeles by the next morning to register on Campus, Hans pays me anyway, and in full. I still feel touched whenI think back on this man's selfless generosity and good sense of humor, smiling each time I remember the shocked look on his face that bright California morning. I can only imagine his real thoughts as revelation of sunlight streams through curtainless windows to emphasize the many imperfections. Often, I wonder if he learned to live with it that way or if he eventually sands out the rough spots and applies a second coat. Hans is not very handy, so Idoubt he will ever do it himself. Nor is it likely either of his other tenantsup to the task. In my own defense, I wish to point out that even though I feel a little guilty taking the money, the paint really was poor quality, as well as the advertised one-coat application somewhat misleading. I did the best I knew how with what I had to work with, except that my implied ability perhaps more than a little inflated. We both learn important lessons by this comical experience. Never make assumptionsabout inherited abilities.

Taking the Interstate 5 south, it is nearly a straight course from Santa Clara County to Los Angeles. Over four hundred miles of semi-arid, sparsely populated terrain of ranchland wilderness. There are the occasional vineyards, less famous than the fertile Napa and Sonoma Valley, California's most notable wine producers. Every few miles there is a commercial ad for an organized wine-tasting tour. I decide to take a detour advertising a pass to Simeon Valley, location of Hearst Castle, a former residence of the famous newspaper tycoon, Randolph Hearst. Believing the attractionnear, I entertain this might be interesting. However, because the pass road narrow and winding, traffic congested, I quickly abandoned theendeavor, realizing this will take me many hours out of my way toward the coast. I will save this excursion for another time.

It is late evening by the time I arrive at the UCLA campus. Grabbing a quick bite to eat and refreshing myself at a nearby gas station toilet, I park on campus and sleep the night in my car. Registration day is the most hectic of the university year. Everyone lost, running from building to building, asking directions, paying fees, and getting class itineraries for the first quarter of academia. Late afternoon, I conclude by stopping at the campus bookstore. English One requires an anthology the size of two standard bricks stacked together; Beginning Psychology (two slabs of hardcover textbooks); and a heavy slab containing an unabridged Larousse French Dictionary. Add to this collection several smaller books of recommended reading. What do I know? I take them all, not realizing that many of these expensive volumes available used. Class officially begins in one week, which means finding another apartment imperative. Two days later, I rent a single-room basement dwelling near Wilshire Boulevard a few blocks from the V.A. Cemetery, which includes utilities and easy access to campus. At least it offers more space than the front seat of my Ford. The next important item on the list is a Smith Corona typewriter, haggled for seven dollars at a Yard Sale. The "O" looks like a "U", the "T" misaligned, and even though more than one Professor frowns at the inked corrections, I never receive an official reprimand. You can imagine my celebration two years later when I find an IBM electric at another Yard Sale in almost mint condition for only forty-five dollars! I will consume a diet of canned Pork & Beans for a month to pay for this fantastic piece of equipment, a technological leap equivalent of going from a tricycle to a Moped.

There is something indescribable and exciting about the beginning days at an institute of higher learning. Everything is so perplexingly new, yet timeless, as though peering into a looking glass spanning centuries. The very halls smell of classical knowledge, retaining the soul of every generation that has passed along these corridors. I feel a sense of undeserving honor to be among them. My old fear of failure begins to resurface. Will I be able to maintain the necessary grade point average? Can I compete with these many minds of elite society cultivated and pruned for this pinnacle of higher education? I am no longer that day dreaming little boy, who only wants to be left alone, overwhelmed by thoughts of the greater world. I am now an adult, hungry for knowledge, and prepared to study all night. Every night if that what it takes! A convictioneasier said than done.

I manage to secure two on-campus jobs. The first begins at 7:00 A. M. in the morning as a canteen server near Pauley Pavilion. The second work shift begins after 5:00 P. M. at a campus cafeteria outside of Royce Hall, lasting three hours. On lite days, I have periods in between allowing intervals of study. When there is a campus event, I slave exhaustively from the beginning to the end of my shift, without a moment to crack open a book. This first quarter willprove the worst, by failing my first English class causing my grade point average to tumble below 2.8, based on an accusation of plagiarism by my English professor.

For the record, I did not intentionally plagiarize. Obtaining the services of a tutor to help me with a midterm paper on the famous Old English tale, Sir Gawain and the Green Knight, I allow more dictation to the final draft than I should have. I actually compose the entire midterm, only chose to integrate many of the constructive suggestions of my tutor. How could I have known that most of her suggestions based on notes taken from a standard extrapolation of the text? In fact, my tutor insists that I use many of her ideas verbatim. Even going so far as to suggest that by not doing so will only guarantee failure. I receive a satisfactory B+ on the written midterm exam, but a failing grade on the final exam taken in class based on the first English epic hero Beowulf. This in-class submission composed so poorly in comparison to my midterm paper, my professor goes back and scrutinizes my first paper more thoroughly.

"You blatantly plagiarized!" He scolds sternly from behind the safe barrier of his paper-cluttered desk, looking like a crippled bird because of a lame arm since birth.

"I swear I did not," I defend.

"Even if you didn't, then it is obvious that the same person could not have written these two papers. My twelve year old daughter can compose more coherently."

He then proceeds to show me word-by-word comparisons from a study guide of at least six identical complete sentences, all being those of my tutor. I try to remain calm, explaining that my tutor insisted I use the final composition and that I believed the source her own ideas.

"As for Beowulf, I simply froze under the pressure. It was my first timed-exam of the quarter, and my mind just went blank."

I then proceed to tell him that I did understand the symbolic nature of the Christ-like hero. How this ancient Gaelic story influenced the root cultural foundation of Anglo Saxony that is the source of today's spoken and written English. I desperately sense that this professor of academic accolade particularly devoted to the early Celtic saga depicting a greater- than- life hero, named Beowulf, against Grendel, an evil demonicmonster. I appeal to this man's intellect and his cradled affection toward western literary supremacy. Pleased with my digestion of his first reading assignment, he awkwardly tosses the two papers into the trash basket with his good arm.

"Okay," he says, "but the failing grade stands. You will need to work very hard next quarter to bring up your average." Adding in an Ivy League tone, "and what I said about my daughter writing better is the truth."

I learn two important lessons from this unfortunate event: never allow someone else to write anything for you, and never underestimate the venomous resolve of a University Professor with tenure. First Quarter, and I am already on probation. I will remain on probation for the next two years with a struggling grade-point average. Yet, I am determined not to give up, remembering the Marine Corps motto, *'When the going gets tough, then the tough get going'*! I do not say I had no fear of failure, only that failure not an option. I believed then, as now, that God capable of delivering through all things and will always show me where to go.

I begin to perceive the concept of academia also a curse of hierarchal blindness shared by most in the field of higher learning. In this world it takes more than one person to change a light bulb: an expert to erect a ladder, another to remove the old bulb, and still another professional to screw-in the new one. Although university has a great deal to offer, common sense practicality is not one of its better attributes. It encourages evaluation of others according to their status of degree, grade-point averages, and specialty in a given pursuit. I am determined not to be blinded by influence of prevailing myopia.

I try more than once to connect with the woman of my future dreams. Continuing to attend church every Sunday, I look for her, but rarely see Debbie anymore. Something has changed between us since Daniel's death. She is a last year senior, while I am only beginning an undergraduate program. Debbie now lives alone in an apartment off campus. I run into her one day between classes and we connect in a good way. I volunteer to help her arrange, and rearrange the furniture, put up shelves and curtains, and all those odds and ends, where women need a little extra brawn to accomplish. I think, also, she feels sorry for me, with desire to impress that we need not to be engaged to share in a fellowship. She emphasizes this by giving me a present of something she calls friendship pudding, a jar containing fermenting fruit kept alive by adding a quantity of sugar every so often. The concept is to allow the fruit to grow until it expands beyond the limits of the container, then transfer half into a second container and pass it on to someone you know. I do not particularly like the taste and secretly toss it in the garbage.

All is going well, or at least I imagine it is. I drop in regularly to see Debbie over the next several weeks, until one night I express my undying devotion. She looks at me without expression, her large cobalt blue eyes drilling into my unrequited heart.

"How do you know that God does not want us to be together?"

"I think I would know," Debbie asserts calmly. "Why don't we pray together?"

We hold hands and close our eyes. Then far away, I can hear the sound of her voice-- not her voice only-- but a message from the Holy Spirit.

"I perceive you are in a snare of darkness bound by confusion," the voicenow that of an angel. "It is a growing mass of confusion, tentacles of desire to ensnare your soul. Thus says the Lord, you must turn from this bitterness now. Allow the light of salvation to fill the darkness with light of joy unspeakable!"

I witness this mass of darkness clearly in my spirit: strands of tangled emotions and fettered passions. The vision ugly, terrifying-- it is me! The old man of the flesh: that part I still have not let go of! Paralyzed, I stand up mechanically and leave without even saying goodnight. The naked truth exposed. There is a beast that lurks still in the shadows of my unconscious self. I feel altogether ashamed that my lust exposed.

Yes, through eyes of the spirit, I see what Debbie has seen all along. I do notknow the chimera in my heart that night or even if that heart my own. I drive slowly, trying desperately to get this bound image out of my mind. At an intersection near the place I call home, the dashboard panel lights go dark and the car stalls, a billow of grey smoke filling the interior cabin. I leap out and pop open the hood. It is a barbeque! A gas line has broken, spewing fuel and igniting. I tear off my jacket and try futilely to put outthe flames.

Fortunately, a fire truck arrives within minutes, extinguishing the fire and limiting the damage only to the engine compartment. I have the car towed to the nearest Ford dealership, walking the rest of the way home. Upon entering my apartment, I collapse on the floor and begin sobbing as a little boy caught in a secret act. Then gripped by another passion, I explode into a sudden violent rage, splitting the dining table in half and punching holes into the walls. I am glad that no one from one of the adjacent apartments comes to check on me. In those days, a lot of Vietnam veterans returned with anger issues, and people have accepted over time that avoidance of confrontation the better course of action. After regaining self-control and surveying the damage, I pray earnestly to never again be infected by that spirit.

The next morning I call my insurance company and discover to my benefit that my coverage includes fire. It will be at least three weeks before the completion of the reparations. In the interim, I buy a 50cc Honda motorcycle belonging to the son of a woman I meet one evening while accompanying Ron on a night outing. It seems the Lord has impressed upon him that his ex-wife will not be returning and that it time to move on. I am not at first too keen on the idea of going out with him on these worldly safaris.

"All things are lawful to those who act in faith," my friend paraphrases scripture, wishing to convince me to be his wingman on an occasional Saturday night excursion. "Little brother it's time you let go of these immature emotions for that sweet little thing in your church. If the Lord wanted you two together, then you would be together What God brings together, stays together, and what he makes asunder, remains asunder. God made his apostles to go boldly out into the world; not to remain hidden under a bushel of fear and indecision."

Ron, married since he was eighteen, admits himself less than faithful in his younger years during long hauls east. But he never actually dated, and feels shy to go out hunting alone.

"The Lord has shown me my heart," I say, sharing a little of the witness with him. "I do not wish to serve that old man of sin ever again.

You are my friend, but I am afraid of losing my way again."

"Remember the parable of the man that received one talent and hid it in the ground for fear of what his master might do if he lost it. Faith without works is dead, my friend. If you believe God has prepared something for you, then it is up to you to reach out: all things given to those who act by faith. This is the wilderness you must cross."

What my friend says makes sense. I have become afraid, uncertain of the magnitude meaning of my spiritual revival since the Holy Spirit first coursed through my mortal being lifting me above all principalities. Recently I have witnessed within me a cripple: a thing undernourished that has been subdued, and not allowed to mature. Had the man Abraham remained secure in the city of Ur, he would not have become the patriarch of communion with the almighty God. Had the prophets not allowed themselves to be led by God's Spirit, then the testament of repentance never would have reached the minds and hearts of the people. Had Christ not submitted to the cross in human weakness, humanity would be lost without any hope of eternal salvation. It is as a light that clicks on in my consciousness. If I am to become a true man of God, I have much growing up to do.

Part of me wishes to remain in the womb of religion, fed milk and honey; but something greater compels me to step out into a spiritual wasteland with only the faith provided to me in the company of my new friend. I have a vision we are two prophets called from different flocks, and sent on a mission in collaboration.

"Little brother," he confirms in his base baritone voice, "the Lord has brought us together in the same circumstances of the flesh. It is not by accident that we share a similar experience of rejection and conviction. By his strength, we will become strong; by his will we will pass through to the promised land."

We have both grown a little misogynistic over the past months, unaware that we are men still in much need of healing. Together we begin a segregated journey into lairs of worldly shadow, with only a pillar to guide us. What we will discover twisted passages in need of being straightened. But this journey through desert place had to be made to refine weakness within: a trek much longer than either of us ever expected. I will not again see Debbie, deciding it better to stop going to the on-campus prayer meetings.

My church in Long Beach moves from the abandoned schoolhouse and into a church at Forest Lawn cemetery. The building rented for our use after the local morning service of another congregation. At least here, the true wellspring of life continues to refresh my soul, renewing the thirst of my faith. Faith is all I have left, as I prepare to embark upon a pilgrimage that will take me far from my new family. I little realize in the moment my role of emissary being prepared for a mission bearing testament of extreme consequence; this traverse already begun.

*I*t will be the beginning of my second quarter by the time

I connect with Rocky again. I call him during the Quarter break after finishing my final exams. I planned to contact him sooner, only those first twelve weeks so overwhelming that I find little occasion for any social engagements. He expresses the usual disappointment, but seems pleased   that I am finally established and have not forgotten him. I suppose I should have called out of etiquette, but choose the wiser course not to start something that might lead to distraction. Now I am ready to engage.

Late November he invites me to his Malibu home for a traditional Thanksgiving Dinner. I omit to tell Rocky about the engine fire of my car, and he seems a little surprised when I arrive on the 50cc motorbike. I meet Inez, his latest young wife, his two-year-old daughter, Elena, and his beloved faithful companion Babe, a mottled-color Pit Bull, spanning four of his previous failed marriages. Inez is beautiful and charming, a true California blonde, only a few years older than me. I find myself consciously resisting the oedipal urge to see this vital woman in any other way than my father's wife. This first evening goes well. It is a unique experience to eat Thanksgiving turkey outside in the open air overlooking the calm ocean under a clear canopy of stars. The full moon appears as a spectacular guardian dragging a shimmering net through the sparkling water. I imagine a myriad of dancing silver fish tangled in a shower of light, so serene a setting we speak little huddled around the dimly lit table, each thinking thoughts. Compared to this natural wonder hovered above the Pacific expanse, words fail, proving insufficient to describe what no human thought, past or present, capable to fully comprehend. It is the clockwork phenomenon constrained in present value, a grandeur taken for granted, witnessed by every generation. The recorded passage of this stellar traveler a reminder of mortality, as it passes unerringly through a gateway into eternity glimpsed only in moment reflection.

"You have a beautiful home, and a beautiful view," I remark, breaking the long silence between us.

"We like it," Inez agrees, hugging her husband's shoulder. "The only problem is that we live so far from anything."

I do not say to her that personally I consider this isolation an asset. A glint in my father's eyes reveals that he, too, prefers the solitude. This is another shared attribute, our minds growing closer in silence.

"Yes, I have everything a man could want," Rocky states contentedly.

"What good is it to possess the whole world, if one should lose his soul?"

The words just pop out, as though spoken by someone else. I know who that someone else is. A long uncomfortable silence passes between us. It quickly becomes obvious to me that the precision of the Holy Spirit has pierced my father and his wife to the heart. I attempt to do damage control, but the more the conversation continues the more adversarial and defensive Rocky and his wife.

It is near midnight by the time I say my cordial goodbyes and return home. I feel altogether perplexed as to what has happened. Traversing the empty Pacific highway, less than a mile from their home, I round the blind point of Leo Carrillo, a knoll of land where the headlight beams swallowed into an ocean expanse. Inexplicably, I am jolted with jubilation, overshadowed by the Holy Spirit, no longer in temporal value. Spontaneously, I begin praising God in the spirit, a feeling of joy mixed with apprehension, followed by a peace surpassing understanding. This vision I will keep to myself through curious reflection.

Ron and I continue our Saturday night excursions. Looking back on it, I suppose we appear an awkward pair to the women we meet. There spans a decade of difference between us. Ron is a large husky man; whereas, I stand short in contrast, both young and with virile expectations. This obvious difference actually turns into a blessing, more than once to sustain our friendship. The women attracted to his type are rarely attracted to me, and vice versa. Seldom are we in direct competition. Gradually, I begin drinking again, not like before, but enough to fit in. My newly acquired favorites are Seagram VO and Courvoisier Cognac, both drinks I manage to nurse artfully for hours with an air of sophistication. In the world of bars and brothels, appearance is everything: a man able to hold his liquor somehow more appealing to a certain breed of woman, than a tea totter. I suppose I should have recognized the author's deceptive signature; but youthful pride easily blinded by the momentary spell of silver lining, oblivious to the greater design of the web.

During the last two weeks of December, I acquire a part-time job delivering mail in Beverly Hills for the U. S. Post Office, due to heavier than usual holiday workload. The hours long, but pays well, and the work easy for a young man in his prime. It also introduces me to how the wealthier classes really live. Bored married housewives in chiffon gowns and slippers often appear at the door with offerings of cookies and milk, and on more than one occasion seductive invitations into their parlors. But I am on the clock, my mind still too pure to consider having an affair with a married woman. Although, I admit there were times when the temptation almost irresistible to the shining silver hooks used by these scantily clad sorceresses to lure my youthful fantasies. But neither wind, nor rain, or snow will prevent me from my duty as a U. S. Postman. The seductive charm of these Sirens, tugs at my young flesh, like I imagine whispers of Dalia in the ear of mighty Samson. And like Samson I will not always see so clearly, or remain always unwavering. God knows my weakness and has in course alreadyprepared a way of escape.

I arrive in the Beverly Hills local post office tired after a long day delivering mail. It is the last Friday of my employment, which I accept with mixed emotion. I receive a paycheck for more than four hundred dollars. This is equivalent of three months' rent, plus change. I race dangerously along rush traffic Wilshire Boulevard in an attempt to make it to my bank before closing. The next day is Saturday, Christmas Eve, which means I will be broke until the following Tuesday when everything reopens.

It is dusk, that time of day when things blend into an unreal twilight, the sprinkle of faded holiday lights beginning to appear like awakening spirits. My mind is five miles down the road. Driven by purpose lacking common sense, I lean on the throttle pushing the small 50cc engine to the limit. It happens suddenly, as in a dream, reminder that time a clock, actions the consequential pattern of motive reaction.

The driver of an older model Black Eldorado slams on the brakes suddenly, because of the bubble light and screeching siren of a police cruiser on the opposite side of Wilshire. I automatically swerve right, my left leg catching on the dangerous projectile of an ornate fin tip protruding from the back ofthat year model, knocking me off my seat. However, I continue to holdon to the handlebar, my body stretched out limply. Somehow, I squeeze between the Eldorado and another car parked on the right, bouncing uncontrollably the full length of the two vehicles like a rag doll in the hands of an angry child. Shooting out of control on the other side, I am the stuntman Evel Kninevel in the air, committed to a spectacular feat. Only this no stunt; nor am I him.

Everything turns in slow motion, overshadowed by a minute perception of a universal connection spanning more than local time and space. I watch the Honda rotate sluggishly in front of me. No sound, no other motion, time itself slowed-down to deadened quiet. I land abruptly on an island beside a newlyplanted tree. Instantly, time rushes forward again, strangers standing around, some asking questions, only I am unable to comprehend their meaning. Then, a Police Officer looms over me holding a flashlight shining in my eyes.

"Are you all right?" He demands, placing his finger in front of my nose and moving it back and forth.

"Yes," I reply firmly and attempt to standup.

Excruciating pain seizes the left side of my body, so intense that I nearly pass out. The next thing I know I am inside an ambulance, being rushed to the nearby UCLA Hospital. Upon arrival my tight-fitting jeans are sliced open on the injured side by one of the attendants and then rushed into X-ray. This is particularly tragic, considering I had just bought them a week earlier. The examination reveals no major fractures. However, my entire left leg has turned black with bruising from the foot up to the ribcage.

"You are lucky, no broken bones," a young intern informs me. "But you are going to be in a lot of pain. Contusions this bad almost always results in a break. Your bones must be hard as rock. You have a lot to be thankful for."

I do not feel thankful. By now, all the banks are closed,   my motorcycle wrecked, me injured and held hostage in a hospital. My immediate priority is to get out of this place, or else all my hard-earned money will go to paying medical expenses. Against Doctor's advice, I check myself out and arrange for a taxi to take me home. Here, there is some misunderstanding. Being cashless, I make arrangements for the taxi transport to be added to my student hospital bill. By now the pain medication has worn off and I am beginning to feel waves of the promised agony. After helping me inside my apartment the taxi driver extends his hand for his due, refusing to leave.

"The hospital will reimburse you."

"You owe me five dollars," he demands with an aggressive Russian accent, stepping aggressively forward.

"I told you the hospital will pay you!"

"No, you pay now," he again demands in a tone becoming even more agitated.

I try to impress on the fellow that I have only an un-cashed check. Realizing the nature of the standoff, I grab a jar of coins consisting mostly of pennies and shove them into his chest.

"Now get out of my apartment!"

I doubt there was more than a few dollars in there, but better that than nothing at all. And I am in no mood for further conversation. I think he realizes this as well. Cursing belligerently in Russian, he hesitantly turns and departs, slamming the door behind him.

Hobbling to my bed, I begin the task of peeling-off the remaining rag of my new blue jeans, and then pass-out in agony.

It is still dark. I awaken in unimaginable torture, needing to use the bathroom. However, when I attempt to move, the pain agonizing, pinning me paralyzed against the mattress. My injured leg swollen to twice normal, altogether black, and looks as something dead. Even the slightest movement is excruciating, the pain pinning me between a solid wall to the right, and the throbbing specter of a dead appendage anchoring left side of my body. I keep saying to myself-- 'you can do it, Marine— *you will do it!*'

In the end, I relieve myself where I lay, and manage finally to doze into a tenuous sleep haunted by fitful images more tangible than mere dreams. I lose all concept of time. Because the curtains drawn, I miss bearing if it is morning or evening, conscious only of darkness to twilight and descent into deeper shadow. On several occasions, the phone located on a table near the door rings incessantly. Each time my whole body jerks, causing intense spasms of lingering pain. I know it is Ron. He is the only real friend I have and is probably wondering why I have not called him over the Christmas holiday. I begin to realize just how desperate my situation. Without water and food, I will die here as surely as if stranded in the bowels of a cave. I reason that since I have no broken bones, my limited incarceration just a question of pain. I need to be stronger than that pain and somehow separate the mind of necessity from the prison of this body. In the dimness I can see the outline of a black engorged stump, once my leg, but no longer a functional part of me. Now it has become nuisance of something dead, but still attached. I know what I must do-- *what I will do!*

"Okay, Marine this is it," I say again. "Either you face your pain like a man, or you die in your own shit!'

This first attempt I nearly blackout and collapse back in nauseating agony. I lay there for what could have been an hour waiting for the anguish to subside. Realizing there no end, only less intense, I determine once and for all the thing I must do.

"Help me Jesus! Make me stronger than I am!" I scream out in prayer.

What I do next is without exception a challenge of mental acceptance greater than anything previous. First, I attempt to roll over on my right side, assaulted by waves of pulsating anguish. Therefore, I devise a more frontal assault. Taking a deep breath, I twist, simultaneously lifting my bad leg using both my arms, and lunge back-first on the floor. I am certain they heard the howl of my tortured screams throughout the complex and in the adjacent building, but know better than to come. Once my mind clears, I realize only half my objective achieved. I am back-first on the floor, but both my legs still suspend on the edge of the bed. Using my right foot, I gingerly attempt to lift the dead weight, hoping to ease it to the floor. This first attempt turns to failure, racked by another wave of nausea. My injury has become a nemesis to my will to survive. I begin to reason with the flesh of my body, as though it exist apart, analyzing the present predicament with detached candor.

"What is pain?" I begin the discourse. "Is it just sensory transmission along network of nerve endings to communicate information to the brain? I reason it is a warning system to protect against existential harm: an automated built-in mechanism to protect the organism from greater harm. Yet-- I demand-- is pain greater than the present need to survive?"

I know the pain real, but also know this not something fatal. Nothing is broken- -nothing that will not get better in time. The solution becomes clear in my mind! I must transcend the moment. Past events have brought me to this place, but the future is where I must go. I will endure by placing my mind and soul into the future, not the anticipation of present dilemma. I hold my breath and with calm precision lift the dead body and lower it to the floor. I see flashes of light pulsating in darkness, the howling of an animal far away, an animal once me, now a thousand years in the past. Once my mind clears, I lift my torso and begin to scuttle backward toward the bathroom using only my arms. I need water, the bathtub being my best bet because it is low to the floor. Time has no meaning, only progress to the immediate objective matters. I need hydration. Now I am in control. I am master over instincts of my body. Above all other considerations, I must have water! After an eternity, I reach the faucet and turn on the cold tap, lapping the life-energizing water through parched lips. It is the most refreshing draught I have ever tasted, filtering down into the withered trunk of my body, replenishing to the soles of my feet; and I can actually feel the fluid tingling into my toes, reviving even to my dead leg. I next find a container of Epson Salt kept under the sink, something Jean instructed me always to keep on hand. Next I fill the tub with tepid water, adding the salt by the handfuls. By now, I am beginning to get used to thepain. Not that the pain no longer there, only somehow less dominating than before. I am now master of my body, and captain of my soul. The rest I place in the hands of my Lord and Savior in a notable day when I will slip from the garment of this mortal. With much difficulty, I manage to remove the remainder of my clothes and pull myself screeching into the shallow basin. Here I remain for over an hour, replenishing the solution with warmer water and adding more salt. The pain somehow changed-- still pain, but less agonizing. I begin moving my toes slowly and even manage to flex the blackened knee ever so slightly.

I discover that to get out of this cauldron slightly more challenging than getting in. Now I just bit my lips and growl, rather than scream. After another hour just to dry off, I wrap myself in a blanket and call my friend and brother in the Lord.

"I had a motorcycle accident and injured my leg," I explain embarrassed. "I can't leave the apartment and haven't eaten anything for days."

"You hang on little brother, I'm on my way."

Within the hour, Ron arrives as an angel of God carrying a bag of provisions, accompanied by his eldest daughter Ronda and younger son Larry, which he has granted custody over the holidays. I am still on the floor when they rush in, moving like a worm inside a cocoon. Fortunately, the door unlocked. I can only imagine what his two children must have thought to see the image of something less anticipated by their young human expectation; witness to a creature crawling along the floor of a darkened lair polluted with the acrid odor of urine mixed with foulness of feces. They say nothing, but I can see the bewildered disgust in their innocent young eyes.

"My Lord— what have you done to yourself?"

Of course, the question rhetorical; Ron as shocked as the kids. He helps me to a chair and immediately changes the sheets for fresh ones. He then prepares a plate consisting primarily of a turkey drumstick, leftover dressing and gravy with a side of potato salad. Also is a loaf of bread, a few canned goods, and containers of more leftovers.

"This should tide you over until tomorrow," he says. "I'm taking home your sheets and what's left of your clothes to wash."

Before departing, Ron goes to the garbage area behind the building and returns with the broken leg of a dining table approximately four feet in length. I stare at this unusual staff somewhat perplexed, then its purpose dawns on me.

"This will help you get around until that leg of yours gets better."

Rhonda and Larry only stare at me in wide-eyed amazement, each sheepishly hanging their heads, as they edge toward the door behind their father, uttering embarrassed mumbles of goodbye.

"I am pleased to meet you both." I say with measured gratitude.

"Your Dad is good man. I hope you two will always remember that."

Three days have already passed since my accident; three days as a journey through Dante's *Purgatorio*. This evening, at least, I eat as a king of the earth and drink my fill from the kitchen faucet thanks to the aid of the improvised walking stick. The next morning I call Ron and tell him he does not need to return right away and to spend the time with his two children. The next day, and the day after, I lie out under the California sun and allow the healing miracle of nature to penetrate. I know now and without doubt I will be okay again.

My car is still at the Ford dealership being repaired, only delayed by a back-ordered part. However, the police have dropped off my Honda, depositing it in the alley behind my building. One of my neighbors has kindly rolled it into my parking area. I never found out the name of this neighbor; only remain grateful for the compassion exhibited by a stranger for a stranger. Except for several deep scratches and a broken turn signal, the overall condition of the bike not as bad as I thought it might be. My first impression upon straddling the seat is a feeling of irrational terror. It suddenly seems larger than I remember, more imposing-- yes, even dangerous! A few days later I decide the time has come to kick start the machine to life. After only a few thrust with my good leg, the 50 cc engine rumbles to life feeling like something untamed and dangerous moving viciously beneath my rest. I feel an all familiar terror begin to resurface, overshadowing me with dread. Part of me wants to get off and never get back on again.

"You can do this— you will do this!" I command, bravely engaging first gear with a toggle of my right foot.

Before I can release the clutch, I begin sweating profusely, experience difficulty to breathe, and imaginethe world around me collapsing into a tightening tunnel. Shutting off the engine, I retire quickly into the security of my apartment, refusing even to look at this menacing beast again for the rest of that day.

Winter quarter begins in less than a week; my Honda the only affordable way I have to get there. Also, I still have my un-cashed check from the Post Office. Were it not for Ron's generosity, I might surely have starved. I am too ashamed to share with my friend the irrational depth of my fear. There are just some things a man must do alone. The next morning I am determined to tame the monster, even if that monster kills me.

"By the same power that Samson slew a thousand with the jawbone of an ass, I will overcome this legion of my fear!" I swear, mounting the small motor cycle again.

This time I do not think what I will do; do not allow my mind to be intimidated by the belligerent rumblings and vibrations. Once more slipping the foot peddle into gear, I slowly release the clutch and am off. The thing lurches erratically forward, threatening my resolve. But I am determined not to be dissuaded. I slowly accelerate to the end of the alley, turn around and travel back to the opposite extreme. I make this circuit for the better part of an hour, never exceeding first gear. Gradually my confidence returns. I begin to feel once more in control. Then I go from first to second, then into third gear. By end of the afternoon, I am Beowulf again-- champion over shadows! And Grendel, the monster of my fear slain forever through metaphor.

The following Monday, I boldly enter traffic on Wilshire Boulevard, navigating cautiously toward campus. I feel particularly venerable, until after the left turn onto Veteran Avenue that runs along the memorial of the Los Angeles National Cemetery. This only fitting since I am always at peace here, preferring to spend many noon lunches studying in this necropolis of fallen brothers.

Premiere of class after Christmas break, I do look the part of a wounded soldier with my camouflage jacket, jungle boots, and worn jeans, hobbling stiffly from class to class. Now I have a renewed appreciation for those classic heroes and villains lurching in ancient halls enshrouded through academia. I have buried another demon within the catacombs. The imagined powerof this principality of paralyzing fear dissolved into future light.

*T*wo weeks into winter Quarter and I receive an eviction notice from my landlord. Apparently, my Honda has leaked oil on the pavement in the parking area. At least this is the excuse. I locate acheaper apartment near the Santa Anta in West Los Angeles, twentyminutes from campus as the crow flies on the big highway. This means I need a larger motorcycle: one capable of California interstate Freewayspeeds. I sell the Honda 50 for seventy-five dollars more than I paid for it, and find a Honda CL 350cc near my new apartment for sell at twohundred. Now this is power! It can accelerate from zero to sixty in less than a minute, which proves ideal for the California speedways. By now, I am fully confident of my ability to handle the machine, an illusion born of youth and lack of experience. There I times I feel indestructible, mixedwith the knowledge that death of the flesh but a mere transition. Often I am reckless, and therefore subject to correction.

The new apartment comes furnished with a stove and refrigerator. Only the refrigerator has a defective compressor, barely able to keep things cool. The building owner, an overweight Jewish man named Murray Small, offers to reduce the rent by five dollars a month if I supply my own icebox. I accept, considering that I rarely eat at home, and keeping things cold more of a luxury than a necessity. I will get to know Murray pretty well over the next five years. I think, in some peculiar way, that we grow a little fond of one another, or at least learn to tolerate each our faults. I soon discover he is having a secret affair with the woman that lives in the unit next to mine. This only because I am usuallyhome during evening hours studying with my front door open to allow air to circulate. I see him arrive, can hear without much imagination their sexual encounters, and then see him leave passing my lighted apartment. In the beginning, he hangs his head shyly, refusing even to look in my direction. After a while he nods greetings and on occasions even lingersfor a brief conversation. I cannot say that Murray and I form a bond of friendship, only that our acquaintance more than casual.

The day I move in, I have yet another unpleasant surprise! Flea season in Southern California is all year round with interval hatching periods. The day I look at the apartment, I see nothing out of the ordinary. But on moving day, I witness a swarm of something a few inches above the shag carpeting. At first, I do not even know what they are, thinking that my eyes playing tricks in the light.

"Fleas," announces the lady next door. "The previous tenant had three cats and two dogs. You will need to bomb the place--maybe twice to be sure."

"What is a bomb," I ask, knowing it cannot possibly be what I am thinking.

"Flea bombs— go down to the drug store. They'll tell you what you need."

I immediately go to the local pharmacy and purchase three spray cans of insect bombs. The directions read: close all doors and windows, place a can upright in each room, and open a tab to release a cloud of deadly spray toxin, evacuating the sealed dwelling for twelve hours. If luckily they are caught between hatchings, without opportunity to lay new eggs, the product guarantees to exterminate completely. Otherwise, I will need to repeat the procedure in two weeks. I follow the procedure and take occupancy next evening. I never see any more fleas, which bolsters my confidence in the effectiveness of some over-the-counter remedies. I call Rocky the first week of February to give him my new address and phone number. I can tell he is happy to hear from me again after so long.

I accept an invitation to his home that Saturday for a steak barbeque. It is another idyllic evening, a little chilly, but still Southern California weather. Elena passes out from fatigue before eight, while Rocky, his wife, and I huddle around an open-pit fire. Sometimes we talk, sometimes just listening to peace in the present, staring quietly into a stunning sky stretched over the Pacific. Most of our conversation centers around mundane events: about Rocky's drive to and from work, about changes in weather, and about the escalating political divide caused by the Nixon Watergate scandal. Rocky comments that he is glad to see I have my car back, since the coast highway a dangerous place. Even an American made tank serves as little protection, but better than exposed navigation on a small motorbike.

At around half past nine, the next-door neighbor begins playing Strawberry Fields Forever from the Beatle's 1967 album Magical Mystery Tour. Before my Holy Spirit experience, this was perhaps my favorite collection of songs, reminding me of my days of promising LSD trips and the escapist promotion through drug culture. But my eyes have been opened to the truth of invisible lies. Now I am able to see the ugly truth behind the mask, the invisible deception embedded in narcotic use and its promoters. I casually mention that I believe there to be subliminal satanic messages in much of today's music quoting from the source of a book I recently read written by Hal Lindsey. I share with Rocky and his wife my firsthand experience into this dark dimension enhanced through numerous drug trips before being spiritually delivered. What I hope might serve as a catalyst to more fruitful discussion quickly deteriorates into another confrontation between religious and secular belief. I feel thrust into the throes of a spiritual battle. It is as if I have inadvertently pricked both in their hearts, inspiring the anger of unseen forces. In the flesh, I wish to concede and change the course of this controversial conversation, only prevented by moving of the Holy Spirit.

"There is such a thing as evil in the world," I say, measuring my every word. "And the evil takes this world by force. But God has sent testimony of his son into the world that the world might through him be saved. This thing is not done in secret, nor is it a religious fable from olden times. I am witness to this salvation and stand before you now a living testament sewn in your generation."

They are both stunned to silence. Inez huffs and goes into the house. Rocky only shakes his head and stares out into the zenith where sky and ocean vanish into darkness. Once again I depart feeling empty and more than a little sad. I wish only peace between my father and me. I somehow feel betrayed by the Holy Spirit and doubt the tactfulness of my speech. On the drive home, I look up into heaven and ask why there must be this contentiousness between us? Why cannot Rocky and I just have a father and son relationship without this spiritual conflict? Answers to these questions will come soon enough.

I most certainly will not hear from my father again for some while. We are both proud men, neither willing to back down. Over the next several months I apply judiciously to my studies. I often think to call Rocky, but what more is there to say? He is a man in all appearance happily married, father to a young child, and caught-up into the same momentum of life as everyone else everywhere on planet earth. Who am I to judge? I continue to regret the unfortunate conversation of this last evening together; but also know that the words spoken not my words alone. Often I feel inspired to pray for my father and his new family, wishing no harm to come to them. The academic challenges continually test my resolve. At least I am no longer on probation, bringing my grade point average back above 2.0. This might not seem much of an achievement, but on the University level means a great deal more than just a passing grade. I will never make it to 3.0; not because I lack dedication, but because my interest of study more diverse, less concentrated on one subject of tunnel expertise.

To my elated surprise, Rocky's wife calls on my father's behalf in late August and extends invitation to attend a private celebration in his honor on the eve prior to his forty-fourth birthday.

"We have other plans with my family on Sunday," Inez states coolly.

"He asked that I invite you for this Saturday. It would be important to him if you can make it."

I gladly accept, hoping that this time we will have an evening of peace. No more conversation that might lead to religious or political debate. By inspiration, I compose a poem for my father, which I hope might bridge our contentious differences. Looking back on it now, I suppose the tone might be perceived as a bit Ecclesiastical, making allegorical reference to life's changing seasons, emphasizing the transient nature of existence and materialism. At the time I am only tacitly aware of the profound prophetic significance in this poem. Rocky reads the verse in silence, his face twitching ever so slightly. Once finished, he carefully folds and stuffs the handwritten card into the pocket of his blue jean coat. He then goes over to Babe's favorite corner, kneels, and begins stroking the motley animal affectionately. The dog stretches stiffly; half opens its eyes, and drifts back into heavy slumber.

The evening goes well, as we all refrain from any subjects that might spark into controversy. So well, in fact, I accept an invitation to sleep over. An hour before sunrise, I am awakened by the sound of groaning sobs. It is Rocky. I see my father weep for the first time. A man overwhelmed by grief, crouching beside the dead body of his beloved Babe, a dog that has been Rocky's constant companion for such an enduring part of his life. I decide it better not to disturb his grief. What more to say than has already been said? Just after sun-up, he wraps the dead animal in an old leather jacket, takes a shovel, and walks alone up into the Malibu hills. I wait for over an hour, finally deciding to leave that I might attend the morning church service. I bid goodbye to Inez and my little half-sister. I feel a little guilty to depart without at least saying goodbye to Rocky, but also think it better to allow my father to mourn this loss in his own way.

"Please give Rocky my condolence for his loss."

"You can't imagine how much he loved that dog," Inez sighs, her beautiful blonde hair moving freely in the bright morning air. "Sometimes I think he loved Babe more than me. I know that probably sounds silly. But I've seen him sit out here and talk to that animal like a person. And he has all these stories how he and Babe used to go running every evening on the beach, how they ate and slept together, and how she understands him more than anyone. It's enough to make any wife jealous."

"I'm sure Rocky loves you more than he did Babe," I reassure. "Tell him to call me sometime when he feels better."

As I drive home, I share my father's feeling of mortality, a living witness to his loss. The day of his forty-fourth anniversary coincides with the irrefutable death of his best friend since so many years. The passing of Babe marks the finality of many ends in Rocky's life, of things in the past he cannot change and of things he will never be able to change. To be honest, I never particularly liked the dog, considering it ugly and nasty looking with an uncontrollable distempered drool that smells a sewer. Yet, as Inez said, he loved the animal with an unnatural affection that seemly defies physical presence. It will be several more weeks before Rocky and I resume communication. He never again mentions Babe, nor the events on the anniversary of his birthday. It is as though this part of his past life never existed, or at most a vague memory. Only he knows with certainty Babe's final resting place carved out secretly in the Malibu hills.

This year's third quarter, I enroll in a disturbing class about the Jewish Holocaust of World War II. I have heard watered-down reports of this tragic history through television documentaries, without ever really considering the full scope of human carnage. It bears witness of what happens to a society stripped of material necessity and protection granted by edict and infrastructure. Yet, this history somehow more devastating: systematic genocide instituted by one's own government and instructed by nationalistic zeal. Models of ethnic segregation conceived by Darwinian observation devised to evaluate and compare Aryan purity based on physical attributes scientifically measurable. Men, women, and children herded first into ghettos, transported like cattle, and naively marched into gas chambers prepared for extermination. Those less lucky become subjects of medical experiments. The more fortunate forced to do labor in Nazi Work Camps dying slowly of disease and undernourishment. What would it be like to be betrayed by one's neighbor, by one's citizenry, and incarcerated by one's government just for being ethically or religiously different? How is it that a cultured civilization capable of such horror in this enlightened age, except there be influence by a mind of greater evil?

The required reading consists of several books written by those, who survived this terrible blithe of human experience firsthand. Touched deeply by the Diary of Ann Frank, a collection of memoirs kept by a thirteen-year-old little girl, I wept in the spirit, praying for her final peace. This personal record describes the last weeks spent with her family hiding in an attic terrified, as their familiar neighborhood changes into a hunting ground of brute men. Nazi Germany metamorphoses into scouring packs of hungry wolves sniffing out Jews in the beginning, and eventually rounding-up any other undesirable not measuring-up to Hitler's archetype of genetic perfection.

Without knowing why, I feel inexplicably connected to these victims, unified in their suffering, and identify with their persecution. It will be one of the most dynamic studies of my academic escapades. I engage deeply the haunting works of Ibsen, witnessing through his eyes the horror unfold. I meld into the thoughts of renowned psychoanalyst Victor Frankel and share the painful revelation achieved through analysis, as he investigates the solidarity of the human psyche's will to survive against all opposition in his book *Man's Search for Meaning*. At end of this class, I listen with compassionate attentiveness to several personal testimonies of the few survivors liberated from the *Death Camps*. They bring pictures of themselves and those they knew, many now dead; bands of vagabond refugees dressed in prison uniforms, reduced to human skeletons, a ghostly living testament evidencing the worse in man's potential to inflict brutality upon his fellow man. It is as though these memories my own; their affliction my affliction. Many years later I will visit the infamous dismantled Concentration Camp in *Dachau*, Germany. Here in this place I will remember these ghosts again.

In course, I meet an interesting girl named Linda Shapiro, as different from me as east is from west. She is very cute, well groomed and sophisticated, adorned with long dark hair that cascades softly along the contour of her lovely back. The most striking of Linda's facial features are her almond brown eyes, large and oval, making me imagine the lands surrounding the Mediterranean. She is a declared virgin determined to save herself for marriage. A few times, we go on my motorcycle to the nearby *V.A. Cemetery* for a picnic lunch. Linda, excited by the ride, is altogether infatuated by idea of being with an ex-marine in a war veteran cemetery. I will later learn that seeing me a rebellion against her father's wishes, whose views stanchly against war of any kind, and especially against the Vietnam conflict. This will not play in my favor.

"It was father's idea that I take this class," she confesses one afternoon as we sit beneath a tree near a neat, flawlessly straight row of white crosses. "He believes that to understand the past is to understand the present. Ever since I was a little girl, he has shown me and my sister faded pictures of distant relatives that died at Auschwitz. I know it is horrible of me, but I just don't care! That was all so long a time ago."

"Maybe because Jews are God's chosen people, they are made to suffer as an example to a world blind to the fact that God the author of everything. I'm sure your father means well, and wants you and your sister to know and appreciate your heritage. Everything past is a long time ago, but that doesn't make the historical meaning less relevant."

"You sound a lot like him;" she says with innocent reflection.

 Something in your eyes that is the same as his. I guess that is why Ilike you."

I like Linda, too, as one might a rare acquisition in time. Maybe because I sense that deep down she wants me that I want her less. Nevertheless, it makes me proud to have this rare beauty on the back of my bike, clutching me tightly, as I speed dangerously through the university lanes.

Near the end of Holocaust Class, Linda invites me to her family's home for a Sunday dinner. I should have known just by the address that my present estate far different from this elite family. My motorcycle engine growls menacingly, echoed through this peaceful Westwood suburb, as an unnatural disturbance, causing people to stop and stare from curiosity or out of dread.

A stoic woman, I presume to be Linda's mother, courteously greets me at the door. She surveys awkwardly my camouflaged Vietnam jacket, keeping it at arm's length, and shows me to the dining area. The interior, tastefully decorated with antiques, rich hanging tapestries, and sparkling marble floors, creates an illusion of grandeur appreciated by the middle-class rich of the nineteen seventies.

"Welcome to our home," reports a robust stoutly built man wearing a yarmulke and seated at the head of the table. "My name is Abe. May I offer you a covering for your head?"

I accept the yarmulke gracefully, not wishing to offend my host. Linda helps to attach the headpiece to my long motorcycle-swept hair using bobby pins. Abe bows his head and recites a traditional pray in Hebrew, bobbing strangely back and forth. His wife and two daughters instantly assume a demur of reverent submissiveness, incongruous to the image of liberated women of the times. However, I will later appreciate that Jewish men like Abe might be the head of prayer at the table; but the true leaders of the household are the women.

I think I am as much fascinated as struck by the strangeness of the ritual. I am reminded of my third academic quarter, when invited to a Jewish feast called Purim to commemorate the victory of Esther over the evil plots of Haman. What struck me most then, as now, is the cultural significance and dedication to events that happened in the past. This family is no different than any other, except united in common bond by genetics, and defined through a hierarchal linage. There is something else about these people distinctly different, something indelibly unique from my personal experience and way of thinking. Abe represents a magnified patriarch spanning generations of remembered chronicles going back to the days of Abraham, first called by God, and given the promise to be Patriarch ofa unique nation. He is humble in a way that fills me with joy and a sense of unspoken kinship. I like this man and his family, appreciate this brief moment of communion, which consists of roasted lamb, fresh green vegetables, and delicately prepared soufflé potatoes.

We eat mostly in silence, with only the occasional comment about the weather, a passing interest in a new addition to the Botanical Gardens at UCLA, and the wonderful wood décor of their home. Often, Linda's eyes glare at me across the table, causing me to wonder if I have said something wrong. I suppose that she feels instinctively the impasse that is to come. I sense nothing at all.

"My daughter tells me you are interested in the history of the Jewish people." Abe comments unassumingly after dinner.

"Yes," I reply. "I was never taught the horrors of what happened to the Jews at the hands of the Nazis. A terrible period of history, a significant event in the times we live. It is a major sign that the Messiah is coming back soon."

"The Messiah-- both my grandparents perished at Auschwitz! No Messiah came to them! Young man, what do you know about the times in which we live and the teachings in the *Talmud*?"

Honestly, at the time I thought that the *Talmud*, the *Torah*, and the *Old Testament Bible* all the same book. Much later, it will be revealed to me that the *Talmud* is actually a book containing collections of cryptic commentaries and interpretations made by Rabbis' through-out centuries dating back to the first Pharisaic order. In my ignorance, I begin to expound on the perfect law of faith and the promise of salvation as shown to me through the grace of the Holy Spirit. This only agitates Abe even more. He shows me a large book several inches thick written in Hebrew mounted atop a pedestal in an adjoining room.

"Contained in this book are all the thoughts and revelations of the greatest Rabbis who ever lived. Are you saying that all the study and teachings of our fathers means nothing? Six million souls were murdered at the hands of brute men— men like you-- men of war; men who were only following orders!"

Now the gloves are off. My first impression of this man turns from respect to adversarial bitterness. I am an ex-United States Marine— not a Nazi— not a butcher— but part of a noble corps serving honorably. It angers me that this man, who obviously has never seen a day of combat, should accuse me of being a monster. It is not the first time; nor will it be the last, but always it stings deeply just the same.

"If it were not for men like me, then no one would have survived the camps!" I reply emphatically, restraining my emotions. "I personally never murdered anyone, and even though I am capable of killing, I choose not to. Before I found Christ, I was a greater danger, but never a murderer. Do you think Israel today would exist were it not by the hand of the Lord in fulfillment of prophecy? Do you think that without men like me, it will continue to survive surrounded on all sides by its ancient enemies?"

I pause and look Abe directly in the eye. I glimpse fear mixed with surprise. The impression he thought to make. now forgotten, as Abe considers many unpleasant possibilities. He has pulled tail of a Tiger, and is now wondering what I might do next.

"Many words do not make a truth," I continue resolutely. "The *Messiah* has come, and is coming again, confirmed through the prophecies of *Isaiah*, *Jeremiah*, and so many others. Salvation is not through knowledge, or by the teachings of men, but by revelation of the Holy Spirit. I am new to the word of God; nevertheless, his spirit has born witness with my spirit that all the scriptures are fulfilled in *Jesus Christ*."

By now, Abe is distressed beyond rational thought. He demands I leave his home immediately, forbidding me to see his daughter ever again. Sadly, I remove the yarmulke and hand it to Linda. I can see the disappointment in her eyes, as if she is saying, 'why couldn't you have just kept your mouth shut'. But it is neither pride, nor prejudice communicated so directly to her father. Abe has heard meaning spoken by the Holy Spirit.

As I ride my motorcycle home, I break into spontaneous praise, thanking God in the spirit for things I cannot possibly understand with my mind. I will not see Linda again, except in passing. Once I bump into her twin sister at the Botanical Gardens and speak at length about what happened that day inside her home.

"I did not mean to upset your father that way," I apologize. "I think that maybe he has the wrong impression of the Vietnam War, and those who fought in it."

"Father once studied to be a Rabbi and believes that Jews should not pick up arms for any other cause than the protection of Zion. If I were you, I would not take what he said personally. I am surprised someone like you would become a born again Christian. What you said that day makes sense. Mother, Linda, and I have talked often about it. Of course, father will have no part of the conversation…still, I am not certain you did not impress him as well."

As we part company, I feel better about the unfortunate incident. Perhaps, I am not born for diplomacy; nevertheless, I have learned something important through the experience. The scars of the world run deeper than I imagine, etched indelible into the memory of each succeeding generation. I learn the meaning of a new term risen from ashes of the *Holocaust*, a future call to arms labeled *Zionism*.

$\mathcal{I}$t is another one of those bright California mornings, the sun pushing through cracks in the lattice, making me burrow deeper beneath the covers, not yet wishing to revive. The phone rings, trumpeting the end of my reverie.

"What do you say we go have breakfast," enquires a familiar voice. "I'm just around the corner. Meet me down in five minutes."

Rocky is in the habit of getting up early, even on weekends. A trait we do not share in common. He claims to be a carpenter, a profession inconsistent with lifestyle. According to his wife, he rises every morning before six, drives to work, not to return until past 6:00 at night. Upon leaving he is always clean, well groomed, with manicured nails, wearing a gold neck chain and copper wristband he claims is for arthritis. Always he returns home in the same condition. If Rocky really was a carpenter, then he undoubtedly qualifies as a breed unique.

I get dressed hurriedly, splash water in my face, and scamper down the stairs where Rocky is anxiously waiting in his silver Porsche. He looks every bit like a movie star, with his designer sunglasses, customized black silk shirt, open at the top to expose his perfectly tanned chest, and crowned with a sculpted hairstyle of the times. I am a crude stone in comparison, but without doubt a chip off the block.

We have breakfast at a place he knows in Venice along the beach called *The Hole in the Wall*, a place that lives up to its name. Located on the ground level of an abandoned dilapidated three-story building, this underrated dining room and kitchen, serves the best breakfast I have ever eaten. Not only is the food excellent, but remarkably inexpensive. Between the hours of 7:00 until 8:30 A.M for just over three dollars, one can order a stack of pancakes, polish sausage, eggs, and toast, more than even I am able to eat, even though I ate it all. I make future notation of this place, and will spend many golden mornings here, gorging myself with the best meal of the day.

Afterward, Rocky drives north on the Pacific Coast Highway. Several miles past his home, he takes a turn onto an unpaved road west toward the beach. Off in the distance, I can see a pocket of homes built along the shoreline, which Rocky claims belong to several movie stars. A man driving a beat-up jeep meets us halfway, a weathered hefty man, badly burned from recently spending too much time exposed to the sun, and dressed like a beach bum.

"How-ya' doing Rocky?" The other driver shouts, pulling alongside our vehicle.

"Ok Steve; this is my son. He served in Vietnam as a Marine,   and is now going to UCLA."

"A Vet," he says, reaching back and pulling three bottles of beer from a cooler resting on the back seat. "How about having a *Heineken* on me?"

"Thanks," I reply, "but you don't need to do that."

The man only smiles, at that moment looking vaguely familiar. Using a pocketknife, he pops-off the caps and passes the cold bottles to Rocky and me.

"Here's to Nam, and all those poor bastards that came back in boxes!"

He bids us a good day, and continues on his way.

"Who was that?" I ask Rocky.

"You don't recognize Steve McQueen? I've known Steve since more than ten years. We used to go drinking together before I got married. Inez doesn't like him much, so he stopped coming over."

"He looks nothing like he did in the movies," I say flabbergasted, remembering the famous actor in Hollywood films such as Ruby's favorites: The Magnificent Seven and The Great Escape, and more recently in The Thomas Crown Affair.

"People change in real life, and sometimes are little like we think they should be. But Steve is just real, and one of the best friends I've ever known."

We continue along the road to the beach homes. The last house in the row belongs to Larry Hagman. Mr. Hagman, along with several of his neighbors, are clearing debris caused by a recent storm. He and Rocky talk for several minutes, only casually introducing me at the end of the conversation. They seem in disagreement over something related to rebuilding a collapsed front balcony. Rocky suggests using reinforced steel beams as supports, an idea adamantly rejected by Hagman.

"That's the problem with all of these celebrity beach homes," Rocky huffs, as we drive back toward the coast highway; "they are built like toothpicks against storm surges. Every year they get knocked down or damaged, but they just build them back again same as before. Even nature tells us not to build too near the water's edge; but people with too much money, and not much sense, never listen."

At the time, I really do not completely appreciate the wisdom of Rocky's words. However, during my years of habitation in Southern California, I will come to the same opinion. Each year homes damaged or destroyed by Pacific storms along the coastline, or raging fires sweeping through dry canyon hills, all dwelling places of Hollywood celebrities and California's *'nouveau rich'* that flock to the Golden State in search of perpetual sunshine and promise of a salad life. Only they discover disappointment by the scourge of over-population, semi-desert conditions, further complicated by limited water supplies and rampant crime. Southern California is both the best and the worse place to live; heaven and hell layered together, a rich Mecca at edge of the world blighted by disproportionate materialism and bloody carnage of violent turf wars. Those wealthy enough to nest in seclusion, often find confrontation with the untamable elements of nature, as destructive as the perils they seek to escape through isolation.

Rocky's next stop is a popular supermarket located on the corner of Trancas Canyon Road and the Pacific Coast Highway appropriated called *Trancas Market*. This food-gathering place of the stars, like any other food market, except that it is a lot pricier. This the place Inez and Rocky first met, the place where they shop every day for food, as do nearly everyone else in the Malibu area. When asked why we are stopping here first, Rocky only remarks that he wants something sweet for the road. Inside the market, a lady shyly approaches Rocky.

"Mr. Bronson, may I have your autograph?"

"Of course you may," he says with stunning calmness, nonchalantly taking a ready pen from his shirt pocket.

I feel altogether embarrassed, but hold my peace. Once outside, I indignantly ask why he pretended to be someone he is not.

"And why not," he snaps back unapologetically. "She wanted to meet a star today, and in her mind she did. What she buys today will be gone tomorrow, but I gave her something she will cherish for the rest of her life."

"But you are not Charles Bronson!"

"In her mind I am, and that's all that matters in the end. She dreamed of meeting someone special, and today is fulfillment of that dream."

It is true that Rocky looks very much like the famous movie star. However, Rudy never would have gone along with a charade of being someone he was not. It strikes me as being pretentious. Yet, the more I think about it, the more I begin to appreciate Rocky's reasoning. What is a movie star anyway, except a figment in one's imagination, an illusion blown out of proportion by a celluloid fantasy? Unless this lady one day should meet the real Charlie Bronson, then she will never know the truth of the lie, and her truth of bragging will be all that matters. I think that deep down I admire Rocky for his lie. Begin to admire the strange workings of his mind that thought it kind to give an unusual gift to a complete stranger.

From here, we drive to the small town of Oxnard in Ventura County and visit the home where Rocky spent the latter part of his childhood. It is a small house located in a poor neighborhood predominately Mexican. Parked in a far corner of the backyard beneath an Avocado tree is a rusted old sagging wreck bearing the rusted license plate I found still mistakenly registered on the rolodex record at the DMV for all these years. An older Spanish speaking woman greets us with hugs and kisses. I know without any introduction that it is Rocky's mother, and my grandmother.

"My name Luis," she says affectionately; "me-- *abeula* to you."

I must admit that expressions of prejudice against people of other ethnic origins still infected my mind unaware. I am only vaguely certain where this comes from, as often I hear a voice from my childhood speaking inside my head and saying things like *'lazy negro'*, *'dirty Italian'*, *'greasy Mexican'*, *'cheap Jew'*, and *'slack jawed SOB'* as a general description of anyone else Rudy uncomfortable with. I am not even sure if Rudy sincerely embraced meaning of these expressions, only that he said them often enough to infect the subconscious of my developing mind. I sometimes find myself wrestling with these demons and determine that by the power of Christ to overcome seat of their established principality.

However, everything about Luis and her present husband fulfills worse prejudice of societal stereotype. Physically they look typically *Chicano*, especially the husband, who reminds me of the Mexican encountered in the Tijuana junkyard. Neither speaks much English; the house, filled with Catholic icons, and could have been any poor class home found south of the border. The culture shock is a bit overwhelming at first. My immediate thought is Rocky looks nothing at all like these people.

As we all sit down at the kitchen table and talk, I become more relaxed, witnessing the simple goodness here. The husband, who communicates better English than his wife, boasts that he is a diesel mechanic, advising me not to waste my time going to University. Rocky snaps something sharply in Spanish, staring angrily into his stepfather's eyes. The other man looks away, choosing to add nothing more to the conversation. Just before leaving, Rocky and Luis disappear into an adjacent room to speak in private. Their voices barely discernable through the thin walls, they communicate in an alien vocabulary, neither English nor Spanish. Rocky's stepfather begins chewing on a green pepper taken from a bowl on the table.

"Would you like to taste a *Banana Pepper* straight out of the garden?" He asks challengingly, passing me the bowl. "This is the real test of a man.

Without much thought, I accept and bite into the delicious looking fruit. It is at first sweet in my mouth, but within seconds, I realize the error. My lips and mouth begin burning, as a river of acid trickles down my throat. Yet, I am determined not to show weakness in the presence of this man. He eyes me for several minutes without saying anything, continuing to bite down on another fresh pepper. I try to quench the flaming discomfort with water, which only causes more burning. Satisfied that I have suffered enough, the man offers me half of a banana.

"This will stop the burning."

Within seconds, the intense burning subsides into a memory. Now I know why they are called Banana Peppers. At this moment, Luis and Rocky return. Luis hugs me goodbye, affectionately burying my face in her bosom. Upon shaking hands with her husband, I observe a twinkle of respect in his eyes. I will see Luis and Rocky's stepfather only once more; and within the context of less pleasant circumstances. To this day, I regret not to have had the opportunity to know them better as people, and notthrough a preconceived judgment of their culture.

Taking a well-rehearsed shortcut through meandering streets until the Santa Paula Freeway, Rocky heads east for many miles to the *Ojai Road* exit. Typical to most regions east of the California coastlands, the terrain here arid and uninteresting, faded dry desert hills rising as exposed mounds between deep crevices carved at the bottom of a diluvium ocean that once rolled over the western seaboard. Appropriately named, Ojai is an Indian word meaning '*Valley of the Moon*'. In many ways it is just that, a terrain detached from time and the fleeting hopes of present course. It seems in many ways a place analogical to the relationship between Rocky and me. My father in so many ways a complete stranger; I the son he never knew. Yet, we find ourselves reconnected by forces unseen, both bound by an anchor of destiny that defies natural reason.

As we snake through the *Ojai Valley*, I can tell by Rocky's expression that there are good and bad memories here, as though he were retracing a route known by instinct, only vaguely familiar now.

"I spent most of my youth in an orphanage near here," he reflects looking ahead. "Also, it's where I made-out with a girl the first time."

"I didn't know you were an orphan."

"Your grandfather died young, as did his father. It seems to be a curse in our family. Fathers never stick around to see their children grow up. I never had any real sense of what it means to share complicity of a brother or sister. Now I find myself to be the sin of my father. I have three daughters from different marriages. But you were the first born, and the only son." He pauses, and looks in this moment painfully mortal. "As far as I know youare the last to carry on the family name."

In the moment I am not altogether sure what Rocky is trying to say. Was it an apology, or a confession? I want to say that I forgive his absence in my life until now. I have a distinct feeling something of greater importance has brought us together, even more important than the fact he is my biological father. Therefore, I say nothing at all. I do not confess that I have reservations to sire a child because of my exposure to *Agent Orange* while serving in Vietnam. Nor that I no longer believe in the duration of flesh or in pointless genealogies.

Suddenly the terrain opens into the panorama of a stunningly beautiful valley rich with Orange, Lemon, and Avocado groves. Ojai, famous for its sulfur hot springs and lush parks, is an Eldorado, a selfishly guarded secret by locals, and to those tourist fortunate enough to stumble into this shielded basin. I quickly understand why Rocky likes it here. Just before a sign that reads *Dennison Park Ahead*, Rocky takes a left turn on *Lyon Canyon Fire Road*. Less than a mile, he turns into a long driveway leading to a lavish estate of a regal Hacienda-style front veranda framed by vines and hanging plants. Insisting that I follow, he steps on the landing and rings the doorbell.

"Mr. Belmonte," exclaims a corpulent Spanish lady from behind the screened door. "The Senora is expecting you. It has been so long, and I see you have brought a young friend. Please come in, she is waiting in the parlor."

The lady of the house sits in the oval circumference of an antique chair, imparting to her an air of majesty. She is wearing a blackveil that obscures her face, but even so, I can make out the refined feminine features of high cheekbones, a regal nose, defined lips that neither smile, nor frown, and a long elegant neck of a lady with presence. The more interesting characteristic are her eyes, which seem to pierce the curtain like distant moons in orbit around shadowy sphere of her face.

Rocky greets her with a kiss on the hand, and a brief exchange in a beautiful language I do not understand. It is the same language I heard Rocky and his mother speak earlier in the day. The way they touch less casual, a familiarity evident in body language, imparting a meaning moreprofound than words. Here is no stranger in Rocky's secret life of youngturbulence, a past with many secrets he will take with him to the grave.

"This is my son," Rocky proudly introduces me, as we seat ourselves in chairs opposite an oval marble coffee table. "He grew-up in South Carolina, and is enrolled at UCLA."

"UCLA— my brother's son graduated from there with a degree in micro-biology. He now works for one of those large pharmaceutical companies on the east coast. If you are anything like your father, you will become very successful."

"I have no interest to become successful in terms of this world." I reply honestly. "I just want to know what the world knows."

An uncomfortable silence passes between us. I can see in Rocky's steely eyes what he is thinking. I know that despite all our similarities, I am a disappointment in a way that matters most to him.

"And so you will," this woman of stoic appearance says approvingly.

The woman that answered the door quietly pours us tea from an elegant gilded teapot. I consider her perhaps the housemaid, an attendant to this lady of obvious means since many years.

"Everything needs constant watering," sighs the lady, gracefully taking a cup of the fresh brew. "It has been so dry lately…" Then, looking straight at me she remarks: "It is so important that things receive their proper carein season. Your name originates before the age of Castile... and before the treaty of Gemika. It means *'Beautiful Spirit'*. You are *Basque*, remember this always!"

I do not know how to reply. Who was this woman, and what did she know about my family name? She makes it seem that I am the last of a kind with some pending responsibility or purpose. I always thought my last name French— at least that is what Jean often told me, which sounds more romantic than whoever these *Basque* are.

"Please excuse me, dear, but I am becoming tired," she says apologetically to Rocky; "I am so glad to have met your son. He is a special young man."

Without any instruction, the attendant goes into an adjoining room and rolls out a wheelchair. Her true position now obvious, she gently lifts the lady of the house from her elegant chair and places the frail body into the chromed-metal contraption.

"Remember always that you are *Basque*," she repeats to me, as the stoic attendant rolls her away.

Rocky and I see ourselves out. When asked about his relationship to this mysterious woman, he evades the question by saying only that they go back very far and that he will tell me more about her another time. This promise he will not keep; this strange meeting remaining forever a mystery.

Our next stop is a cemetery in Ventura near the ocean. Rocky has a plot already picked out, knows exactly where and how he wishes his remains buried. I think this unusual since he always avoids conversations concerning death and the soul. The chosen plot on a small knoll beneath a tree where an ocean breeze breathes ever so lightly with a distant view of the Pacific Ocean. It is idyllic, a pastoral place suited to repose into eternal bliss.

"This spot cost almost as much as my car," he brags proudly, as though he is presenting the future site of an extravagant new home.

"Sepulchers of the living appear magnificent, but within holds the corruption of death. The Pharisees, too, believed in the importance to house their own bones, while ignoring the importance of the soul, which neither dies, nor is subject to mortal consolation."

Rocky reaches out, takes my arm gruffly.

"All that anyone can know for certain is what can be touched and known through the senses. I used to be poor like Luis and her husband—poor like you! I am not poor any longer. Why shouldn't I be buried as well as any president or king?"

"The ancient Egyptians took great care to insure the continuance of the flesh after death," I report candidly, remembering a book I read for a classical literature course. "Herodotus describes in detail how the body is prepared for burial: removing all the organs, even the brain sucked out through the nose, the shell stuffed with spices and resins as a technique of preservation. Today, all their efforts have produced only shriveled mummies. The flesh was not made to last; but you have an eternal soul made of greater stuff than this."

"How do you know that?" Rocky demands angrily. "How do you know that there is anything after death?"

"Because the Holy Spirit has born witness to my spirit that it so, Rocky. I swear that of something as important as life after death, I would not lie to you."

Rocky says nothing back. He has a way of retreating into silence, of pretending that all things exist in a neat package. Then I wonder if perhaps he might be sick, if perhaps he has brought me here because he knows something about his health that he is not saying. He could be secretive that way. Therefore, I decide not to press the issue further, agreeing that this place as grand as any Beverly Hills mansion.

He drives to a place near the *Malibu Pier*, where we have an early dinner at a newly opened establishment called *Alice's Restaurant*, named after a song by *Arlo Guthrie*. Unknown to me at the time, *Guthrie's* comical satiric song has its roots in fact. There actually was a restaurant owned by a woman named Alice in Great Barrington, Massachusetts, who lived with her husband in an abandoned church. *Orlo* and a friend, arrested for littering, fined fifty dollars, and are later rejected by the draft because of their conviction. *Orlo* makes the unfortunate experience an inspiration for the famous song; which also becomes platform for a successful anti-war protest against America's long involvement in Vietnam. Although I do not altogether agree with the simplistic politics presented, I will always enjoy the ballad style of the song as sung by the original artist.

I can only describe the environment as modern hippie, with a touch of true California glitter sprinkled to attract the wealthier elite. The waitresses all have flowers sprouting from their hair, all pretty young women that seem to hatch everywhere from the Malibu sands, each seeking a nest of their own near the sea. The menu lives up to the spirit of the restaurant's name with a variety of fruit and vegetable salads, and combination meat platters called *Alice's* special this or *Alice's* special that. The mother establishment of this franchise is called just *Alice's* located in nearby Westwood. Two business partners looking to raise cash for a movie project opened the establishment with the help of outside funding. This particular *Alice's Restaurant* in Malibu represents a business split each owning a profitable share of their brilliant concept. Maybe this *Alice's* is not as original as the original, but creates a fun environment with excellent food and presentation. I will come back here many times in later years when money less of an obstacle.

Rocky takes particular interest in the twenty-two year old bartender with long auburn hair and striking green eyes made even greener by a florescent glow in this place. She claims to have an agent with plans of becoming a famous movie star like *Audrey Hepburn*. I must admit that she looks a little like the actress, the same petite demure, and the same impish smile. *Audrey Hepburn* has always been my favorite on the big screen. In fact, when I think about it, she is a lot like Jean when she was young, possessed of a humble beauty that shows the kindness of a good heart.

It is dark by the time we leave. The fact there is a new moon and patches of fog made our passage even darker. The Porch headlamps slice surgically through the grey matter with my father confidently at the wheel, neither of us saying a word as we slip from layer to layer of the twining mesh along a twisting highway.

"I saw you take the number of that girl." I say finally. "So what," he replies tersely.

"So, you are married to a beautiful woman and have a young child. You know where something like this can lead."

"Don't give me any of your *"Holy Roller"* crap! What I do is my business, and I don't need a moral advisor to decide what is best for me or my marriage." He is no longer my father, but now dangerous and as vicious as any man. "And buckle your seatbelt!" Rocky adds at the end.

All day he has continuously reminded me to buckle-up. I usually comply since this his car and because it seems so important to him. However, there are no seatbelt laws in California at this time, nor am I in the habit of wearing one. Out of principle I refuse, demanding to know his preoccupation with the devices.

"I was not much older than you driving just south of *Big Sur*." The tone of his voiced changed solemn. "It was a night similar to this, dark and low visibility. A Chevrolet convertible flew pass me carrying a bunch of teenagers. Around the next bend, I watch the car swerve out of control and tumble down an embankment. I stopped, but they were all dead, scattered like broken dolls among the rocks bordering the ocean. One of these kids-- I think was the driver-- lay on a rock at the edge of the tide looking blindly up at me, his neck twitching in death. I never got that image out of my mind. I always said that if even one had been wearing a seatbelt, then maybe someone might have survived."

I can see a dark highway in Rocky's terrified mind, the mangled bodies, and the young man with a death twitch just as he describes. I can see something else as well: a curve on a dark night and lights shining into destiny. A sudden heaviness overshadows our presence, a sense of being timeless and seeing forever.

"Rocky," I say somberly; "there is a place in the highway of your life where you will not see the other side. In this place is your destiny reserved-- a place and an hour this seatbelt will not save you. Now is the moment of your salvation. Enter in at the open gate, for the hours and the days on this earth are a record not of our choosing. Hear now the calling of the Holy Spirit."

The silence that follows will last until Rocky drops me home. It will be several months before we see each other again.

$\mathcal{B}$eth Newhouse is stunningly beautiful, with earthy seductive brown eyes, long raven hair, and olive smooth skin glistening sensuality. She stands at the end of the pool table in a sometimes biker bar a few doors down from my apartment. I drop in this particular evening to speak to the bartender, a scruffy looking man named Spade, who sold me the Honda 350 CL, to ask a mechanical question related to the motorcycle's carburetion adjustment. Unfortunately, I learn that Spade has quit his job and moved back to Arizona. I might have left immediately had it not been for this statuette beauty carefully aiming the eight ball into a side pocket of the only pool table in position to win the game. Our eyes meet, igniting a spark, and we both recognize immediately a connection made. I make challenge for the next game and rack-up the table. Maybe it is the way she avoids real eye contact, or how she never gives a straight answer to any question that further tantalizes my curiosity. Although I provide some competition, she wins with a long bank shot, so I buy her a beer. Later Beth Newhouse is a snug fit pressed against my back, as we speed through congested boulevards and down familiar alley short cuts that only a motorcycle can traverse. After a spin to the beach and back, we return to my West Los Angeles apartment and make love. This relationship is not destined to go very far. I do not know it at the time, but Beth is hopelessly in love with an older married man.

Nevertheless, we share nearly two weeks of romantic bliss. Beth is a fun party-girl, as seasoned as she is attractive. We become intimate both as friends and as lovers. Had I been a little more experienced in ways of this world, I would have left it there and not gotten emotionally involved. Beth becomes a teacher to etiquettes completely new to me. Particularly humorist is the first time she invites me for a romantic candlelight dinner at her new apartment. Placed strategically on the floor around a low coffee table and marking the center, is a covered steaming pot. Over-stuffed cushions placed along the circumference create an exotic Malaysian ambiance, each richly embroidered with ornately saddled elephants, jungles of lotus plants, and scrolls of Sanskrit mantras. In the background, music instrumentals play a Hindu melody, reminding me of a classic audio book recording I often listened to as a child titled *Around the World in 80 Days*. In this Jules Verne novel, the main protagonist, *Phileas Fogg* and his faithful servant *Passpartout*, rescue the *Princess Aouda* from a sacrificial death to Sati, while on their way to Calcutta. The tale embodies many of these elements, laced with mysticism and adventure, including a little romance latently appealing to my emerging puberty at the time.

Beth disappears into the bedroom and changes into a sexy gown. She then proceeds to uncover the steaming pot and fishes out a large green plant with thorny leaves, depositing one on my plate and another on her own.

"Perfectly done," she comments, and smiles delighted.

I scrutinize the thing for several minutes. It is definitely a vegetable. I thought that Jean had prepared every garden variety in existence. Yet, never have I seen a thing even remotely like this one.

"Go ahead," Beth coaxes, sliding a bowl of melted butter and garlic toward my plate.

I should have confessed that I had no idea how to eat the thing placed before me. My pride approaches this new challenge as any other: the bullish determination of a Marine. I pull off one of the thorny leaves, put it whole into my mouth, and begin chewing. My first thought is how Beth could think this foul tasking weed ready for consumption? It is like eating the bark of a tree that has been soaked in water. Nevertheless, in chivalrous consideration, I consume, not one, but several of the leathery leaves.

"You must really be hungry," Beth looks at me astonished. "I never saw anyone eat artichoke that way."

"In the south we eat all kinds of things," I reply between chomps. "I'm sure my mother made artichokes at least once, or at least something like it."

Beth says nothing in reply, but begins delicately detaching a leaf from her vegetable, dips the meaty end into a tub of garlic and melted butter, eating only that part by scooping it out with her teeth. I decide maybe this definition of a more female approach to dispatching the rude plant. However, I am a man, and eat like a man. Finally, I reach the center-- or what Beth refers to being *delicious heart of the artichok'*. I can hardly call the mass of yellowish-green fibers resembling texture of dog hair delicious. I immediately gag on the first bite from the course strands that stickin my throat like tiny fish bones.

Beth can no longer bear it. She reaches into my plate, cuts around the circumference of the green fibrous mass, and removes it like a sorcerer's cap. She then slices out a section of the meaty hub, dips it into the tub of garlic-butter, and places it into my mouth.

"This is the heart of an artichoke," she whispers affectionately, and then begins to laugh robustly.

We both laugh through the rest of the dinner; and even later, we spontaneously break into simultaneous chuckles without ever mentioning the true butt of the joke. Beth is fun that way, and as romantic a partner I may have wished to find in any woman.

The following week I meet a Jewish couple named Isaac and Rebecca, considered Beth's best friends. Isaac is in his final year of law school, tall and lean. Rebecca, on the other hand, a little overweight, is employed as a high-powered sales person and territorial manager for a pyramid company called Shaklee Products. She can hardly wait for her husband to begin his career so that she might quit her job and become pregnant. Married extremely young, Rebecca sacrificed her academic potential to take a job straight out of high school to help put her husband through law school. Now that he is nearly finished, I sense some boredom on Isaac's part, but more I sense regret. Rebecca feels it, too, and spends much of their brief visit belittling him, while reminding everyone how much he owes her.

"The only thing he knows to do is study. God forbid that he raises a finger in the house! Still, he's my teddy bear and will make it all up to me someday."

Isaac only grimaces, as he watches his wife gorge compulsively on a bowl of chips and candy placed on the coffee table. Rebecca is the type to eat her frustrations, but also remarkably ambitious with an enormous power to influence. She gives me a phone number to call in order that I may learn more about the Shaklee products. Because of her, I will attend a sales seminar and briefly become a Shaklee sales agent. I also will end up becoming my best customer by purchasing the concentrated protein shampoo and delicious Shakley chocolate protein powder, which makes an excellent quick breakfast.

"Isaac and Rebecca were the children of promise to Abraham," I say amazed by the coincidence of their names. "This promise continues to this day with the rebirth of the nation Israel, reunifying Jews scattered in the earth as a sign to other worldly principalities that God's word unfailing. Through this same seed is born Jesus Christ the hope of salvation to all mankind."

"Except for Becky's uncle being a Rabbi and my Bar Mitzvah, we aren't very religious. But I'm pretty sure Jesus Christ was not a Jew." Isaac advocates.

"Salvation came first to the Jews through the patriarch Abraham, a covenant made by a seed of promise, as recorded in the Book of Prophets. Since this same Messiah is the promise to all mankind. I am a living witness to that promise. Jesus was indeed born a Jew, according to the traditions and beliefs of his generation, and he died and was buried a Jew in accordance to custom. This same Messiah came in the fulfillment of prophecy made to every generation And will surely come again as prophesied. It is not through the teachings of religion, but by the spirit of God that salvation manifested into the world conditioned to think myopically."

At this time in my life, I believed that all Jews knew at least their history, as recorded in the Old Testament Bible, as translated from the Torah. It never occurs to me that this young couple might be ignorant of even the most fundamental facts of scripture. I see Beth tense up, fearing that I might insult her friends. Perhaps, without meaning to, I have.

I can only say in retrospect that I sincerely liked this young couple, and felt in the moment a shared affinity for the bond of matrimony they represent. Without great surprise, I will later hear through the grapevine of the Shaklee community that Isaac and Rebecca divorce childless after he graduates from law school. I wish I had said more, although I am not sure if it might have made any difference.

The last night Beth and I spend together flourishes with expectation that only young love can have. We kiss passionately; make love, cuddle and fall asleep in each other's arms. At a little past four in the morning, the phone rings. I am still half-asleep, but I remember distinctly to this day remnants of her conversation to someone more special to her than just a friend at other end of the line.

"Yes— yes, I do you, too," she sighs. "Of course I will be ready." She promises hanging up the phone and then begins dressing.

"You must leave," she commands without affection, turning on the light. "I don't have time to explain. Please just go."

"Baby, is something wrong?" I mumble groggily.

Beth retreats into her usual silence. Only this time, it is less mysterious, more sinister, and less seductive. I slip on my jeans and shirt, as she puffs anxiously on a cigarette. I sense an uneasiness that I have not felt from her before. I leave with neither of us even saying goodbye. I call her several times during the day, but there is no answer. The next evening after my last on-campus work shift, I ride past her home. It is dark, the curtains drawn, and no one home. The next day the same, and on the third day, I get a message that the phone number no longer in service. Angry and concerned, I knock on the door of the building manager.

"She left without notice," he says perplexedly, shaking his head. "She was such a nice young lady, too. I think that big Italian had something to do with it. Did you know her well?"

"No," I reply, stubbornly proud. "We met only a short while ago."

Beth Newhouse vanishes just like that without leaving a trace. It will be a few years before I see her again at a luncheon spot in Marina Del Rey. She looks exactly the same, seated with co-worker of a Bank of America. Beth is in still in the accounting office doing what she does best. Even her way of dressing unchanged: she continues to wear the same style of clothing, jeans and a halter-top blouse. It is like going back in time, a time I have since outgrown. We will see each other a few times and both realize that time in our lives gone; left in a past of lingering ghost and lost dreams of things that once might have been.

After Beth's inexplicable disappearance, I decide I no longer want a relationship, preferring to concentrate my energies into study. It is during this period of reprieve that I meet Bruce, ex-army, also a believed at the time to be a Vietnam veteran. Even though we sprout from different branches of the military, it is refreshing to be acquainted with someone whose experience of reintegration similar to my own. Bruce is a tall and lanky individual with long unkempt hair and sports a scruffy John Lennon styled beard and mustache. He is like me, also a loner. Only he continues to indulge in the use of marijuana homegrown in his own apartment. Even though we will eventually become good friends, I think he never truly confides in me, mostly because I refuse to partake in his wampum offerings, or maybe it is because of my faith in a God he does not wish in the moment to believe exists. We are also from different background of military participation, each product of very different experiences. Even though neither of us admits it, there is a basic competitive difference between Army and Marines. For these reasons, neither of us completely trusts the other.

I first run into Bruce once or twice on campus while working at the food court. I recognize immediately that he is a Vet by the style of his clothes, particularly the green t-shirt he wears beneath a descriptive faded army green t-shirt.

"You served overseas?" I ask the embittered looking scarecrow hunched into a paperback titled *The Principles of Quantum Mechanics*.

"Yeah— did my time-- guess that you did too?"

"I was with Second Battalion First Marine Division outside of Da Nang."

"I was in Korea. If you ask me, America ought to keep out of people's countries and wars. The world would be a lot a lot simpler place."

We end up talking for hours, sharing details of our adventures, both in bitter denial that anything happened beyond the triviality of our duty. I like Bruce immediately. Mostly because in character he is a lot like me; he hides well pain of his frustration. But the truer self of this man glimmers below the surface, like deep scars in the grain of unfinished wood.

One rainy evening as I am powering toward home along Wilshire Boulevard, I see Bruce chasing after a departing bus. He looks like a half-drowned cat, his beard and mustache slimy, water dripping from his fogged horn-rim glasses. I am no drier. The sudden early February storm has caught us both by surprise.

"You want a lift home?" I ask, pulling up beside him.

He looks hesitantly at the vibrating machine considering the alternatives, then swings behind me, directing me to a beach apartment on the Venice Boardwalk. I can feel him shivering as he clutches my shoulders tightly. I am uncertain if it is the nervousness of fear or the cold. Once we jump on the Freeway splitting traffic, his nails dig into my flesh like pruning hooks. Upon arrival at his building, Bruce stiffly dismounts his perch and falls down. To both our surprise, his right sneaker has melted on one side where he has rested it against the exhaust pipe. I can see the displeasure in his face. But whose fault was it? We both laugh at this ironic quip of an extracted due for a free ride.

"Hell— I never liked them all that much anyhow," he grunts. "You want to come up and dry off a little?"

"Sure."

Bruce lives on the fifth floor of an old hotel converted into apartments facing Venice Beach. Like most residences along the shore, it has roaches, smells damp, and with poorly insulated windows. But what a fantastic view he has of the ocean sunset when it is not raining. He expresses gratefulness that I offered him a lift home, even if we are both soaked to the bone. I stay for more than an hour, allowing the worst of the storm to subside. Bruce and I hit it off pretty well. Perhaps, because we both come from humble backgrounds and because neither of us could have afforded to go to university without a V.A. scholarship, we find common turf. But mostly because we both just want to know what the hell is going on in the world.

Through Bruce, I meet Ed, an Ivy League graduate of NYU with a degree in screenplay writing. Ed is well spoken, conceals his insecurity inside determined dreams of high success, and has a noticeable bald spot on the top of his head. This he compensates with the burly mane of a full beard and lives in a run-down beach apartment on the border of Santa Monica. Ed will strike his fortune in the film industry, even if it means his integrity. His best friend is Charlie Hutchins, a talented Shakespeare actor, short and slightly overweight, whose real source of income comes from playing the part of a hamburger in a Wendy's commercial. Although, I am unable to see it at the time, Charlie is the most successful; and will turn out to be the most noble of my new friends.

Then there is the indomitable Jennie Kelly, a lovely creature, petite and seductive, who lives in an upscale renovated apartment building two addresses down from Bruce. She reminds me of a 1920's starlet abandoned by time, continuing ageless as so many other relics in Venice. Like a territorial lion, Ed has already confirmed Jennie as his own. He could have had as much chance catching the wind. As for Jennie, she only toys with him much like her two Siamese cats might torture an exhausted mouse under her bed, often using Bruce, or some other man to make Ed jealous. She is a graduate of a large technical University, a genius, and one of the first women to pioneer the new age of mainframe computer programming. I never knew exactly what Jennie did, only that after a day at work, she arrives home exhausted, removes her professional business attire, and slips on a flowing dress or sometimes cut-off jeans. She can often be seen staring out the window of her third floor apartment, looking like lovely mad Ophelia searching the sunset horizon for some fabled love to return. Tragically, Jennie has really been in love only once with a handsome artist named Kip. After surrendering herself heart and soul, her dreams shattered by the revelation Kip is Gay; and has always been Gay. Just one day out of the blue, he leaves her for a man. Bizarrely they continue to remain friends, even after this personal betrayal. But each time Kip comes to visit her, eventually only to leave, the torment shows obvious in Jeannie's face; and so returns, too, her need to make someone else suffer. I do not think that Jennie ever truly allowed herself to love again, as though that part of her dead and beyond resurrection. I like Jennie immediately, and would have competed with Ed and Bruce for her affections had it not been for an event that happens the first evening we all go out together.

It is a half hour walk from Venice to Marina Del Rey along the Boardwalk. Jennie knows the location of a partially enclosed outdoor terrace converted into a Jamaican Reggae dance bar. I pick up on vibes that Jennie also likes me by the way she keeps moving to my side during the walk, probing me with questions about my past and future ambitions. As I said, she is a cat, always toying with something, a nature oblivious to any disturbance it might cause. Except that Jenny also has a computer brain, which makes her calculatingly dangerous. This does not go unnoticed by Ed. He moves on her opposite side, attempting to disengage her interest in me. At one point, she makes enquiry about my Vietnam experience.

"Did anything good come from your war?"

I perceive in this question a glimmer of humanity that struggles deep in the frozen depths of Jennie's blue eyes.

"Yes, I found salvation in Christ. War takes everything, and when nothing is left there is only a choice between heaven and hell. I would say that eternal life is the most important truth one can discover in this earthly passage. The rebirth of a human soul is worth any present sacrifice of the flesh. I would not trade one day of darkness for the wondrous revelation given to me by the Holy Spirit, which bears witness daily with my spirit the knowledge of salvation."

"I am an Atheist. I do not believe in God or the soul. Life is now. Life is experience and knowledge of things that are; and those things that can be proven by mathematical equation."

"Atheism is only the limits of reason and what can be understood through reason. I am here to tell you, Jennie, that there are things of spirit and truth that are beyond the shadow of reason and models of mathematics."

Ed snickers something in her ear, and both laugh at the private joke. I have already had this discussion with Ed and Bruce, whose views similar to those of Jennie. I know they think me foolish to hold such traditional beliefs in this new age of individualism and humanism. Nevertheless, if God has made me a prophet to them, then I will be their prophet, even if they think me the fool.

Once at the bar, Jennie and I begin dancing together. By now, my ego puffed out as an over-ripe egg ready to hatch. That's when Jennie swats the mouse, as only Jeannie can. In the middle of a song, she turns away from me and begins dancing with a total stranger, a tall handsome black man with young pecan colored skin and an afro. I uncouthly cut in, but instead of parting, they move to the side and continue to dance together. He is, in my mind, a bobbing cobra. Jennie another kind of serpent caught in his hypnotic gaze. I suppose I should have been more concerned for the cobra. My pride gets the better of me. I boldly step between them, grab Jennie roughly by the arm, and demand an explanation.

"Don't touch me!" She shouts and pushes me away. "No one owns me! I will dance with whom I like, and do what I like-- go away!" Then she turns toward Ed and Bruce standing near the bar; "all of you—just go away!"

Without saying a word, I storm out on the boardwalk to get some air. Ed and Bruce soon follow, two dispossessed hounds. Oddly, as the three of us walk home, a greater bond of friendship brings us closer together since we now share the sting of a common nemesis. I have more compassion toward Ed's frustration and choose not to contribute to his future emotional distress. In a way, I pity him, considering that he stands alone in the viper's pit. As far as I am concerned, Jennie Kelly is now officially off my future menu. I will continue to remain her friend for the sake of the group. In time, even Bruce surrenders the chalice of competition. In the end, none of us will have her, not even Ed, though he will continue to try.

A few years later, after she and Ed permanently end their relationship, I will go out on a real date with Jennie Kelly. Afterwards, we end up at my new Santa Monica apartment. To be honest, I suppose I still have lingering feelings for her. As we sit on the floor near the burning gas fireplace, I think there might still be a chance for romance with this eccentric beauty.

"Would you contribute your genes to make my baby?" She inquires matter-of-factly, her cobalt blue eyes piercing coldly into my soul.

"I don't know if I'm ready to get married just yet." I reply honestly.

"Who said anything about marriage? I think just that your genes with mine would produce a beautiful and highly intelligent offspring. I am ovulating, and now would be a good time to conceive."

"Jennie, I like you, but to father a child is a big responsibility. Why don't we wait and date for a while, at least until we get to know each other better?"

"There is no time. I am leaving for Hawaii next week. It is now, or never."

I feel ill. This woman is a heartless robot disguised in human flesh.

We talk for over an hour-- rather we negotiate. Jennie has taken an indefinite leave of absence from her place of employment, deciding to move to the island of Oahu and live in a villa, where she plans to have her baby. She wants me to help her conceive, but does not want me in her life, or have anything to do with the baby. I consider the whole idea another Machiavellian example based on values of selfish design. It is an amoral suggestion, altogether lacking in human expression. But, then again, Jennie Kelly was not completely human; or at least not what I consider human. When it becomes obvious that I have no intention to contribute my sperm on these terms, she rises to her feet and unemotionally prepares to leave.

"Here is the telemetry for my future location in Hawaii," she says mechanically, placing in my hand a business card with a phone number and address printed on the back. "Come visit sometime."

It can always be said that Jennie Kelly programmed to know where she is going. I will unexpectedly see her again sooner than I think.

$\mathcal{T}$he weekend of Easter Sunday, I receive another surprise invitation to Rocky's Malibu home for a Saturday night barbecue. The past winter has been long, my course studies mentally demanding. This particular evening the odors of spring pour down from the Malibu hills, mingled sweetly with a gentle evening breeze from the Pacific. It is another one of those idyllic nights, which makes one happy to be alive; happy to be in the company of family and friends. Rocky, however, appears troubled, talking less than usual and drinking more wine than his habit. Inez retires into the house with my half-sister, Elena, just before eleven, leaving a silence that settles inside Rocky somewhere far over the horizon and in oceans deep.

"I always wondered how you might turn out after your mother left," he sighs somberly. "More than twenty years and it seems just like yesterday. Now you are a man, and an ex-Marine. I never thought that my son might go off to Vietnam."

"Me too, Rocky… but I am glad that God brought us back together."

He shifts uneasily in his chair and exhales. It is difficult for me to know for sure how Rocky really feels about our reunion. I think in one way he really is glad, maybe even proud of how I have turned out. Also, I believe that my testimony of Jesus Christ and immortality of the soul disturbs him deeply. Of course, how can I blame him? It is uncanny how the Holy Spirit moves nearly every time we get together, as though he is being haunted, as once I was haunted.

"You know I used to be an altar boy… that was before I saw what really goes on inside of churches after the doors are closed."

"There are many doors that lead to destruction, but only one door that leads to God, and but one Sheppard that calls our soul to repentance and peace. Jesus says, 'I stand at the door and knock: if any man hear my voice, and opens the door, I will sup with him, and he with me.' Only when that door is open can a man enter into salvation. It is not by flesh and blood, but by the calling of the Holy Spirit. Don't let that door close, Rocky, without entering in while there is still time."

I actually do not know why I say this. I can see clearly the Lord standing at the door of this man's heart. Not the man that is my father, but a man blinded by sin as once I was. I know Rocky struggles against the Holy Spirit. I also know it his decision and that I have no power to wrestle the demons for him. He asks that I sleep over and leave early the next morning to attend Easter Service held at my church in Long Beach. It is my regular habit to attend church at this time, a devotional need for fellowship, partaking hungrily of the milk and honey necessary for spiritual growth. The idea of missing Easter service unthinkable; nevertheless I feel compelled to accept my father's kind offer.

It is still dark outside when Rocky awakens me. He is kneeling beside the couch where I rest, sweating profusely, and appears panicked and confused. I have never seen my father this way before, and to see him now more than a little disturbing.

"You know that church you go to every Sunday," his brow slick with perspiration; "Will you take me and my family there this morning?"

"Yes," I reply without hesitation and immediately arise and begin dressing.

Inez is not too keen on the idea, but accepts after insistent persuasion from her husband. It is strange that these people of obvious means would choose to be chauffeured in my older model car. This bright sunny Easter morning we all cram into my Ford Fairlane destined for a little church nestled in the Forest Lawn Cemetery. We could have traveled in Inez's new Bronco parked in the carport recently won, as a last year's contestant on the *Price Is Right*. But it seems somehow expedient that I be the one to navigate the more than ninety miles round trip. Few cars on the freeway, the sun already high in the sky by the time we arrive. Because it is early, we need to wait for the congregation of a previous church service to finish before our group can enter. This is a transitional location only.

Already a change in spiritual direction is afoot, only I am unaware at this time. Those in charge of church finance are busily negotiating plans to build their own establishment. A church building I will never enter or even know the location. I have faith these earthly ambitions rooted in a foundation of good intentions. However, my personal belief not based on establishment of a worldly edifice or calculated collections instructed by business practicality. I will be called into the path of another ministry less to do with organized religion. Over time, moving of the Holy Spirit diminishes, creating a schism between those with new agendas to establish an earthly temple and the original congregation of those spiritually revived. Nearly all the grassroots supporters drift away like seeds blown in the wind to more fertile soil. The McDonald family will be one of the last pioneers to leave; but even they return to their native Arkansas in search of another revival after Karen marries a Cowboy.

This particular Sunday our presence is more a calling of destiny, than course of future politics. Along with others from my church, the four of us sit on a concrete platform supporting a greater than life statue of Michelangelo's David, reproduced from the four meter tall original located at *Piazza DellaSignoria* in Florence, Italy. I will one day see this magnificent sculpture firsthand, and be no less impressed by the human anatomy embodied in   this magnificent sculpture. My father and his wife have little interest in artwork of antiquity. In many ways, they are far more modern rock and roll in their style of dress and thinking than me. Rocky and I may have a lot of similar taste, only he is more refined to the times. In every respect, Rocky possesses the successful demure of a fallen Malibu star.

Just before noon hour, the church doors fly open releasing a flood of practitioners signaling the end of the first service. Like a hoard of hungry sheep, our congregation files into the brightly lighted chamber to commune in the spirit of Christ our living Lord on this special day commemorating his resurrection and our resurrection. There are too many people for the four of us to sit together. Therefore, Rocky, his wife, and daughter are seated in a pew nearest the altar, while I find a place a few rows back. Not since my conversion has the Holy Spirit moved with such force. I extend my hands toward Rocky and his family, praying in the spirit for the unveiling of their eyes and their hearts.

The dictionary meaning of the word salvation is 'somebody or something that protects or delivers another from harm, destruction, difficulty, or failure'. Rocky has everything the world can give, in need of nothing material. Except his soul dead, dried up and drained of essence. I see in this man some of the man I was, a man bound in darkness so great he does not even know he is bound, starving for fulfillment. I am acutely aware the Holy Spirit is calling him and that I have been sent as a messenger. I earnestly pray his pride will not blind him to the grand significance of this moment in time. I feel an intense jolt. Opening my eyes, I witness the miracle of Rocky and his wife, hands raised, passing together toward the altar and kneeling before a heavenly congregation. It is an extraordinary revelation in the spirit, a time divided by time with eternal significance. It humbles me to see this man of worldly position humble himself before the Lord. Yes, it is a miracle of great blessing to witness the progenitor of my earthly presence step willingly into flowing stream of the Lord's salvation!

There remains a prevailing silence as we drive back to Rocky's Malibu home. I feel a sense of relief and wellbeing, a peace that surpasses the understanding. I think that Rocky feels it, too. We are on the coast highway, nearing the curve of *Leo Carrillo Beach* a mile from the road leading to their Malibu home up on a hill overlooking the ocean, when Rocky turns to me.

"All I want to say is you were right about everything," he says, his eyes moist. "I also want to thank you."

"No, Rocky, it is not me who spoke to you these many months. It has been the Holy Spirit all along. I feel only joy for you and your wife. But I have no recompense in this; rather, it is the same mercy shown to me. Give God only the glory. Salvation is through grace, not by works or wisdom of any man. I thank my God that I have been obedient for your sake. As a man, I kneel at the throne with you glorifying the author of our new faith, but don't imagine me more than this."

We do not speak again the rest of the distance. Inez remains noticeably quiet the entire trip back. It is unclear to me what the events of this day mean to her. She confesses to have had some past dealing in witchcraft, believing this to be the main source of their material success. I do not know the course of her ultimate destination, nor is it my place to judge. I pray only that the spirit of the Lord continues to guide this sister through this life's many shadowy passages. I decline an offer to stay for an early dinner, expressing need to catch up on my studies for impending midterm exams. How much they remind me of Rudy and Jean standing side by side, soon to vanish in my rearview mirror. On the drive back to my West Los Angeles apartment, I feel an irrational sense of relief, but also emptiness, as though my purpose accomplished in a scheme of greater events. It is a feeling particularly strange and unsettling, considering that the relationship with my father has just begun.

The next several months require even greater dedication to my increased study load; and then acquisition of a summer job that requires I work almost every weekend in the Long Beach district. The next Fall Session, I opt to take a Children's Literature class, which I imagine easy, but will demand a lot of reading from a bound anthology of nearly 1300 pages. Besides this I need to read other assigned classics such as Charlotte's Web, Wind in the Willow, and Kipling's The Jungle Book. It will be one of the best classes I will take since introduction to Shakespeare.

Rocky and his wife invite me a few times, but I find myself mostly unavailable. Interestingly, we never again have conversations as we had before. It is as if the message delivered and the rest up to them. It is my understanding that they attend church service on occasion in the Malibu area. On the other hand, I stop going to church altogether when a new pastor starts giving sermons based more on need of money for a new building and less moving of the Holy Spirit. I am not offended, exactly, only less blessed. I give praise that those doors still open the day Rocky and Inez accompanied me there. The few times I do see Rocky, I observe greater peace in his life, the rest I surrender to faith. Rarely do we consciously observe the hand of God working through his angels in mortal dispensation. But the Lord showed me a miracle through these events, and many others since. I stand humble with the Apostles, giving sincere testament of his abiding presence in the affairs of men. And there is still a meaning not yet finished.

*T*he beginning of Winter Quarter sends me scrambling for a new job. Responding to a notice posted by the campus bookstore, I acquire a temporary position to replace someone away on a sabbatical. Between November to December, U.C.L.A. reduces to skeleton operation lasting until after the holidays. In mid-January it starts up again full force until the summer break. I am happy to secure this job, even if for a while because of the easy convenience to and from class. Many of the employees here are Graduate students, easy going, interested only in proficiency. Like most student jobs the pay is minimum wage, the hours long, and includes some weekends. Often it demands that I load my car with several boxes of textbooks, lug them to different campus locations, and sit through long boring lectures to offer them for purchase at the end. Rarely do I sell more than a dozen, hardly worth the sacrifice of a Saturday night. Nevertheless, it is pay, which means survival until my next V.A. check arrives in three months. It seems that for every rare weekend I do have free, Rocky and Inez are busy with other plans. Even Ron and I see each other only on occasions. Since, even gas money remains tight, Ispend nearly all the time in between reading, sometimes watch television,   or on occasions forced to tinker with my motorcycle.

A week prior to the Christmas holidays, Ron calls and asks if I might manage to get off work for a weekend trip to Vegas. His primary interest is to attend an evangelical event; but also he wants to test a new gambling system he believes came to him through a vision. Being a truck driver, he often stops over at Vegas to try his luck. Sometimes he wins, sometimes he loses; but more often, he loses. Through some complicated math, he now believes he has a winning formula. I am not very interested in playing the odds, failing to see the allure.

"I don't think so, Ron. I couldn't even afford to pay my meal on the flight right now."

"You don't need to worry about that. I already booked reservations for two, flight and hotel, and back home Sunday night. Jennifer from work was supposed to go; only she canceled out the last moment. Women— they sometimes do the darnedest things. Come on little brother. You never have seena city until you see Las Vegas at night."

It is true I have never been to this fabled city of lights and entertainment. I once got as near as Reno, but never to Oz itself. I call my supervisor at the bookstore and manage to convince him of a pending urgency, needing my personal attention. I do not lie exactly, nor do I reveal the whole truth, only that a friend desperately needs my assistance. I am a good employee and am allowed to go on the condition that I work extra shifts the following week and weekend.

Las Vegas from the air sprawls across and expanse of flat desert as a dazzling oasis, brightest at the nucleolus, spreading out in all directions, only to wane on the horizon into gray matter of nothingness. We take a shuttle to the hotel, where fortunately, there are two beds. We arrive just in time to attend an evangelical conference held on the suite floor. The main message is that God wants to bless his people with material wealth, and that there is no sin in wanting to be rich. It seems an appropriate message within present context. I suppose I never thought about it before. As a born again Christian, I already feel rich beyond measure. To be perfectly honest, something about worldly materialism, I find repulsive, even detestable. I try to maintain an open mind for the sake of my friend, but deep down I am disturbed by this American dream interpretation of God's gifts to men. Something about the whole concept adolescent and delusional, reminding me of an event related in the book of Acts of the New Testament Bible about Simon the Sorcerer. This man thought to purchase power of the Holy Spirit with money, believing this power something acquirable through material transaction. The Apostle Peter rebukes him, emphasizing that the true gifts of God have no part in worldly commerce. It seems to me that desire for this world's eroding riches allegorical to children playing in a sandbox squabbling over toys thought precious in the moment. Often too late one sees the world as it really is through eyes of an adult, realizing only then all those things desired only conventional extravagance bearing little true significance. I now see through those adult eyes, having received a revelation of the true treasures given in the fullness of season. For this reason, I am uninspired by this *'God to riches'* sermon, but decide in this present to hold my peace.

Ron and I consume a late meal and afterwards wander along the main strip lined with flashing lights of casinos. I know nothing about gambling. Ron suggests I try one of the Crap Tables, while he enthusiastically tries out his new system on the Black Jack table. He advises me to play the Pass or Don't Pass based on rolls of the dice by other players. Even though I never fully understand the odds, I end up raking in several hundred dollars on the initial one hundred dollars I brought with me. I have watched enough movies to know that the smart thing to do is cash out while ahead. To my delight, Ron has also won a pile of money. We are two Kingpins loaded, with more available cash in our pockets than either of us ever had before. Ron has also met a cute redhead during his winning spree, a woman in her late thirties clinging possessively to his arm. After this success, Ron decides to take a separate room two floors up. The next day I rent a new car, and that evening the three of us book dinner reservations at *Caesars Palace*, purchasing tickets for a dynamic performance by Anne Margret. A year earlier, this famous personality had the misfortune to fall off a stage while performing at the Sahara Hotel in Tahoe, shattering the bones of her face, as well as several other injuries. Ron expresses a boyish infatuation for this luscious actress, commenting that she *"looks just as beautiful as before."* I remark that his new consort very much resembles the woman on the stage.

Caesars Palace well deserves its name, a sprawling compound of matchless grandeur that recalls the splendor of a once proud, but fallen empire. The entertainment Coliseum is an enormous chamber, encompassed by a sentry of tiered balconies jutting out toward the center stage, some dominated by private poker tables with a minimum hundred-dollar cash buy in. Ron's attention keeps wandering toward these. I can tell he wishes to be there. But what is the salary of a lucky truck driver to these titans of success? Well-dressed businessmen, who think nothing of wasting stacks of crisp new one-hundred-dollar bills, while at the same time watching an entertainment performance. I think the idea that Ron feels ostracized from this elite society resurrects memories of his youth growing up a poor half Indian, whose mother an alcoholic and whose father buried in a pauper's grave at an early age. Deep down my friend enormously tormented by the illusion of this world denied.

Because he is my brother in the Lord, I pray that Ron finds resolution in his heart and soul.

After the spectacle, Ron and his lady depart for other activities, with the plan that we will call each other the next day in plenty of time before our late afternoon flight departs for LAX. That night, I drive around Las Vegas, exploring this city of lights, which has given me so much. At close to midnight, I stop into a relatively new casino called *The Circus Circus*. Here I am handed a five dollar free chip, a free drink, and escorted to a Crap table occupied by two gentlemen and a woman.

"You throw the dice," the woman urges.

On the first throw, I win a five-dollar chip against the one given to me. On the third roll, I lose both. I decide to buy a hundred and fifty dollars of chips with the remaining one hundred sixty dollars left over from my previous winnings. I am now playing for real, as free drinks continued to appear. I seem to remember buying a few more chips offered by the cute flamingo girl that kept plying me with free drinks. Inside of a couple of hours, I reach in my pocket and realize that I have only one chip left. Each roll of the dice has represented five dollars of hard-earned cash in the real world. But in this mock existence, where nothing as it seems, I have squandered them away like pieces of board game plastic. Then I glimpse the true face of Oz, the deceptive wizard behind the veil manipulating the levers of blinding greed and empty dreams. Here the exposed truth of Las Vegas: skeletal fingers that drive humanity since Adam and Eve cast out of the garden! Now I know first-hand, and behold true face of darkness within the light.

I wish in that moment to escape this city of glitter and make the decision to drive my rented car out into the surrounding desert. Several miles outside the Vegas city limits, I take an unpaved turnoff that leads to a knoll in a dry uncultivated field. Getting out of my vehicle, I look back at the shimmering presence greatly diminished beneath a host of burning stars. Strangely, I miss already the warmth of humanity, a cradled genesis filled with vitality running to and fro as a distant caged animal bound by diver iniquity. I realize here the frontier of a stark wilderness marking fringe of civilization and that I am irresistibly also part of those lights reflecting in the distance. I could no more exist in isolation, than I could exist without sustenance. I am bound to the whims of present condition in contradiction to greater awareness. In time, I will be reconciled to the measure and consequence of this meaning.

It is easy to become disorientated in the desert, particularly at night, a little like being on a ship out at sea; every direction looks the same. I head toward the distant glow, only to reach the edge of a large impassable gully. I navigate miles turning in all directions through this unkempt field, discovering one barrier or another. After many exhausting hours my gas tank nearing empty, I find a rocky, but passable exit to a small country road. Not the way I came, but at least a paved path. This leads to a larger road and eventually to the 15 interchange. To my dismay, I am more than thirty miles from the Las Vegas City limits. At least now, I am no longer lost. Finding a gas station, I empty my pocket of the last few dollars. I am lucky the gas station attendant accepts one the gambling chip as payment.

Ron and I come back from Las Vegas both winners. I am a hundred dollars poorer, which I consider a small price to pay. I have learned something that will instruct me for the rest of my life. Nothing comes free; and all that glitters here on earth only a reflection. Ron retur to Las Vegas alone two weeks later and loses his shirt. I suppose his system has a few unpredictable flaws. He stops gambling after this, saying what all gamblers say in the end: *"What happens in Vegas stays in Vegas."*

$\mathcal{T}$he frostiness of a California November bleeds down from the Malibu hills, mingling with the slightly warmer air nearer the ocean. It is considered chilly, but nothing like the winters back east. A week before Thanksgiving Rocky calls to invites me for an outside barbecue the same week I receive my paycheck, so I volunteer to buy the steaks for a change. It has been nearly seven months since I last saw Rocky and Inez. I think we all made a little apprehensive by the quick passage of time.

Saturday afternoon after a half day of work, I go to the local market for the purchase of three T-Bones. To my delighted surprise, there is a special on something I have seen only in the movies. Buffalo steaks, slightly higher in price per package because of their size, yet are cheaper

per pound than T-bones: large, dark red meaty cuts, as one imagines steaks of the old west should be. I take three, certain that these will be an exotic change from prime beef.

"Buffalo," Rocky comments, and takes a deep whiff to make certain of freshness. "Buffalo is something you don't see every day."

He then covers the dark slabs in his special marinade of wine vinegar, fresh garlic, and wild herbs gathered from the hills behind his house. I must admit I feel proud to present this rare delicacy to my father and his wife. However, Inez refuses to eat anything she does not recognize; and Buffalo is not on her butcher's list. She and Elena opt for a hamburger instead. The first several bites cannot be described as delicious, only different. By the time I gnaw down to the bone, the meat begins to take on a gamy flavor and feels heavy in the stomach. I am sure the experience the same for Rocky; yet he makes no comment. Nevertheless, there is something special about eating buffalo with my father under the brilliant stars of a western night sky, an experience I will remember always. We talk little this evening, even the Holy Spirit still now. This moment remains sacred in my mind, a last supper shared between my father and I.

Upon leaving I notice my gas gage reads nearly empty and I have spent the last of my cash on the buffalo steaks. I decide to go anyway and try to make it back home by faith alone. I reach bottom of the hill and prepare to turn south on the coast highway. I remain here for several minutes lacking conviction to embark on the more than twenty-five-mile trip home with less gas than it will take. Is the wisdom of this act based on faith or foolishness of pride? After all, Rocky and I are friends. Surely, he will not mind lending me five dollars for a week.

"I realize that I don't have any money for gas," I say apologetically when his wife answers the door. "Could Rocky loan me five dollars until next week?"

Inez disappears into the house without inviting me in. She then begins whispering something to Rocky in a tone that sounds agitated. I hear at the end words that cut deeply.

"See-- I told you he is here for money!"

Rocky appears, wearing only his pants and with a five-dollar bill in his hand. He looks uncomfortable, glancing behind as he hands me the cash.

"I am loaning this to you." He announces loudly. "But you know I don't owe you anything."

The spoken callousness of these words revives within me a lifetime of rejection. Words always whispered behind my back representing plans within plans that I know nothing about.

"No, Rocky, you owe me nothing at all. I'll be sure to get this back to you soon as possible."

I could not have felt more hurt than if he had just told me to get lost. Deep down, I know it is not just about the five dollars. Rocky and his wife have conferred that my purpose of being here about material acquisition. In all this time, I never asked him for anything; and in my one hour of need, he throws it in my face as he might to a stranger. The next morning I get up early, withdraw money from my bank, and drive back to Rocky's Malibu home on the hill.

"Here's the money I owe," I say coldly to Inez, handing her a crisp five- dollar note. "I wouldn't want Rocky to pass a day without receiving back what belongs to him."

I depart as unceremoniously as I arrive. I do not care if Inez thinks me angry. I am angry. And I know it will take a while for this anger to subside. Weeks pass, and still no news from Rocky. Of the less pleasant things we have most in common, pride our greatest nemesis. Now I wish I had been a little less stubborn. Not that it would have made any difference, only that I might have seen Rocky at least one more time.

One Monday morning several weeks later, Rocky drops by my apartment on his way to work. I am taking a shower at the time, but instinctively feel the presence of someone inside my dwelling. Rarely do I lock the front door, which in retrospect not exactly prudent living in this rough neighborhood in West Los Angeles. I race out prepared for battle; however, no one is there. On the marble coffee table is a hand-scribbled note that reads:

"I dropped by, but don't have time to stay. I'll call you later." It is signed, *"Your Dad."*

This is the first time Rocky ever acknowledges himself in this familiar way. For him, it is almost affectionate, so I forgive him instantly in my heart for our last encounter. I race off to my classes feeling good, a feeling that I belong; and that I have a father, who accepts and loves me, even at expense of his pride. It is not that Rudy a bad father, only I could never really reach him; nor did I feel him able to reach out to me. Things will be different between Rocky and I for now own. I see him for the first time as truly human. A man able to forgive; and a man I wish to forgive. Together we will overcome male conditioning of our generation that has made us both hard and less trusting. Now we can make things different, perhaps even learn how to truly love one another in weakness, as well as in strength.

I suppose this to be the unspoken affinity unique to a father and son. I remember as   a child sometimes feeling jealous of my little brother because of some invisible link shared by him and Rudy. Now I have some glimmering of what that connection is, my former jealousy elevated to enlightened comprehension.

It is past eight by the time I arrive home, exhausted after a busy day, the grime of freeway traffic clinging to me like gray husk of approaching night. A phone rings incessantly, an urgent distant unrequited screaming from the surrounding darkness. It is my phone.

"Hello," I answer tiredly, upon entering my apartment and simultaneously dropping the heavy bag of books on the floor beside my study area.

A voice sobs on the other end of the line. At first, I do not understand the meaning, thinking that it might be a wrong number. Then the words cut clearly into my soul. It is the voice of Luis Escalera, Rocky's mother.

"Your father killed tonight in car accident."

She continues to sob incoherently and hangs up. I sit down in my study chair stunned, but also strangely at peace. It is as though in some greater scheme, I have witnessed already this event, seeing it clearly since the beginning. Yes, Rocky is dead in present existence, passed into shadow, no longer constrained to the elements, no longer endowed with mechanical force. Yet, I know he is alive in Christ, and I am witness to the salvation of his eternal soul. I begin praising God in the spirit. I praise the Lord for the mercy shown to my father... and to me. These many months, and I never suspected how near eternity; how fleeting this moment called life. I thought Rocky and I had all the time in the world-- not once considering the tragic event of his approaching hour...an hour destined to all in course. Even though I glimpsed his destiny, I never put it together. Now, it is all so clear... so very clear.

I receive notice of his funeral held on Friday. It is a dreary February day, rain and fog since early that morning. The solitary drive along the coast subdues my mind with thoughts lingering between present and past. I stop at the sharp blind curve that marks the point of Leo Carrillo Beach. This is the place where Rocky met his fate; the impact so great that shattered pieces of the Porsche body still litters the narrow shoulder like slithers of broken glass. Years later, I will meet with a lawyer in San Francisco, representing Inez and her daughter in a wrongful death lawsuit. Only then will I see photos of a mangled Mustang with the engine crammed into the backseat. A solitary picture of Rocky, still harnessed into his bucket seat, the entire assembly ripped out, leaving him lying face-down in middle of the Coast Highway. The Porsche had completely disintegrated by the unimaginable force of the impact. I cannot help but think it ironic that he should die this way. But more perplexingly that I had seen this event in a vision, a premonition of warning to my father of a time and place preordained. This vision not provided to change the event, but to bear witness of greater context. For it is destiny of all things to perish in course of time, but only the blood of God's Messiah shed in a time divided by time provided in season to a purpose known only of God. This is a faithful saying, but my spirit continues to bear testimony to this fact.

According to the official police report, a British rock group calling themselves *Deep Purple* rented a house just two doors down from where Rocky and his family live. That fateful night, someone attached to the group decides to drive into Santa Monica in a new rented Mustang. My father is returning home from work, tired, and perhaps thinking about what he will eat. One mile from the turnoff to his house, he rounds the blind point of Leo Carrillo Beach, a precarious bend in the coast highway where the lights of traffic in both directions shine out to sea. Rocky always did drive his Porsche too fast. The combined speed of both vehicles clocked in excess of one hundred and twenty miles per hour. When Rocky sees those lights bearing down on him, he instinctively swerves right. The driver of the Mustang, being from England, instinctively swerves left. Both conductors killed instantly.

I think the funeral particularly depressing. In accordance with Catholic tradition, it is a solemn ceremony presided over in Latin. The Priest holds a censor of smoldering incense and parades around the richly polished wood of an expensive casket spreading smoke through the congregation. No resurrection here; no sense of spiritual revival; only superstition, wailing of the flesh and everlasting blackness of the grave. It is a closed lid affair, poor Rocky's body too badly mangled for the mortician to reconstruct. I suppose that in a way I am glad for this. At least, I might avoid the hypocrisy of viewing a made-up manikin, pretending to be a man once I knew.

This ritual of the living accomplished, we follow a train of three hearses to the Ivy Lawn cemetery, halting near a mound of fresh earth with a concrete and lead grave-liner lowered into a hole in preparation for the coffin. It all seems so morbid, a futile attempt to edify the flesh and bone carcass, as though this empty dwelling still contains living essence. It reminds me of ancient customs of mummification to preserve the physical form through statutory provisions in an attempt to appease the piety of pagan ritual and assure an afterlife through mortal preparation. This not the promise of the God I know and serve. Other than the symbolic disposition of bones during Patriarchal times, there is no ordinance related to processing of the dead as guarantee of resurrection, except the sanitary avoidance of putrefaction. The idea my father's smashed remains entombed inside a babushka doll to the edification of living fantasy, deeply disturbs me. So much resource wasted to erect proud monuments to those erased, when so many in present conditions enjoy neither food nor shelter. Even the name of religion profaned through an example of opulent extravagance glorifying the flesh in death, rather than proclaiming the living new testament of a similitude magnified through resurrected Christ.

I wonder if Rocky might feel the same way today, considering this all planned many years prior to his spiritual revival. If there lingers any consciousness after death, then Rocky will be sorely disappointed, sealed into a darkness of many layers, without the caress of an ocean breeze or chirping of birds, as they build their nest above his preserved shattered skull. Without the grand splash of a summer sunset, he did so love in life; or taste of ocean salt swept from churning winter waves.

As for me, there remains no doubt in my mind that God able to recall the very atoms of every living thing when the time comes, not one atom displaced or forgotten. From bellies of the deep or of particles scattered to the four corners of the earth, from ashes-to-ashes and dust-to-dust, all things called into remembrance, regardless of where the eons scatter them.

After the funeral, we all gather at the home of Luz and her husband in Oxnard. As I walk into the living room to offer Inez my condolence, two lawyers bushwhack me.

"Would you be willing to sign this affidavit wavering all claims to estate of the deceased?" One of the sharks pesters, dangling a pen in my face.

I look around, but there is no protest from anyone in the room. Not Rocky's sister, not his mother, nor his wife say anything, each eyeing me to see what next I will do. It all becomes so clear. This ambush planned long before I arrived, a plan of design made within plans. Luz and her husband, Rocky's sister, and his last wife have formed a conspiracy with these legal vultures to abolish me from any paternal claims. It is another deep stab of betrayal, altogether emptying my bowels of any willingness to fight. I feel surrounded by hungry carrion perched over Rock's cold grave ready to devour the morsels left over. In this moment I decide that I want no part of this last supper.

My purpose here now fulfilled, I angrily sign the waver and depart immediately, never to return. I will, however, run into Inez and her daughter a few years later while walking along the Santa Monica boardwalk. We exchange cool greetings and talk briefly, not once mentioning Rocky or what really took place after his death. In my mind, they will always be my father's wife and daughter, for whom I wish no harm or distress.

I get caught in a torrential downpour swept in from the ocean on the drive home. Upon nearing the dangerous point where Rocky lost his life, I break into praise. My father has escaped a death far worse-- has achieved a crown of greater glory than attainable through the promises of this world! The blue flashing lights of a patrol car appear behind me and I pull over only meters from the accident site.

"I clocked you twenty miles over the limit," the officer reprimands, asking for my license and registration.

I explain that I am returning from the funeral of my father, and that just a few days ago he perished tragically in an automobile accident. I hope the truth of this explanation might be enough for him to have compassion and give me a break.

"Then he would be glad if his son didn't die the same way."

I am back in present time again. The following week I pay the ticket in the knowledge that time pauses for no one: the future a winding highway racing errant toward destiny; the past dead and buried, already vanished in the rearview mirror of traveled distance.

Part Seven

Illuminations at Perigee

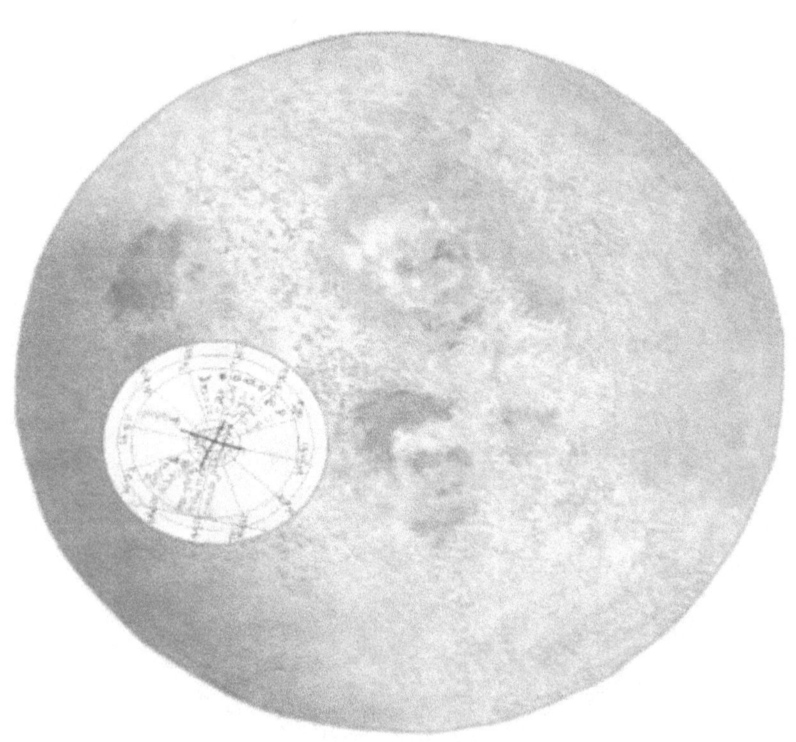

Shadows of Light

They so darkly beautiful there
as pearls strung together
night illuminated in reflected light
blind in a vision of mortal doubt
the world sees with eyes plucked out
to watch them appear without seeing
without conscience without meaning
they as souls spun within the moon
swirled in zenith of a lunar noon
they to whom light as fleeing
the wonder and lightness of being
spirits reborn without sorrow without sin
they to whom dreams in believing
there may be more to hope more to lose
more to light than in heavenly shoes
more to shadows than approaching night
to see more than through fading sight
sparkle of angel dust in their hair
they the children born of air
they so darkly beautiful there

*R*ocky has been gone since more than a month, perished in time, as all things once plucked from the vine. I choose not to dwell on what is lost, but rather accept the change I cannot change. Ron and I begin hanging around at a bar on Redondo Beach, where the drinks cheap and the women more aged. I become friendly with the bartender, a bald-headed Greek, who also served in Nam during the early sixties. He claims to have a metal leg as a souvenir from the war, but never shows it. I think he has taken a liking to me, because he has a tendency to push the female patrons in my direction. Mostly, they are older, yet still in their prime. Grateful, I buy him a drink from time to time with a grandiose toast to the days of Nam. Unlike Bruce, this ex-soldier is not bitter, even after sacrifice of an appendage to a fruitless campaign. He wears a gold ring in one ear, which makes me suspicious that he might be gay. I must admit that I am a little homophobic at this time in my youth. Perhaps my manhood a little more fragile than I am willing to admit. However, later in life I will get past this stigma. One night after a round of Seagram, he tells me he has a 1959 MGA to sell in running condition. I shrug off the idea, considering investment in a sports car beyond my budget, saying only that I will think about it.

The same night I meet an attractive lady named Charlotte from Texas. She and her husband are visiting L.A. for a few weeks on business. Actually, it is her husband doing the business, a wealthy rancher along the Pan Handle, also rich in oil wells. Charlotte and I talk for hours, buying each other drinks, gazing fondly into each other's eyes. Though married to one of the wealthiest men in America, she is miserably unhappy and lonely. They are childless, both with teenagers from previous marriages. Past midnight, Ron comes over to inform me he is ready to leave. I hand Charlotte my phone number and ask that she call me before returning to Texas. She promises she will, but I am doubtful I will ever hear from this interesting lady again.

The following Saturday, I prepare to head east on my motorcycle for a Safari into the California badlands beyond Riverside County. This is a buffer zone between the civilized populous and the dry desolate expanse representing the vaster portion of the Golden Gate State heading east. I rise early in the morning, stuff my backpack with necessary provisions, oil my twelve-gage double barrel shotgun purchased through the Camp Lejeune Commissary before shipping off overseas, and sling the blackened Bowie Knife over my shoulder. I wear my jungle camouflage hat and jacket as good measure. This is no picnic trip. As the desert creeps westward year after year, drying up the precious wells, entire farming communities disappear into draught with only a few skeleton foundations of what were once houses and barns. Even the sturdiest animals perish, but not the pigs. This tough omnivore capable of surviving on anything, even able to adapt to these harsh conditions, free range without competition and are dangerous. Pigs are known to attack and eat other animals, as well as each other, becoming dangerous predators in the wild. They even change physically, growing long dangerous sharp tusk, their hair becoming matted tangles of razor thistles from traveling through thick underbrush of tumbleweeds. In fact, these animals are physiologically closer to the menacing Wild Bores of Africa and South America, than the domesticated variety that most of us recognize on tended farms. It is for this reason that the state of California has issued a bounty of fifty dollars a head with the proof of two amputated ears removed from the carcass of a dead animal. I have never been that much of a hunter; but for this kind of money, I am determined to learn. After all, how difficult can it be to kill a few pigs?

I arrive at a designated area on the map, less than a mile from a failing farm, still occupied, as evidenced by a curl of white smoke escaping from the chimney. These badlands act as a buffer zone between the true desert and the lower irrigated regions. The underground water table once collected enough to sustain an existence, but that water is drying up. Soon the wilderness will creep back in and reclaim the land. Stashing my gear near a shrub patch beneath an identifiable rock formation, I begin scouring the area. You would think the task easy to spot a prey in this semi-arid region, where one can see for miles in all directions. However, the vastness is deceptive, with tangled brush of tumbleweeds snared together and anchored by sharp thistle plants of a dead orchard, now choked by a maze of blind corridors running through them. Washed out gullies and hidden revives act as natural borders, eroded by flash floods and the sharp edge of unobstructed windstorms. This is indeed no-man's land, where outlaws of the old west, as depicted by the writer *Louie L'Amour*, evade capture by hiding in plain sight, often to disappear into grave of a dry gulch, their remains dispersed by vultures and starving scavengers. I shiver to think of the many dreadful possibilities that can ambush a man out here alone.

Late noon, and still nothing, except a straggled Coyote off in the distance that saw me long before I see it? I have brought a binocular acquired at a yard sale for a dollar. One of the lenses is missing, but the functioning lens proves sufficient as a one-eyed telescope. Considering the vast distances out here, the apparatus serves some practical purpose after all, well worth the investment. I have no watch, but judging by the position of the sun, it must be well past noon. I therefore crack open a can of sardines, washed down with a swig of warm canteen water. I begin to think that perhaps this all a waste of time. Maybe the animals already hunted to extinction, considering the bounty more than a few weeks old. No doubt there are many hunters, more proficient and better equipped, that have taken advantage of a profitable expedition.

As the sun nears the western horizon, I think I see movement not more than fifty yards from my position. I scour the area with my eye piece and decide it a mirage, a shadow only, blending into the dead surrounding terrain. But no, it is not a shadow! Appearing on a small knoll closer now, stands a beast six-- maybe seven feet long and weighing not less than 300 pounds. I can just barely make out what appears to be gnarled tusk protruding from the monster's jaw. Grabbing my loaded shotgun, I jump-up and start my motorcycle. My plan is to cut-off the creature's route of escape by coming up from the rear, forcing it against the shrub patch. This is exactly what the thing wants; only I lack experience to predict what happens next.

I see myself as a modern-day buffalo hunter hunched in the saddle of my ferocious 350cc CL motorcycle, shotgun ready on my lap. As I approach the startled animal, less than ten meters away, it turns and bolts toward the tumbleweed barrier, disappearing into an invisible corridor. The passage, though narrow, is wide enough for me to follow. The desert sage walls on both sides whip across my hands and clothing as sharp barbs, the pain nullified by the adrenaline of the hunt. Accelerating, I approach to within a couple of meters of the grunting wild hog. Taking the shotgun in my left hand, I aim down at the head and fire. I do not know for sure if I grazed the beast, or missed altogether. I remember the recoil of the blast greater than anticipated, and that the animal squeals horribly, pivots left and continues running into a side corridor. Applying the brakes already out of the question, I bust through a dry crackly barrier and find myself no longer on earth. I witness everything happening remotely, acutely aware of each detail, as I move through the air in slow motion. I manage to leap from the whining motorcycle, at the same time releasing the shotgun. I next hit hard the tapering face of an eroded hill, sliding down an embankment unharmed. My bike, however, fares less well. The front forks so badly bent that to ride is out of the question. Gathering my scattered equipment, along with broken pride, I decide I am lucky after all. The dry gulch, at least twenty feet deep, scarred with sharp rocks and veins of deep crevices, promise certain death to the wayward cowboy. I have somehow beaten the odds, surviving by a miracle, withonly a few minor cuts and bruises, mostly owing to the relatively softembankment eroding into pebbly sand on the opposite face. But in the moment, my greater concern is how damaged is my wonderful motorcycle?

I push the crippled machine along the ravine incline, until it eventually empties into a flat plain. A couple miles in the distance, I can make out the skeletal shape of the farmhouse seen upon arrival. Circling around to pick up the rest of my supplies, I head this direction. It is nearly dark by the time I knock on the front door.

"What you want?"

The voice is less human, more a growl, than articulated words. The door slings open, revealing an old man with a lantern extended in one hand, the other concealing something behind his back.

"Sorry to disturb you," I say humbly. "I wrecked my motorcycle while hunting. I was wondering if I might leave it in your barn for a few days, or until I can come back with my car?"

"Hunting— hunting what? There ain't nothing here worth hunting."

"Wild pigs— the *California Department of Fish and Game* is offering a fifty-dollar bounty on each hog. I almost got one today, but it was too smart for me."

"Them critters don't do no harm. Besides some of them are on my property and belong to me. It's good you missed." The shriveled corpse takes a deep breath, and then exhales. "Go ahead and stick the damn machine in the barn, but don't you come back hunting on my land again."

He slams the door shut with the finality of a haunting ghost. I push my damaged bike into the shadowy interior of a slouching structure, as much rickety as the owner of this land. Some part of me rebels against the idea that this dried-up husk of a man claiming propriety of a wild pig two miles from his house. He makes it seem that he owns everything as far as the eye can see. Then, I consider that maybe it is I that does not see context of the greater picture. Maybe, by the true laws of nature, he does own everything as far as the eye can see. After all, this man represents the last living soul in these dying parts. Who am I to challenge the vague borders of this formidable principality?

A desert mile later, I cross the continental Interstate 10, a slither of civilized passage running east and west through this vast wilderness little changed since the days of Wagon Trains. The setting sun melts into the distant horizon, leaving a warm trail in the western sky tracing the only way home. Without further hesitation, I begin the more than fifty-mile trek back toward the L. A. basin. What is a fifty-mile force march to one still a young Marine in his mind?

I hope in the beginning to hitch a ride. However, after an hour, I give up trying. Two Highway Patrol cruisers pass me by without even slowing down. I have become a nomad in a no man's land. In retrospect, I suppose I must have been a frightful sight in my military camouflage and jungle boots. Black grease, dried blood mixed with dirt mottling my face and hands. Add to this a loaded shotgun cracked open over my backpack, a menacing Bowie Knife slung over my left shoulder, the dangling handle within hand's reach. All combined with tense exhaustion of a disappointing expedition. No doubt this day I fulfill everyone's nightmare of a deranged Vietnam vet, filled with anger and blood, prepared to do battle with anything unfortunate to cross my path.

Yes, in reality, I am angry—mostly angry with myself for traveling into this empty wilderness on a fool's errand, only to wreck my motorcycle. Angry because I thought to make a quick buck by murdering an unsuspecting animal adapted to its environment, and with plans to leave the carcass to rot. Mostly I am angry, because I realize I have brought this judgment on myself, and that it is just after all. Then I ask God is it also just that Rocky had to die so soon? We were at beginning threshold of truly knowing one another as father and son-- now that opportunity gone-- forever erased and immutable!

"Why?" I demand, shouting into the encroaching infinity of desert sky. "Why now-- and why like that?"

"It was the way prepared. The only way— a way prepared since the beginning." A small voice replies within.

Day light begins to disperse and settle upon the distant horizon, as cars pass with headlamps turned on. My mind and body slip into a mechanical mode, detached from the moment. I begin spontaneously to recite Marine Corps march cadences. A host of stars fill a moonless sky, remaining distant, and no nearer than when I first perceived their existence. Except for the occasional flare of a passing vehicle, the blackness complete. Soon I am aware of nothing, except the rhythmical shock of one foot followed by the other, striking the asphalt pavement with automated precision. I am on just another force-march, just another objective to be reached.

How much time passes is unclear; the outer darkness pressing steadily into crevices of my distressed soul. A horde of several Harleys roar past me and pull over on the shoulder about a quarter mile ahead. Here are the true nomads of this outer darkness expanse, legions of restless souls, roaming these western highways and byways in search of an elusive freedom and peace unobtainable to their natures.

They might be friendly or they might attack like wild dogs just for the fun of it. Headlights shine in my direction, winking in and out by eclipsing bodies. I continue to march in a straight line toward them, one hand resting on the hilt of my Bowie, prepared for battle. As I approach within ten feet, a large silhouette steps in front of the blinding light, scrutinizing the situation and me. He then makes a motion with his arms, whistling shrilly. In unison, the bikes grumble alive and the pack vanishes into the night. Were these Angels, or some other motorcycle club that populate the passes of this Wild West frontier? I often wonder what their true intentions were: if they had thought to do me harm, or just maybe offer a ride to a fellow phantom of the highways? Whatever the scenario, I suppose they prudently decide to be on their way and let this lost warrior find his own way.

The air begins changing ever so slightly, becoming grey matter, as myriad of stars fading into an ember canopy-- all signs of early morning. Shapes and contours morph once more into living context; the hibernating world no longer dead. I have marched all night, covering a distance of perhaps forty miles. A few hundred meters ahead, I see the cloverleaf interchange connecting Highway 15 north and south, rising out of the surrounding terrain like the bones of a giant fallen mastodon. Exhausted beyond endurance, I find a place amid the columns of concrete and lie down at the base of a pillar that helps support the massive structure. The rumble of increased morning traffic, early commuters rushing through hubs of commerce disturbs me little. I am too tired to notice the litter of discarded cans and bottles, empty cigarette packs, and garbage withoutdescription, all discarded onto this grassy hollow populated by a solitary withered shrub. It makes no difference to me that I am on foot in the middle of nowhere, a vagabond belched from the bowels of a shameful place in history called the Vietnam War. With these thoughts and others, I promptly succumb into dreamless slumber.

I awaken to the hot morning sun stabbing my mind and obliterating a nightmare I do not wish to remember. I am still exhausted, but determined that my body will follow the command of my will. Attempting to rise, I fall, racked by agonized throbbing in my feet. Loosening the boot strings, I manage to stand after a few attempts, realizing this day I will not be able to trek another day's journey home. I spot a Denny's restaurant on the other side of the Cloverleaf and decide to limp there for a coffee and a bite to eat. Once inside, I am struck with the revelation that just south on the fifteen is Torrance, home city of my friend Ron. Today being Sunday means Ron might be home, probably preparing for Church service by now.

"Good morning," answers a familiar robust voice.

"Ron… I'm sorry to call you like this, but I have a problem."

I then sheepishly relay to him events of the past sixteen hours. "Don't worry little brother. I woke up last night and the Holy Spirit had me start praying real hard for you. Now I know why. Stay where you are. I'll be there quick as I can."

Ron as true a friend as one might have in this life is there to save me again. He is in my mind to this day an Angel sent from God, loyal to the end. God will eventually provide to this man a loyal and loving wife, the devoted companion he so longs for. My greatest hope is that he looks back on these tumultuous days and thinks of me with certain fondness as well. We were both young then, filled with dreams, and a burning desire to serve the Lord of our new found salvation. We both also had many things to learn, which eventually splits us along separate paths.

I am sitting near the front window nursing a cup of cold coffee, when an hour later I spot a familiar canary yellow pickup sliding down the north-bound exit. In the bright sun, it reminds me of a golden chariot with kind Prometheus, giver of fire, at the helm.

"You look like a real killer. No wonder nobody would give you a lift." Ron remarks, as I climb into the cab.

"I went hunting, not a social event."

"Friend, there's no need to get all puffed-up. I'm just stating things the way they appear."

"I'm sorry, Ron. You are right. I feel like I did first coming back from Nam. I think I need prayer."

We both begin praying in the spirit, immediately breaking into joyful singing, the peace of something greater over-shadowing the finite of our beings. The dark thoughts of the preceding day and night vanish into a timeless realm. My soul unbound, I am lifted above the cares and tribulations of this present hour. My wise companion insists on going back and picking up my motorcycle. Then, I must have fallen into sleep, because the next thing I know Ron is asking if it is the next exit.

The farm house sags unchanged in the abandoned distance, a relic from another time, soon to be erased from living memory. We knock on the door, but no one answers. The windows, nearly opaque with age and cobwebs, reveal only shadows of a table and chair. Standing against one wall is the specter of a grandfather clock, but no sign of a living occupant.

"Are you sure this is the right house?" Ron skeptically inquires.

"I'm sure. Over there is the barn where I stowed my bike."

It is still where I left it, damaged, but not without a promise of repair. Together we hoist the crippled machine into the bed of the pickup, press a couple of dollars into the front door jamb of the house, and head to my home. Once there, we again hoist it back to the ground and roll it into the garage. As he leaves, I cannot thank Ron enough. He comments that I should be able to repair the damage without it costing too much.

After he is gone, I examine more closely the extent of what must be done. I might make the motorcycle functional again by just changing the front fork. I know a used motorcycle parts shop nearby and will negotiate in the coming week a complete fork assembly, including the shocks, for thirty-five dollars. It will be a challenge to change them myself; but what choice do I have? As always, I will get the job done, and be left with a couple of pieces that remain a mystery as to where they belong. Although the Honda runs almost as well as before the incident, there is a little too much play when negotiating tight turns and vibrates badly at speeds over sixty miles per hour. Nevertheless, I manage to use it like this for almost three years, which says a lot about state-of-the-art performance of most things. What I had hoped to be a profitable weekend turns out to be a costly lesson learned.

I shower away the grime of the past two day, eat a simple meal consisting of a canned-tuna sandwich, and prepare to turn-in early. Then the phone rings.

"Charlotte," I say surprised.

"My husband and I are going back to Texas next week. I would like to see you before I leave."

"Or course— I didn't expect to hear from you so soon! But I would like to see you, too."

"I hope it's not bad timing."

"Not at all," I lie. "I just finished showering and was about to get dressed."

"Don't put too much on," she chides impishly, "except maybe just a pair of boxer shorts."

This is all I need for a second wind. I give directions on how to navigate to my place and wait expectantly like a young school child. Charlotte arrives in record time driving a red Cadillac convertible. She is older than I remember, yet elegant in a way that one might discover in the bouquet of an aged wine. I know what she wants; and I want it, too.

There is such longing in Charlotte's eyes, virtuous desire mixed with worldly passion creating a hunger through repressed desires. Trapped in a loveless relationship she does not know how to escape, she has taken a bold step to find freedom. I am her Adonis ascending naked to over-shadow nakedness of flesh and soul. It is something imaginary, but also very real in the moment. It is as though we are both dying embers floating aimlessly in a vast universe, brought together for the climax of this moment. I see in this woman's sad blue eyes a prisoner bound in tightened knots of a passionless existence. As I near orgasm, I hear the groans of Charlotte's promised freedom released at last.

"You are beautiful," I whisper into the trailing night.

I must have fallen immediately asleep. My body made so tense by events of the past thirty hours, releases like rubber into profound depth of relaxation. I have no idea when Charlotte leaves, or even if she may have tried to revive me. No doubt, she thought it odd for me to pass out this way.

I can only imagine her perception of this untimely rendezvous. Perhaps I should have explained my exhaustion before we made love; maybe Charlotte might have stuck around for a little longer. But maybe, too, she still would have vanished before morning light, as all pleasant dreams do. I will never see or hear from this woman again. Like all ghost and fantasies encountered along the way, this woman named Charlotte passes into a faded counterpane of rich memories forgotten... until just now.

I decide to buy the MGA, even against the advice of my friend. Because of lack of worldly experience, I think the idea of owning this iconic vehicle appealing to my youthful vanity, without considering that a sports car demands constant attention. I sell my Fairlane for $475.00 to a man with a wife and two kids, and pay $350.00 for a car that has been stored in a garage for the past three years. My bartender acquaintance neglects to tell me that he has lost his driver's license and not started the car since. My first unseen expense is to invest in two six-volt batteries linked in- series and mounted into compartments behind the seats either side of the rear drive shaft. Because British cars are positive ground, I damage the coil by connecting the system incorrectly. This costs me another $18.00. The car starts, but runs unevenly and stalls during acceleration. I invest in a Haynes Owner's Manual for another $7.00, and after extensive reading, comprehend the engine equipped with a dual SU carburetor system, requiring oil poured into reservoirs on the top of each unit. They are both bone-dry.

Now the British 1600cc engine starts effortlessly. As Rudy would say about any good sounding motor, *it runs smooth as a sewing machine'*. I spend several days making tidy my new ride. It takes me many hours of driving to get used to the four-speed floor-mounted stick drive, plus reverse. In time, however, I learn to appreciate the practical sporty design.

The aluminum body is in good shape, except for perceptible wind ripples running along the aerodynamic length when viewed from a certain angle. It is a grey motley color, reminiscent of a battered World War I *Sopwith Camel*, and with a heavy vinyl soft-top that I raise only when it rains. In fact, I often feel like an intrepid aviator skirting around corners or zipping daringly through traffic in this peppy low-center-of-gravity machine. As soon as I get a little extra money, I invest $29.95 for an *Earl Scheib* metallic-blue paint job.

A week after the paint job I unexpectedly need to change the rear muffler at another cost of $20.00. It takes me all day one Sunday in the alley behind where I live to pry off the old rusted piece. Installation of the new muffler goes relatively quick, only I break one of the rubber supports. Unwisely, I use a coat hanger instead of buying a new support for two dollars. A decision I will later regret.

Bruce has met a girl named Catherine, who attends *U.C. San Jose* and studies Bio-ecology. They often fly back and forth for visits. Presently, neither has the money to fly. Bruce proposes that we drive up in my car, splitting the gas.

"Vallerie has a cute sister named Tamera," he coaxes enticingly. "She thinks you two might hit it off. She's a real looker."

Being part Lebanese, Bruce possesses the qualities of a natural salesman. Not that I need that much selling. I like Vallerie since the first time meeting her, but more plutonic, than desirous. This is partly because I consider she is my friend's special interest, but also because Vallerie is not my physical type. I wonder if Tamara might be any different. Nevertheless, the idea of traveling up the coast highway in my convertible sport car appealing, since this particular weekend I am free.

Before noon on Friday, we stuff our few belongings into the compact trunk and skirt up the Coast Highway. By half past four, we straddle the precarious ribbon of a two-lane road that climbs into the elevated region of Big Sur along the scenic ocean route.

"Smells like a forest fire," I comment, surveying the wooded hills to our right.

Bruce grunts agreement, also scouting the dry tree-covered terrain. To the left precarious cliffs drop hundreds of feet into the pacific; to the right a green mountainous barrier separating the coast from arid plains that spread eastward of the Santa Lucia Mountain Range. Highway 1 cuts along the contour of a twisting range reaching an elevation of approximately 300 feet above this stretch of coastline. I remark that the higher we climb, the stronger the odor of burning wood. Suddenly Bruce begins yelling frantically something about there being a fire.

"Yes, I smell it, too." I yell back above the roar of engine and lashing wind.

"You are on fire!" He shouts articulately, pointing down between my legs.

I am now aware of crimson-yellow flames spreading along the floorboard. I swing over to the narrow shoulder, leaping into action. I tear off my shirt and manage to get the flames out before the seat also catches fire. My shirt now only a smoldering rag, but at least my MG saved. Ripping-out the burned carpet, I discover a charred narrow hole, at least three inches wide and almost a foot long, running from under the seat to half the distance of the floorboard. The cause is immediately clear. Because I used a coat hanger to support the muffler, I failed to take into account the distance of the pipe from the bottom of the car. Because the MGA floorboard constructed of airplane plywood sheets screwed to a metal frame for lightness and flexibility, it is subject to an unsuspecting vulnerability. The extreme temperature generated by the super-heated exhaust pipe caused the wood to combust. Now that the drama passed, Bruce and I look at each other and begin laughing hysterically.

"That's what I call a hot seat," Bruce snickers.

"At least we know that Big Sur isn't going up in flames."

"Hurrah for the forest, but looks like we have a problem. How are we going to go without it happening again?"

Bruce is right we do have a problem. Even though most of the surrounding area burned away around the pipe, there is still chance that the extreme heat of another hundred miles might be enough to ignite the wood again. Upon searching the trunk, I find a piece asbestos cloth on top of the spare wheel. A mystery of providence that it is even here. Nor do I remember ever seeing it before. Miraculously, it is exactly what I need. Using a strip of wire scavenged from the side of the road, a remnant from a semi-truck blow-out, I tie the heat-resistant cloth around the affected area and we are on our way again.

We arrive in time for dinner. Tamara is much prettier than I expected, much younger, and a virgin. Chronologically, our age difference less than 3 years; only I have been through a war, and with life experience that exceeds most in my generation. I like Tamara, but make it clear from the beginning that I think it best to avoid an intimate relationship. Perhaps it is because Tamara professes to be a virgin and waiting for the right person to come along. Deep down I respect this attribute, wishing that I had waited, not desiring to deprive another of love's potential. As sweet and lovely as Tamara is, I know within myself that I do not love her, perceiving this intelligent vital woman as I might one of my sisters.

The next day we all go on a picnic along a rocky shore southwest of Santa Clara where the turbulent ocean waves form tide pools. The water too cold to swim in; yet, the shallow pools, warmed by the sun, prove to be perfect reservoirs for sunbathing. Bruce and Vallerie become romantically intertwined, which make Tamara and I a little uncomfortable.

"I think I will go exploring," I announce.

"I'll go with you." Tamara insists.

Surprisingly, Tamara is rather agile, as courageous as any boy, capable of skirting along the narrow black shoreline rocks. Discovering a small inlet beach at low tide, we stop here to rest.

"This is a beautiful place," Tamara ventures. "It reminds me of an episode on Gilligan's Island."

"Funny— I was thinking about Robinson Crusoe."

"I guess because it is isolated like one might imagine an island to be. Do you like isolation?"

"Maybe I do a little. I feel somehow more near to God and less trapped in machinery of this world."

"No man is an island unto himself. That's just the way we are made. I sense you are lonely."

Tamara is right. I am lonely, but I do not feel alone. I share that the thing I truly seek is fulfillment, only I cannot presently explain exactly what this means. We end up talking in this place for a long time, until change of the tide begins. Upon our return, Bruce and Vallerie are waiting; everything packed into my MGA, ready to return home. The two girls prepare a delicious vegetarian meal, which we eat under the stars on the back terrace. The next morning Bruce and I leave early for our return journey back to Los Angeles.

I completely forget about those hours spent talking with Tamara by the end of summer break. A few days after mid-term exams that inaugurates the middle of my new quarter, the phone rings heralding pleasant news.

"Hey, guess who's in town." Bruce announces coyly.

In his usual character of suspense mixed with sordid human expression he confirms that Vallerie and Tamara are visiting on a week vacation. He adds that I am invited to join them on the Boardwalk for a local excursion. I decide a little socializing welcomed pressure release at end of an intense academia quarter. That night we meet-up at a local dance bar, joined by Ed and Jennie. I must admit Tamara to be fun, her innocent appeal inspiring a genuine attractiveness. The following Friday, I invite the gang to my apartment for food (which I am informed must be dishes excluding any meat products). Although this a culinary challenge, I proudly produce a meal acceptable to the most ardent vegetarian, consisting of Jean's special Pinto Beans, minus the fatback meat, Eggplant Parmesan, and Avocado dip to go with Taco Bell corn chips. After enjoying this hearty repast, we all lounge around for a night of local T.V., beginning with a rerun of MASH, followed by Kojak, and ending with an episode of Twilight Zone hosted by Rod Serling. All except Tamara and I end the evening by smoking a joint. Tamara protests her desire to stay longer, but departs with them upon Vallerie's insistence. I should have suspected then that trouble coming.

With my employment at the UCLA bookstore renewed, I decide to take it easy and enjoy the summer break for a change. Maybe the job pays less well than I might have found elsewhere, but the hours are easy, transit close, and provides at least enough to live on.

One evening a week later, I arrive home to find a candle burning on my marble coffee table and a note that reads: "A surprise is waiting in your bed." Tamara lies naked, smiling shamelessly, as Lady Godiva spread beautifully over the familiar sheets of my place of repose. I am altogether speechless, and also flattered. Tamara's depth of affection for me is now unmistakable, as I fight a battle within against desire for this lovely creature presenting herself naked, and wisdom of better reason. I realize only now that our meanings not the same. Aware of the delicateness of this moment, I feel a deep empathy for this girl of innocent affection, not wishing to inflict a scar of rejection.

"I am truly honored that someone as lovely as you would want me to be your first love," I say tenderly, trying to be as diplomatic as possible. "It is not that I don't find you attractive… it is just that I am not the one for you... the one you are waiting for."

"But I want you. Since the first time I saw you I can't think of anything else. You must surely feel something for me."

"I do Tamara. Just not in that way. You are so young and innocent.It would just be wrong for me to take advantage of your affections. You need to find someone who will love you and be worthy of your love. I know that deep down you want a relationship to last."

"You have no idea what I want!" She snaps, jumping up and pulling on her clothes. 'Don't worry— I will find someone else-- someone with a heart!"

I attempt to reason with her, but she storms past me and out the door. I must admit this experience unsettling, making me feel empty and ambivalent about what it is I really do want. I lie down in my empty bed, the odor of Tamara's perfume still lingering, and wonder if I might have handled the situation differently? Would it have been so terrible to at least embrace, maybe stroke Tamara's soft hair, maybe even kiss her a little? Was Tamararight-- am I devoid of natural affection? I tell myself it is for Tamara's own good and that one day she will be glad for this present frustration.Deep down, I do know the truth. Were Tamara not a virgin, I would have taken her. The reality being that I am afraid of true commitment. To defile her would mean an allegiance of responsibility I am presentlyunwilling to accept. Nevertheless, I remain confused, and sad for the loss of a friendship.

In the following days, Tamara makes a point to avoid me. No longer invited to casual get-togethers with my friends, I begin to feel like the odd man out, but do not voice protest. After all, what is there to say? I will experience this segregation again many years later after my divorce, turned away by friends and family. Those once near to my heart forced to take sides and establish barriers of allegiance. Now, as will be then, I have no camp, unable to mount a defense or offer any apology that might make any difference. It is not my fault Tamara in love with me. Why should I be blamed for a young girl's infatuation; and should I have compromised my more noble values just to fulfill Tamara's tantrum desires? I decide I have done nothing worthy of rejection. If my friends judge me on such shallow grounds, then they are less the friends I imagine. Of course, I never really knew Tamara's version of events. Still, I think that friendships should remain impartial, and not allow loyalties to become pawns of irrational partisanship.

I am better off alone, preferring my thoughts to be my own, and not the influence of others. Because I attend church less often I devote more of my Sundays going to the beach, tinkering with my motorcycle, or just sitting alone in my apartment reading for pleasure. This is partly because of a real lack of resources; but mostly because of a new material creed festering within a congregation of ever fewer familiar faces. It is not that I am against the idea of a community wanting better accommodations for themselves and their children. However, I feel that Christian service should be a symbol of outreach into the highways and byways of this world, shining a light of salvation to those lost and without the knowledge of God and the anointed Christ. Once it becomes a members only private club symbolized by an earthly edifice, then it is no longer an instrument of the Holy Spirit.

This is also the summer the McDonalds move back to Arkansas with their daughter Karen and her new fiancée. They are one of the first families to depart. Then Jim, an ex-policeman, along with his pretty wife June vanish to regions unknown. These two folks show particular kindness to me, extending invitation to their Long Beach home for dinner on more than one occasion. June confides in me one night while I help her with washing the dishes that she is less than happy in her marriage. I try not to read into the meaning of this confession, saying only that her husband a good man tempered by Christian values. Once they even give me a Kirby vacuum cleaner. I mistakenly presume this to be a free gift, until Jim appears one day at my door demanding it back. I am more than a little embarrassed. In retrospect, June did hint that she might wish to have back the machine one day. At some point I planned to return this powerful household appliance, but neglected to make it a priority. I never see Jim or his wife again after this forceful retrieval, and continue to hope to this day that their fragile relationship weathered the future migration to parts unknown.

One Saturday afternoon, I catch the eye of an attractive woman in one of the aisles as I restock a shelf. She possesses a picturesque prettiness that I like. Only by her hands do I discern her a little older than she appears. Her hair dyed rich auburn, which serves to accentuate the hazel in her eyes.

"Do you have the works of Marquis De Sade?" She purrs with a slight European accent.

Unfamiliar with the author, I excuse myself and make inquiry of the manager. As it turns out, we do carry a volume titled The Marquis De Sade, a biography.

"Thank you," she smiles, placing her hand affectionately on my arm. "You wouldn't believe how difficult it is to find any of his works in this country. Are you familiar with any of his writings?"

"No," I confess. "I have read the Count of Monte Cristo, as well as some translated works by Moliere. I would love someday to read them in their original language. Maybe after I take enough French, I will do this."

"Of course," she replies condescending. "Meanwhile, what does a nice young boy like you do for fun?"

I may have pretended naiveite, but I know what she means. Since it is time for my lunch break, I ask if she will join me for a beverage at the canteen. During the course of conversation, she entices me to join her later to see Shampoo, a new Hollywood movie starring Warren Beatty. I would have gone anywhere with this lovely madam. I begin to formally introduce myself, but she stops me, insisting on no last names and adding it better this way.

I meet her after work at the front entrance and take a seat in a new powder blue mustang convertible with pristine white interior. We first grab a bite to eat at the falafel stand on Westwood Boulevard, then off to a local theatre. Throughout the movie, we intimately make out like a couple of teenagers. I only vaguely remember the plot. The main theme being about a flamboyant hairdresser portrayed by Warren Beatty and his numerous sexual exploits. I suppose this mystery woman perceives me as some bulging stud worthy of conquest.

After the film, we head straight to my apartment and engage in unbridled passionate sex. There is something very erotic about an intimate encounter with a total stranger: a prevailing mystique that endures through veiled anonymity, always unattainable. In a situation such as this, one might do or say anything, the total use and mutual exploration of another body without premeditation. She demands that I take her from different positions. I obey without question. I cannot say the experience altogether pleasurable, nor is it without certain gratification. One observation certain: it is different.

"What is that?" She enquires startled as we reposed, noting a stuffed green Iguana perched dominantly at edge of my cherry-wood dresser.

"That is a friend to keep me company when I don't have a beautiful woman in my bed." I state coyly, giving her an affectionate squeeze.

This unusual decoration has haunted my dwelling for more than a year, ever since I saw it poised stunningly at a garage sale, deciding I must have it for a sacrificial price of four dollars. It is in death so life-like, so primitive and also inspirational. Yet, for some reason I never thought of it as being truly dead. I often spend hours just studying the intricate detail and design of the green leathery skin, the delicate fabrication of its clawed feet, and long tapered serpentine tail. Most fascinating are prehistoric spikes sprouting along the center of the creatures back known as *tuberculate scales* making it seem presently alive. I cannot say why I have it, or why for so long this taxidermy lizard entranced my interest. Then I just forgot about it, until tonight, which makes me wonder why I ever wanted the thing in the first place.

"Does it have a name?"

"No. He is called just Iguana. Like us, he has no name, no past, and no future. But if you tell me something about yourself, I will give him to you."

"Really— you would give that to me?"

"Only, if you tell me why you are here, and why all the mystery."

"Why does it matter? We are here, and it is good. Today we live, and tomorrow we die. Does anything matter beyond the present experience?"

"It matters when I feel well with someone like I do with you now."

"What if I told you that tomorrow my life ends?"

"Are you sick… dying?" I hesitate in alarm.

"I am getting married."

I think I am more shocked than anything else. So here is the finality of truth. Tomorrow this woman is getting married to a fiancé, who loves and trusts her-- someone that has no idea the last act of fidelity of his bride to be is to spend a night of infidelity with a total stranger. This revelation hurts me, makes me feel cheap. Maybe I even feel a little jealous. But mostly, I feel sorry for her husband to be.

"Are you sure you are enough in love to get married? I believe marriage should be sacred between two people."

"So do I-- this why I want to do it all before. He's nothing like you. He's so prim and proper. Never would he go see a movie like Shampoo, or entertain the idea of a stuffed Iguana. And never would he make love to me like you did tonight. But he is rich, and I love him. In real life one can't have it all."

I try not to show my true emotions, as she chauffeurs me back to the bookstore to pick up my motorcycle, the green Iguana placed in prominent contrast on the white leather backseat. I decide that cold-blooded kind should remain with kind.

"I will always think of this as the night of the Iguana," she says with a devilish wink once I am seated on my motorcycle.

The powder blue Mustang disappears into the night and is lost in the surrounding metropolis. I remain for several moments pondering the events of the past several hours. I feel somehow unclean and used. This night I have reaped the ugly emptiness found in the pages of a *marquis* novel and been solicited to fulfill the harlequin romance of a shampoo dilettante. I cannot help but wonder the long-term success of this strange encounter before matrimonial bondage and if the Iguana might adapt after all.

The next weekend I run into Bruce and Ed on the Venice Boardwalk. Bruce informs me that Vallerie and her sister scheduled to return to their home in San Francisco basin on the afternoon bus. As we are talking the two girls arrive, each carrying a bag containing healthy snack foods and juice to accommodate the eight-hour trip up the coast. I greet them both cordially, venturing to say little. What was there to say? Then the car horn of a taxi blasts from an adjacent alley. Vallerie embraces Bruce and goes ahead.

"Good bye my wise friendly scarecrow," Tamara says, hugging Bruce around the waist. Turning to Ed, she says "Goodbye my brave and noble lion," tugging affectionately on the thick mane of his beard. "And you have no heart," she whispers, tapping several times my chest.

It is a strange goodbye: a resonating farewell touching me with apprehension that there is some truth to the observation. After the sisters gone, I laugh with my two friends, pretending to shrug-off the rejection. Only at the end do I realize just how lovely Tamara really is and find myself hoping she might find her true love somewhere in the Land of Oz at the end of a California rainbow.

$\mathcal{F}$or the first time, I am genuinely ready for a new quarter to begin. This summer I have received a taste of what routine living all about, now fully aware I am not a person made for routine. I suppose I will remain forever torn between desire for a sedentary existence and the reckless behavior of putting everything on the line. Ed, Bruce, and I hang around more often, getting together for early breakfast at the Venice Hole-In-The-Wall breakfast house or just sit under a boardwalk gazebo to watch pretty girls pass. It is during this period I meet Charlie Hutchins, a short pleasant individual, who plays an anthropomorphic character in a Wendy's hamburger commercial.

"Can you tell which one me?" He probes showing me a flyer with several persons dressed in hamburger and french-fry costumes.

I easily point him out, selecting his distinctive robust figure from the line-up. Charlie is actually a very serious and talented Shakespearean actor belonging to a troop at a Hollywood playhouse. According to Charlie, Wendy's Hamburger pays his ticket, but Shakespeare remains his one and only true aspiration. I will attend at least one of these productions billed *The Taming of the Shrew*. Charlie cast as *Batista Minola*, father to Kate and Bianca, shines as a true gem amid the constellation of seasoned actors. Through the course of the play, I become enamored by the young lady that portrays the part of *Kate*.

I write her a poem, send flowers, and make several desperate attempts to meet her. Upon the good fatherly advice of Charlie, I abandon my obsession, allowing this *Kate* to remain forever lovely upon the stage of my imagination, a shimmering image glimpsed remotely in the face of the moon. I will not ever really bond with Charlie; nevertheless, he will turn out to be one of my more loyal associations.

Because I spend so much time hovering around Venice Beach, either in the surf, or on the boardwalk, I grow acquainted with many of the strange apparitions that dwell timelessly at the edge of the sea. There is Mad Lidia, the roach queen, who wanders around like a xenophobic hag talking to herself with live cockroaches in her hair and on her clothes. According to rumor, a summoned city health inspector once entered her residence, discovering thousands of the proliferating insects. Lidia proclaims them pets, ordering the intruder to leave. I do not know what eventually happened between this disturbed woman and the city council, only that Lidia continues to haunt the Boardwalk even many years later. This human tragedy reminds me of what happened to the enormously wealthy recluse, Howard Hughes. This brilliant man of fame lived to the end of his life in squalor, dying of malnutrition, fearful of the world beyond fortress of his penthouse prison. Even a gilded cage a jail to a soul incarcerated.

I meet a fellow that calls himself *Tiresias*, a wild-eyed transvestite prophet. One minute he is calmly intelligent, and then flies inexplicably into a wild tirade, shouting that Cerberus, the three-headed dog of Greek mythology, will rise from the ocean and destroy the habitations of humankind. On at least one occasion, I have an interesting conversation with this man. Turns out, he is married, the father of two daughters, and in the past a successful business executive from the Beverly Hills suburbs. One morning he awakes, puts on a dress and hiking boots, then walks nearly ten miles to Venice Beach, where he continues to remain as a familiar fixture to those that live here. He claims that in a dream he has witnessed the end of the world. I share with him my testimony of Christ's salvation. For just a moment his countenance changes to one of comprehension; then his eyes grow wide. He then begins to cry madly that the heads of *Cerberus* will rise as a full moon out of the sea wearing many faces to destroy the earth. I often find myself praying for this man. It is my hope he might find relief from the demon that so easily besets him, keeping him restrained to this narrow corridor of existence. I also pray his prophetic vision less true.

As the air changes and begins to grow cooler, I take this tormented soul my green wool military blanket and poncho as some protection against the coming rains. Then he is gone, just vanished from the scene. After much inquiry, I learn that a woman accompanied by two younger women arrive one afternoon and spirit him away after much pleading. It remains my hope that this mad prophet found his way back to a wife and family by striking again the serpent of his sanity.

The most intrepid character of all to haunt the Venice Boardwalk is a young mulatto man dressed in a white tunic. This Genie skirts around on roller-skates, a white turban covering his head, and carrying an electric guitar connected to a portable amplifier on his back. He has the most interesting blue eyes. His fame is to arbitrarily skate up to a passer-by and begin playing a Hendrix style melody, while singing unintelligible lyrics. I think him in the beginning-- like so many others here-- a fallen outcast, just another earthbound spirit doomed to wonder aimlessly along this stretch of beach at the far end of the cosmos. As it turns out, he is a rather pleasant fellow, very perceptive, with grand ambitions of one day becoming a famous musician. We talk on several occasions, but I must confess I never embrace his musical style. Through the years, however, the name *Harry Perry* will become legendary among many circles. It is my understanding that this fellow has since authored several records and performed cameos in big Hollywood productions. To this day, I wonder if he is still skating up and down the boardwalk in his white karmic outfit sharing his special brand of human contact to whoever will take time to gaze into the captivating azure calm of his eyes... and just listen.

A day in late September, I go to the beach for the last time before the water temperature changes and the hot Santa Ana wind blows from the east releasing desert heat that heralds the end of Southern California summer. I place my towel near a pretty body sun tanning face down and immediately hit the surf. I can bob in the sinuous currents for hours. This particular day the waves are idealfor body surfing. It is nearing sunset by the time I stagger back to dry land and collapse on my towel. The young woman still lies in the same position without moving since my arrival. The first thought is that it none of my business; nevertheless, something inside me says the situation looks wrong.

"Excuse me," I hesitate, "are you all right?"

There is no response. I reach out and touch her on the shoulder, still no reaction. Moving to the opposite side of her face, I see a pool of vomit dribbling from her mouth. Immediately, I lift her up to check if the woman still breathing.

"I don't feel good," mumbles a weak voice.

"Do you want me to take you to a hospital?"

"Hospital... no, I want to go home."

I gather our few belongings and usher her toward my car. Realizing she is too weak to walk, I carry this wraith the remaining distance in my arms. I try to get directions for her dwelling, only she is too incoherent. So, I take her to a cafe instead. After several cups of coffee and something to eat, her conversation becomes more lucid.

"My name is Shari. I'm sorry to put you through all of this. If not for you, I guess I might have spent the night on the beach."

"You passed-out on something. I saw several blue pill casings in your vomit. I think you planned for more than just a nap."

"That does not matter now," she deflects, as one skillful at avoidance. "A hero came along and saved me. You are not sorry that you saved me... are you?"

Shari is lovely, representing all that I like physically in a woman. Nevertheless, I remain cautious, believing her unstable. I should have listened more closely to my primary instincts. After eating and exchanging phone numbers, I give Shari a lift home and briefly meet a white Terrier named Jasper that greets us as we walk in. I glimpse a solid black kitten, which darts under the couch refusing to venture out, and on the coffee table lingers a swollen gasping goldfish in a clouded bow of water.

"I think it time to change the water for your goldfish."

"It belongs to a friend," she replies disdainfully. "But I suppose you are right. It's not her fault she is trapped."

We see each other a few times as friends only, sharing a cup of coffee and desert, or just taking a ride together in my MG with the top down. In early November, we decide to take a trip together to the Grand Canyon. A few days before our planned departure, I hear an unpleasant sound coming from my car engine, like bits of metal bouncing in the combustion chamber. Then the car begins running rough with black smoke issuing from the tail pipe. Upon reading my Chilton Manual, I determine the problem to have something to do with the head valves.

Methodically, I dismantle the carburetors and surrounding components, release the torque on the six tension bolts, and remove the engine head. I see immediately the problem. One of the valve guides has inexplicably decayed, a piece wedging open an exhaust port, another fused into the top of the piston. I take the head down to a parts store within walking distance that also has a machine shop. For a reasonable amount, I commission to have the valve and guide changed. I make mention of the piston and ask if I can leave it like that.

"It will cause a hot spot and uneven running, particularly at high speeds." The machine shop mechanic warns.

Therefore, I order a new piston as well. This is when I make a fatal decision. I reason that since I have the engine open, I might as well change the rod bearing caps as well.

"Are they standard or over-sized?" The man inquires checking his order manual.

Since the car has over fifty thousand miles and considering a factor of wear, my logical quantum assessment is to take the over-sized. I do vaguely remember being asked something about the micrometer measurement; but why should that matter? Within a day, I reassemble everything and by evening ready to start the engine. At first, it runs fine, but within a few minutes begins making a loud clanking noise. For some insane reason I decide to drive the car down to Torrance, twenty minutes away.

Ron probably knows only a little more about mechanics than I do. Like me, he has a history of making the occasional repair, but few things internal to the engine. Although the idea foolish, I feel the need for psychological comfort, hoping my friend has a better suggestion than what my gut is saying.

The temperature gauge is redlining by the time I pull in front of his apartment building, the engine fatally smoking and coughing. Ron has lived here since his unwilling eviction from Scarf Street after the building condemned. I think we both miss the simple innocence of that time and place: an island of rare peace in the maelstrom of life, a place we will not know again.

"What seems to be the problem, Little Brother?" He asks, swinging open the door.

"I don't know Ron, but there is something wrong with my car. I just barely made it here."

Ron comes outside and tells me to restart the engine. Instead of turning over, it only makes a decisive click.

"Smells mighty hot—what in tarnation did you do?"

I relay the events of my brilliant repair, leaving out no detail.

"So why did you decide to put over-sized bearing caps? Did the guy at the machine shop tell you that's what you needed?"

"No, I just figure that once an engine has a lot of miles that it would need oversized bearings."

"I'm afraid you have a real serious problem here. The engine has completely seized. No telling how much damage is done."

This confirms just how dire the situation. In my effort to improve the engine of my car, I have altogether destroyed it. Ron gives me a lift back home and I spend the next day contemplating my situation. Then I remember something I saw in one of the adjacent garages several months earlier when Ed came by with his Fiat. We had gotten permission from my landlord to use one of the garages in the alley to store the Fiat when he flew to Marilyn to visit family for two weeks. Through the slats, I remember seeing another MGA in the adjacent stall, very similar to mine. I go to the next building and boldly knock on the door.

"Excuse me sir, but do you know who owns that yellow MG parked in the second garage?"

"Yes, that would be mine. It don't run no more since the transmission broke, the suspension is finished, and has been in a few fender benders. Used to be a spiffy vehicle-- then again, I was younger and full of spiff, too."

It turns out to be a 1960 model, one year younger than my car. I explain the unfortunate mistake I have made, stating that I want the car just for the engine block and main shaft. He is more than happy to take a hundred dollars for the whole thing as long as I take it away. Ron hitches a toll bar to his truck, and together we haul it to a field of open semi-desert terrain belonging to a mutual friend named Bill Keys. We next tow my car to the same location. The first thing I do is remove the seized motor from my car, and then extract engine from the 1960 canary. Except for a little surface rust, it cleans up well. As far as I can tell the main shaft, bearings, and pistons look in fair condition. I remove my engine head and bolt it onto the scavenged motor, along with my starter, alternator,and transmission.

In retrospect, I am just lucky that the water pump and other peripheral parts good, since it never occurs to me to change them. Bill Keys has a torque wrench, as well as other tools, making thejob easier. The most annoying part of the ordeal is whimsical nature of the elements. The wind blows relentless, stirring up dust devils of fine sand that gets into everything. I award a great deal of accolade to this generation ofBritish engineering for the toughness of their engines and the materials used, despite the notorious weakness of the oil gaskets. This is all before the world import of cheaper Korean and Chinese steel. I doubt that later engine designs might have fared well the inexperienced ignorance of a young backyard mechanic.

Bill Keys' wife Helena, an opulent sweet lady from Hawaii, exhibits particular kindness towards me. The three days I toil reassembling my car, she saves me a place at the dinner table, often sending one of her three children out with a cold drink.

"You so skinny," she berates often, piling my plate with an extra helpingof Polynesian style cooking. "I used to be skinny like you before I get married.

Bill was good handy man like you-- but now so lazy! All he ever does is come home from one of his trips and watch T.V. On the road, and watch T.V. is only thing he care about. You eat and make some woman good husband too."

There is something seductively sad in the opulence of this woman's face, a demur speaking regret, like a disturbed pool revealing a longing for something new. I do not wish to entertain the undercurrents in these troubled waters, pretending ignorance.

Helena accepts her situation gracefully; placing all of her frustration into tending on the needs of their three children. In many ways, I feel pity toward Helena; pity the isolation so apparent in the dilated circumferences of her large oval eyes, sad and stagnant, reflecting youth drained many moonsago. As with most long-haul truckers, Bill is seldom home, nearly always tired, and probably less at home here than on the road. According to Ron, he makes good money. This makes me to ponder if all the money in the world enough to stoke the hearth of a romantic relationship after the kids grown and home becomes just another house.

To my delight, the scavenged 1960 MG engine starts immediately, sounding better than before the change. I thank Helena for her hospitality and rush back to my L.A. apartment. It is Friday of a long weekend, which means I have four days to drive to the Grand Canyon and back. After a quick shower, I call Shari, telling her to be ready within the hour. She is more than happy to comply, wishing only to escape.

The October weather particularly mild, we are on the road before 8:00 P.M. heading east. Shari brings along her shaggy dog Jasper, which later reminds me of the canine companion to a character named *Tintin* created by the Belgian cartoonist *Herge*, a classical hero of a daughter I will one day raise and love as my own. But in this present, we three are passing through night of a new adventure on a lone western road with stars surrounding. After the first hundred miles, I distinctly smell the odor of burning motor oil. My first thought is that this normal, considering the newly reconstructed engine dirty with residue. Then I notice a drop in the oil pressure gauge. Stopping at a gas station, I confirm my oil level low by nearly a quart. I am leaking oil! The most obvious culprit is the oil pan gasket. I persuade the young gas attendant, who knows nothing about mechanics, to allow me to use the service bay. Fortunately, this year of MG has easy access to remove the oil pan without too much dismantling by just undoing one of the motor mounts and raising the engine slightly. With a small bribe, the kid finds me some gasket material. Using the original as a template, I cut a new one. Two hours later, I funnel back in the oil and once again hit the road before midnight. Again, the oil pressure begins to drop. Pulling into another gas station, I diagnose the leak not from the oil pan, rather from two rocker inspection ports located on back side of the motor just below the two SU carburetors. These are made of a special eighth-inch thick cork, the original torn and mangled, as a result of over-tightening. At least now, I know with certainty the problem. Purchasing additional quarts of oil, I determine to drive all night to Kingman Arizona where I might find a foreign auto parts store.

Shari curls up catlike on the narrow bucket seat and sleeps soundly most of the way. As is her habit, she has taken a sleeping pill to make the journey pass more swiftly. Jasper appears comprehensive, his shaggy white head protruding between the seats and resting protectively against Shari's feet. Arriving in Kingman a little before sunrise, I locate the only import car parts in town and park at the entrance until it opens. At half past eight, I awaken to the sound of Jasper's barking, the harsh early Arizona sun etching into pitted swirls on my windscreen. To my delight, the gaskets are in stock, which also comes with directions on how to install them properly. The trick is to place gasket cement on the engine side only and allow a few minutes of drying time before tightening the center cover bolts. The procedure quick and simple, a detail inconveniently omitted from the repair manual, which serves as substance for one of those wise scenarios: how nearly lost a kingdom for the want of a simple horseshoe nail.

This problem solved, I awaken Shari and we go to a recommended restaurant and share an imitation South-of-the-Border style breakfast for two. The restaurant owner, a greasy corpulent fellow, kindly gives Jasper some scraps from the back. Shari has neglected to bring food for the animal. We are back on the road again an hour before noon, and less than three hours from the Grand Canyon. We may be angels delayed-- but by the grace of God, we will get there! This is my first and most important lesson in the Zen of auto mechanics superseding quantum theory: *never fix something not broken; but if you do fix it, make certain you understand the proper torque measurements provided in the specs!*

*D*esert places are both familiar and unfamiliar, stretching out in all directions dotted with cactus sprouting out of an antediluvian landscape once the floor of a now extinct ocean. A combination of extreme fatigue, withering heat, and unchanging terrain, I begin to hallucinate, hearing sounds and seeing things not there. Sometimes a loud noise swoops overhead, as though a jet landing beside us. Twice I swerve to avoid something in the road that disappears just as suddenly. I hear people mumbling inside the car, a woman's frantic screams coming from under the hood, and feeling presences huddled in the space behind my driver's seat. Over time I will learn that the open desert has its own host of spirits of the air. This particular trip I can feel them— almost see them, occasionally glimpsing their ethereal essence. By early afternoon, we reach Flagstaff, still an hour and a half from the South Rim of the Grand Canyon. Jasper makes it clear that it is time for a stop. After relieving himself, the dog begins leaping excitedly, licking my legs and feet. I admit that I have begun to become attached to this animal. Shari, in contrast, cold as a fish, but at least her dog overflows with unbridled emotions of gratitude. Grabbing a quick bite at a little restaurant on the outskirts of town, we go around back and again find scraps fit for a hobo. Perhaps all this human food less than good for a pedigree; but Jasper is no pedigree. Like me he is content with whatever he finds, content to dine on leftovers, as though the finest cuisine. I will miss Jasper most by the end of this journey.

It is a scenic drive from Flagstaff to the mountain resort overlooking the Canyon expanse. The road narrow and at a constant incline until reaching the peak of an alpine forest. We book a room overlooking the abyss, both glad to have a shower and a bed to stretch out on after so many hours cramped in a small sport car. In my exhaustion, I neglect to raise the soft top, deciding that a little dew will not hurt anything.

This night I attempt to make love to Shari for the first time. This turns disastrous for both of us. Because of some consciously forgotten trauma in Shari's past, she is unable to physically consummate with a man. Her entire body turns rigid, her vagina involuntarily contracts tightly. I never observed this kind of reaction before, gripped by a depression of brooding disappointment frustrating to my anticipated desires. Shari confides that she prefers the company of women and that I am her first male friend. How can it be that this lovely feline inaccessible and without substance, no more satisfying than a made-up store manikin? I am reminded of a Greek history class about an exotic population on the island of *Mytilene*, a society of only women led by the poetess Sappho, who in one of her lyrics wrote: *"Love is a cunning weaver of fantasies and fables."* So this night we just talk, hold each other affectionately like brother and sister, with Jasper curled between us as a watchful chaperone.

Next morning, the world transformed unexpectedly. An

accumulation of frozen rain and snow a couple inches deep has fallen overnight, a drift layered over the seats and burying the gearshift of my unprotected MG. I rake-out the snow using my hands, discovering the shifter linkage frozen in first gear. It will be more than half an hour before I can start and drive the car. Just as suddenly the snow melts into water under a brazen Colorado sun, thawing-out this alpine wonderland. Shari and I begin throwing snowballs at each other, Jasper running excitedly between us, snapping at the flying missiles. I throw one just for him, which he catches with a splatter.

"That's not nice," scolds Shari, taking the bewildered animal lovingly in her arms.

"Now he knows what it is like to catch a snowball!"

We both break into laughter, with Jasper running around in circles, sniffing and digging holes, reluctantly licking the strange white substance, careful to avoid taking into his mouth another cold shot. After lunch, the lodge announces it is sponsoring a hike down to Indian Gardens, a Cottonwood grove that defines an oasis several thousand feet below our present elevation. These stoic desert landscapes the traditional habitation of a Native American population named the Havasupai, meaning People of the Blue-Green Water.

Their descendants now herd together on an impoverished reservation located in the southwest part of the park. Often one might pass them huddled in pairs on the side of the hot dusty roads selling their turquoise and handmade Indian blankets. Size and distance are deceptive in this region of vast terrain. From the top, the oasis appears a patch of green; the expanse beyond, a short stretch of desert ending abruptly, dropping off into the lower lip and into the stream of the Colorado River.

Shari prefers to remain topside with Jasper. I prepare a flask of water, using a discarded soda bottle, and begin the treacherous descent with perhaps a dozen other intrepid souls. The way proves more harrowing than I imagined, often steep and precariously exposed, skirting along narrow ledges affording a magnificent panoramic view of the Canyon's colorful distant north face. I find myself wishing I had brought my combat boots on this trip, instead of these frail, slick-bottomed sneakers. Nevertheless, I am determined that a pair of inappropriate shoes will not deter my intended purpose. It takes nearly two hours to reach the oasis. The Cotton Woods that resemble shrubs from the top are actually towering shade trees, not less than thirty feet tall, sheltering the source of a fresh water spring spreading into small pools and running off into an underground fissure. For many this is excursion's end. Some have brought tents and sleeping bags to make a campsite. There are a few rock hounds, who begin rightaway scouring the surrounding desert for unusual specimens. There is one fellow with whom I had brief communication on the hike down only interested in collecting cacti samples.

Refilling my water bottle, I accompany this gentleman from beneath protection of the pleasant oasis shelter and venture into a blistering wasteland. We talk a little, mostly about his compelling hobby to collect spores and cactus plants, which he grows in a climate controlled hothouse behind his home in Buffalo.

"It is amazing that even in this inhospitable environment life abounds," the man comments, dropping on his knees beside a small Barrel Cactus.

"Yes," I agree. "God has born wisdom in all things to flourish everywhere in the timeliness of season."

"Science calls that evolution."

"I do not disagree that there is evidence in the world of Natural Selection, but I do not altogether accept the scientific definition proposed by evolutionist."

"Then I guess you think the world was made in six days."

"I do not think six days impossible, since time only a model of measurement based on present observation. What is the acceleration value separating two stars and who can say definitively if this velocity truly constant and has always been the same quantum? I do know without question that there is a God of creation and that the earth we know example of his handiwork. Even these rocks and the plant species you find so interesting; and even this Grand Canyon is here by accident. I am more surprised that a man of your obvious inquisitiveness has not speculated on the many obvious contradiction of logic inherent to Darwinian Science as presently postulated."

"I have more faith in science than in the idea that everything a product of some grand intelligent design."

"Then you have a faith based on knowledge. My faith is based on experience. I tell you plainly there is more design in that rock you are holding than can ever be riddled through any science."

He shrugs uncomfortably and goes back to excavating his specimens. Therefore, I bid him a good day and continue my solitary challenge. From this vantage, I can no longer see the canyon, only the edge of the opposite North Rim. This is as true a desert basin as any I could have imagined. Following the wisp of a barely discernable trail headed in a straight line, I cross a wilderness made of hard-packed earth, the ground eroded by unimpeded wind, uneven and rocky beneath a scorching midday sun. Embedded on the surface are numerous fossil remains of crustaceans dating back to a time when this entire region wasted at the bottom of a sea. How different the world must have appeared then. Since science would have us believe in a time table of millions of years, then why these many fossils evidenced on the surface? And why have not the greater forces of nature, capable of chiseling granite rock faces, yet unable to erase these much softer petrified remains?

After a force-march lasting nearly two hours, I arrive at the South Rim edge overlooking a majestic gaping chasm many miles wide. A few thousand feet below flows the cool ribbon of the Colorado River, snaking between sharp vertical walls and around overhangs of enormous protruding boulders.

The Grand Canyon is a spectacular geologic wonder of the world, in some places more than a mile deep, and more than eighteen miles at its widest range. Feeding out of Lake Powell, the canyon river flows into Lake Mead, adding to the reservoir of Hoover Dam. It extends nearly 280 miles from Lee's Ferry at the Arizona and Utah border to the Grand Wash Cliffs outside Las Vegas Nevada. This great national monument founded in 1908 by President Theodore Roosevelt, and eleven years later designated a state park. I might add that this gallant leader of the Rough Riders, before elected the 26th president of the United States, remains one of my early childhood heroes. I think that in many ways this blustery legend reminiscent of my Uncle Junior, Rudy's blood nemesis, a swashbuckler career Navy man and intrepid adventurer to ends of the world.

The Grand Canyon, although not the deepest, nor grandest on planet earth, is unique in that it represents in graphic detail the geologic table cut into precise layers visible to the eyes. The famous geologist Charles Lyell, father of the Uniformitarian Theory, and a subscriber to Emmanuel Comte's uniformitarian ideology, interprets such stratification as evidence of a very old earth undergoing constant formation by slow and predictable changes over time. His close associate, Charles Darwin, author of the Origin of Species, and considered the patron saint of the evolutionary theory, additionally constructs his ideas upon these same principles. The problem I have with all this is the assumptive quantification of these foundation theorems. Lyell admits in personal diaries that his theories to rationalize time and events all stem from a traumatic incident witnessed during his early childhood. A horse hooked to another carriage in front of the one occupied by the young future Scottish geologist spooks suddenly, causing the other carriage to cascade down the side of a mountain killing the occupants. Lyell chooses to pursue a course of definitive predictability to describe existence. He does this by constructing a model of scientific theorem, including only evidence supportive of a pastoral and scientifically contrived timetable. He ignores mountains of records supporting potential of cataclysmic events, suggesting that these thousands of entries aberrant discrepancies, because they do not agree with the hypothesis of his predictable model.

To my mind, this a bit like saying: *"As I think so I am"*, which concludes that better a philosophy designed through uncertainty in mortal reflection, than to embrace the unpredictability of random causality. It has been my experience that any one event may be interpreted in several different ways. Every hypothesis dependent on the discriminate inclusion of facts based on model construction and tools used to interpret the evidence. Documented history suggests that Darwin incorporated Lyell's steady-state theoretical conclusions to validate his own speculations. Using compelling evidence observed in natural selectivity of species to adapt, Darwinian Theory adds bias to the definition by incorporating principals of a speculative timetable to establish norms supportive of evolutionary projections riddled with missing links and present-day contradictions.

As with the desire of geologic science to rationalize cosmic existence by funneling observation through syntax of limited data collection, so I think this also true for organic life extrapolation. Now I am not altogether negative to laboratory disciplines utilized through empirical observation, but am suspicious of science as a doctrine of rigid principals. I do believe in the ability of species to adapt to environmental changes; but am logically reluctant to consider the collection of fossil bones spread-out on a table of millions of years *(this is a number preceded by nine zeros)* conclusive evidence of accidental evolution. It seems to me just as ludicrous to believe that inert elements stimulated into complex cell production over time by a non-quantifiable chemical reaction. This had to happen, not once, but hundreds, perhaps even thousands of times. So in my mind, either the code of life already present in unified blueprint form, supporting the idea of intelligent creativity, or else the random stimulation of chemical reaction occurred so often as to become a pattern of design, which basically comes back to the same conclusion.

I postulate this idea as intellectual corundum only, already personally knowing the answer. I state here, without any reservation, I know indisputably God-- *yes God of the Holy Bible*- the author of all these complexities observed and others that new age of computerized science is just beginning to comprehend. Further, I know without doubt that all observed phenomenon not accidental or the attribute of some natural process too gradual to be categorically observed through present census just awaiting another burst of evolution to occur.

Undoubtedly, I will be labeled a Creationist with a myopic view of the universe as a quantum condition made according to a pattern of infinite design. This definition proposes that every atom contains a unique thermodynamic signature, which emanates from an energy source existing outside of normal space and time. A condition further supporting the idea that faith is more a spiritual condition, than a theorem of belief. This comprehension ascribes foundation meaning to the phenomenon of miracles in defiance of natural laws. As stated in the Holy Bible: *it is a gift of the Holy Spirit, not based on human intellect, least any man should boast through mortal reason.'*

In present state, I see no conclusive evidence to the contrary; but do perceive claims of adamant protest mounted by academia to protect institutional concepts. Well organized programs of indoctrination instilled through many institutions in society. These programs based upon egotistical conclusions of a Godless world that has spontaneously blasted from a collapsed singularity with no beginning and no end. Through process of many academic debates, so readily engaged by scientifically enlightened communities, providing grants and awards to minds with aptitude to unravel the atoms, but unable to create even one.

And still there is no consensus to the question: *Is intellectual reasoning evidenced through empirical science proof of an absent God; or is God intellectual proof of existence evidenced through the rational of unseen principals discovered daily in empirical science?*

As I stand at the brink of this stunning expanse of natural wonder, I am overwhelmed by a feeling of insignificance. This is indeed the exposed skeleton of the jewel in the universe, a living testament of majestic inception. But seeing it like this reminds me of something else as well.

As a child, I constructed a mountain in our backyard out of mud, sand, and small rocks. I leave it all summer, allowing the structure to harden and pack tightly by action of wind, rain, and sun. By the end of fall, it remains petrified hard as stone. Under pressure of a garden hose, it dissolves away in minutes. In the beginning the water just bounces off, but after persistent pressure, the action begins to penetrate the shale, breaking-off chunks, and eventually eroding completely the structure. My fortified summer mountain melts quickly into a crumbling maze of small tributary canyons.

It is not impossible to imagine this microcosm of cataclysm occurring on a grander scale, as testified here by this canyon. Imagine just for a moment the tremendous forces assaulting planet earth, as described in the *Book of Genesis* the day that Noah and his family entered the Ark, as waters of the deep burst forth from subterranean caverns. Add to this, unprecedented rapid atmospheric condensation, causing oceans to shift and mountain ranges to push up, bending and folding into rock stratum from the enormous pressures. No other reference in worldhistory describes the catastrophe that happened on a planetary scale in more graphic and scientifically accurate detail than recorded in theBook of Genesis found in the *Old Testament Bible*. Moreover, there remains indisputable proof of this global event found on all the earth continents. Evidence that affirms such a calamity occurred in a recent geologic past. Records of jumbled fossil remains inexplicably jammed together within subterranean caches, supposedly spanning eons of evolution. Even this Grand Canyon, threading a mighty river along the Continental   Divide, is a conduit of melting glaciers that eventually feeds down into the Gulf of California and trickles into the Sea of Cortez, as a tale of many endings. It is by all means a book easily read; but as with any good   detective novel, a plot supporting more than one possible conclusion.

It is dark by the time I reach the cool mountain lodge, exhausted, yet victorious. Shari has already eaten, prepared to turn in early. I am too tired to eat anything more than a vending machine sandwich. I shower, drop heavily beside Shari, and fall immediately into dreamless slumber of the dead.

The bright late morning sun floods the room; Jasper incessantly licking my face and hands. Judging by the clock, I have slept ten hours, and feel I could sleep another ten hours. However, after several cups of coffee and a satisfying Colorado style country breakfast consisting of a three-egg Denver Omelet and a Burrito, I am ready for another day of driving. I can sense Shari sad to leave. This has been more than a vacation for her. This has been the fulfillment of a dream, a great escape of a golden bird from a sequestered cage. I will discover later the true nature of this cage.

While traversing the hilly country road heading toward Flagstaff, I hear a distinctive pop followed by a *bong* sound coming from the rear of my car. Pausing to listen, I hear another, and then another. The steering begins to wobble slightly, becoming more noticeable, so I pull off the road for a quick examination. Several wire spokes surrounding the center rim on the rear driver's side wheel have broken. Evident is a tangle of mangled splintered spikes in one quarter of the circumference. Clearly I cannot go further without risking an accident. I have a spare, only now remembering that my spare is flat since taking ownership of the car, with a wide gash on the tire wall from a previous blowout. What I need to do now is change the good tire to the good rim. I jump immediately into action. Jacking up the car and removing the center locking hub, I take off the damaged wheel. Within just a few minutes I am holding both wheels, one in each arm.

"Lock Jasper in the car and come with me," I instruct Shari.

"But what if something happens and we don't come back?"

"We will come back. I need to find a gas station-- and fast! Jasper will be fine. And besides, he will make a good guard dog of our belongings."

Shari less assured, detects in my tone that I am in no mood for a debate. It is already well past four o'clock, with less than two hours of daylight left on this side of the mountain, and I have no idea what time the regional gas stations close. A command decision must be made, and I have made it. Jasper whimpers a little, instinctively accepting his duty, and curls passively on the driver's seat to wait for our return. Fortunately, less than ten minutes later a pickup appears over the horizon with an Indian couple in the cab and three small children in the open bed. I manage to flag them down and explain my situation. They are kind enough to give us a lift seven miles to the only gas station between here and Flagstaff, declining my offer to pay them a few dollars for their trouble. The three children think Shari and I rather curious. They keep touching us both and then breaking into laughter. I am not altogether certain why they find us so humorous. Maybe because we are both pale skinned in comparison; or maybe they just think it strange a couple hitch-hiking alone in this isolated terrain, with me carrying two wire wheels belonging to a sport car.

To my relief, the gas station still open. The owner is also Indian, a big man with long grey hair and sharp penetrating eyes. He and his two sons are in the process of removing an engine from a farm tractor inside the garage. Upon seeing the broken spokes, his first reaction to me is an adamant no!

"The tire machine will collapse the wire wheel," he insists. "I will not be responsible for that. And I don't have the proper tools to do it manually."

"I have no choice. We are stuck in the middle of nowhere. If the wheel gets destroyed, then it gets destroyed. I just need the tire from the damaged rim put on the good rim. It has to be done."

Nevertheless, he refuses even to try. Therefore, I push him aside, flip him a ten-dollar bill and center the damaged rim on the hydraulic press. I hear one, then another (perhaps more than three) of the spokes break as the heavy metal arm presses down along the outer circumference.   A loud plop, and the tire collapses into the center, allowing easy extraction. Now it is time to try it on my good rim. With some experience from the first wheel and by using the rubber from it as a buffer, I apply less pressure, alittle more gradual. With aid of a large screwdriver (*the same caliber that once stabbed into my head as a boy*) I manage to leverage the hydraulic force a little more evenly. To my relief, the worthless tire falls away. After the transfer complete, I notice that several of the spokes are badly bent because of the applied pressure, but have fortuitously survived the strain. For another five dollars, one of the sons agrees to give us a lift back to my stranded vehicle.

With last rays of light from the setting sun, I tighten back the middle hub-nut and we are on the road again. Jasper now uncharacteristically quiet just hopes not to be abandoned again. I have always wanted to see Phoenix, so decide to continue south and stay overnight in a cheap motel with plans of taking the Interstate 10 back to Los Angeles. My budget is already blown; what did one more night matter? Besides, I am still exhausted from the expedition of the previous day and need another good night of sleep. Shari is now giving me the silent treatment because of the way I handled the earlier crisis by leaving Jasper alone locked in the car. Maybe she is right. Maybe we should have taken him along. However, in my mind all is well that ends well. But Shari has never read Shakespeare, which is much *ado about nothing*.

We arrive back at Shari's West Los Angeles apartment at half past eight the following evening, tired, and happy to be home. A bullish woman meets us at the entrance, anxiously flinging open the door.

"Where have you been?" She demands of Shari. "I've been worried sick since two days!"

Shari says nothing, but runs into her bedroom followed by this guardian warrior. Their voices rise and fall, with intervals of silence. I honestly have no idea what is going on. The woman, too young to be Shari's mother, acts toward her with matron severity. Nor are there any physical markers to suggest they might be sisters. Yet, there is a familiarity between them, which seems more than casual. Jasper remains loyally at my side, as though he knows already the coming ax. Then out steps the angry bulldog, eyes glaring with such contempt that even Jasper runs under a nearby table.

"Shari wants you to go!"

"I'm not going anywhere. I want to speak to Shari-- now!"

"Shari and I have been together for three years. She's mine, this is our apartment. Get out, or I will call the police."

This revelation hits me like a ton of bricks. All the signs were there, only I refused to see them. Nevertheless, I do not respond well to threats. I am determined not to be pushed around by this angry lioness. If for no other reason, than to give me some needed closure.

"I want to hear that from Shari."

This stout woman takes a position between the bedroom door and me. Jasper begins whining, a physical confrontation appears inevitable.

Then Shari steps out clutching a small black cat.

"I'm sorry. I should have told you," she whimpers. "Please, accept this as a gift and go."

She gently places the purring kitten into my arms, kisses me on the cheek, and moves to the side of her girlfriend. There is something painfully surreal about all this. Jasper ventures from under the table and begins licking my feet. He somehow senses the gravity of this moment. Without saying a word, I turn and go out the door, embracing the warm purring ball of fur, as though it is the collapsed center of my broken heart. It is one thing to have loved and lost-- but to lose the woman I love to another woman! I am in a stir of many conflicting emotions. I feel angry, hurt, but most of all I feel a profound sense of defeat.

Arriving home, I sit down in my favorite study chair and stare out the living room window at eclipse of stars framed between the roof of an adjacent building and the overhang on my front veranda. The crest of a quarter moon peeks shamefully at the corner. This is naked reality of the now. I am here and will remain here for as long as God determines... maybe forever. I know that above all else, I need to let go of the anger.

It is early morning when I awaken, the autumn sun streaming through the kitchen window, igniting golden eyes of the young kitten still perched on my chest. I have in my life a new friend and companion. I name her Shadow, not because she is black, but because she represents a nebulous part of me in forgotten deeps: when once was a girl named Shari, vanished into antiquity, a myth only... the memory fading... never more.

*I*f nothing else, I become a better student. Shadow is all I need in life. She snuggles up to me in the morning and is here when I return home in the evening. Shadow also has the annoying habit to bring a dead bird or rodent in through the open window and drop this undesired gift at my feet or on my chest while engrossed in study. Nevertheless, I forgive these small indiscretions, realizing them to be acts of affection. In time, I develop a strong bond with this feline, as fulfilling as any relationship. Of course, it is not without certain distractions. For example, one morning I awake to the snarling of two large Tom Cats in my bedroom with Shadow cornered at the foot of my bed. I boldly leap-up and attempt to shoo-away the vicious creatures. Instead of scurrying away as expected, one of the Toms actually attacks. I grab a pillow intercepting the creature just in time. A few bouts against the wall, the surly wildcat leaps out the door and is gone. Shadow pounces into my arms still shaking from the ordeal. Three months later, she bares three kittens in a corner of my bedroom closet, but for some strange reason eats the newborns. So dark the mystery shrouded in the heart of the animal kingdom.

Ron has met a woman named Lorrain, a lovely dark eyed vixen with jet-black hair that severely contrasts with her lily-white skin. She is a true knockout in the dimly lighted context of a nightclub swooning with alcohol; however, less so in the bright light of day. They keep insisting that I join them on Saturday evenings of barroom intrigue. After several invitations, I finally agree to join them at a Country and Western dance hall in Long Beach.

At the entrance looms a uniformed Goliath, standing more than six and a half feet tall handling a nightstick. Upon closer examination, I perceive there is something very odd about this bouncer. His slightly slanted eyes magnified by thick coke-bottle spectacles, a face void of any emotion, and wearing an oversized police cap pulled over flattened ears. His head small, bobbing hypnotically, attached to an enormous body that sways rhythmically back and forth. This poor fellow is in fact a mongoloid retard, resembling a teetering bowling pin doll. I pity the drunkard that antagonizes the statutes of orderly conduct, not wishing to be in the path of this human locomotive on a Saturday night when the spirits high. I can only imagine the carnage.

Country and Western is not exactly my first choice in music. Nevertheless, it is danceable, the melody secondary to the true reason for being here. Close to midnight, I spot an elegantly dressed woman sitting alone at a table. My first thought is why such a lovely creature not be with someone. I watch her decline two invitations to dance. I finally decide to take my chances and ask her for a twirl. To my delight, she accepts. We dance for nearly half an hour without saying much other than polite introductions. Later over a beer, we become better acquainted. Her name is Glenda, a girl of Spanish descent, presently sharing an expensive condominium with a friend somewhere in New Port and hiding from someone. I like looking into Glenda's eyes, an allure into her soul, large and sad, like sullen dark pools deceptively deep and mysterious. Just how deep and how dark, I will soon find out.

Our first official date, I pick up Glenda on the corner of Hollywood and Vine. This rendezvous point is of her choosing; her way to remain clandestine and aloof. We will know each other for nearly three months, without me ever acquiring her phone number or knowing exactly where she lives. Though I think her pretty, I feel a sense of unrequited frustration in this woman. She is as a chance encounter on a dark road, as a wild deer transfixed in a moment of surprise, and then gone in a heartbeat.

I do not really wish to capture Glenda; rather, I feel to save her from some indescribable oppression that looms spectral in her countenance. On the first of several dates we grab a sandwich and soft drink at a Drive Through, both overdressed for the occasion. Glenda makes insistence we get our food here, saying that she always wanted to eat out in a convertible. Afterward we drive up to a lookout point on the Hollywood Hill and eat on the hood of my MG under the stars poised above the twinkle of city lights spread out as far as the eye can see. At some point, our hands touch and we begin caressing. Glenda is hot and I perceive she wants to go all the way. At the point of vaginal penetration, it begins contracting in a way now familiar since my last experience with Shari. My immediate reaction is another rejection. Then something inside me says no, this is different. Instead of withdrawing, I relax and continue to rub up against her clitoris. After nearly an hour, Glenda's body explodes into spontaneous orgasm. I cannot explain why, only for some reason my physical satisfaction secondary in this encounter.

"That was wonderful," she giggles warmly. "I never knew a man could be so affectionate... so unselfish. I felt your soul inside of me, and feel now released."

"Release from what?"

"It's not something I want talk about now. Just hold me and pretend this moment is forever."

I embrace Glenda until the moon high overhead. Then hurriedly she demands we go. I drop her off on the same corner with the promise that she will call me soon. Two weeks later, the phone rings in the middle of the night.

"Hi, would you like to meet me for a glass of wine?"

I can tell Glenda already drinking. I drive ten miles to a small restaurant bar near Redondo and find her talking to another man. Upon seeing me, Glenda dismisses her suitor, motioning for me to come over. After a drink and a couple of dances, we drive to an all-night golf course and make love on one of the greens. This time we experience full intercourse; this seemingly inhibited woman proves to be a real tiger out of the bag. Nevertheless, at the end of the evening, she again insists I drop her off at the same bar where we met, saying only that she will call me.

I see Glenda only twice more over the next six weeks, each time at a different location, each time discovering another unorthodox haven to make love. We are as two teenagers sneaking off to some new romantic adventure. The secretive nature of our rendezvous begins to bother me. Even if we are not in love, surely we can go even once to my place and have sex in a bed. When I confront Glenda with this suggestion, she turns ice cold, saying only that would ruin everything.

"Why must you be always in control?"

"You have no idea what it means to be controlled-- to be controlled every day of your life!"

"What happened to you, Glenda? Why are you like this? Are you married?"

"I was married when I turned fifteen-- and before that I was raped by my father! I have only known rape since I can remember. That's why I could never have a fulfilling relationship with a man... before I met you!

I knew you were special that first night. Don't you see it has to be this way? My husband is a very rich and powerful man. I would be left with nothing, even if he did let me go."

"You could leave and make a new life for yourself."

"And do what? Could you support me?"

I can barely support myself and I still have almost two years of university to complete. The question in my mind is not about supporting Glenda, or even to have a more conventional relationship. I just want to be a man with a woman I can call sometimes. I no longer wish to be used as entertainment, while she remains trapped in corundum of abuse manipulation.

"Sooner, or later you must choose between living in a cage or to live free. I have only unlocked the door, but I can't make you fly."

"Then you will make me dream someday... to fly."

I guess that even a dream of freedom enough for her. Glenda too long has been conditioned through contentment in mind and body. She could have more, except it would take a step of faith; now the hour of her soul's reflection. She tells me she is going away on a trip with her husband and for me not to expect to hear from her for a while.

Fortuitously, something unexpected happens a week later. Bank of America sends me a crisp new credit card with a limit of $500.00. This gift will prove to be my near downfall. I feel now even greater loneliness, isolated, and far from family roots. With Christmas holidays quickly approaching, I decide in a moment of spontaneous rashness to purchase a round-trip airline ticket to Greenville for less than two hundred dollars. I calculate I can pay off the expense in a few months.

Jean falls on my neck weeping. Rudy stiffly shakes my hand, and my brother and two sisters crowd around me as the lost prodigal, now returned. It is the best homecoming I ever had. I decide not to celebrate this Christmas with my family empty-handed. My new credit card makes it possible to shower them all with gifts. I therefore spare no expense, choosing something special for each one. On the eve of this joyful holiday, I can see a sparkle of well-being in Jean's eyes, as the spirit of the lord descends over us all. Her family is made whole again, peace on earth, and goodwill to all men.

The next day, after a famous turkey dinner with all the trimmings, I venture to take a walk around the old neighborhood. At the bottom of Von Holland drive, I run into my old friend Bill Hawking sitting on the front porch of a run-down rental.

"Hey man-- what are you doing back in town?" Bill shouts, running over to me. "The military had enough of you?"

"I've been out since the past three years and now living in L. A. attending university. Did you ever get on the police force?"

I remember this beingBill's younger goal in life.

"Naw-- I failed the physical. Mike and me are roommates now. He took off up the mountain to find Indian smoke should be back real soon. Come on in and have a beer."

I accept the invitation to come in, but decline the beer. We talk for nearly half an hour, but Mike fails to show. I bid Bill goodbye, and trudge back up the hill. Just before evening dinner, a ford Mustang pulls up into the driveway and out jump Bill and Mike. I must say that it gives me pleasure to see my old friend again. Mike may have been a rogue, but he is an entertaining rogue, a one-of-a-kind jack.

Good-hearted Jean insists that my two friends stay for Christmas leftovers. All children-- no matter how big they get-- remain still her children. Over the next few days, the three of us bond as men in our prime—no longer boys dreaming of girls or thinking of promises over the horizon. We hold conviction of the future in our hands, howbeit, with different visions. Over the next few days, Mike outlines an ingenious plan by which he and Bill will accompany me back to Los Angeles. I am to cash-in my return flight and the three of us take a road trip across country. I am a little apprehensive at first, considering my friend's shady past.

"That person ain't me no more," Mike assures me. "And besides, my little brother Hawkeye here will keep me on the straight and narrow."

Bill promises sincerely, as is always his better nature, and he and his older brother determine in excited agreement that the golden state of California their new future frontier. How could I deny them the opportunity of escape their dead-end lives?

Five days before the start of Winter Quarter, the three of us pile into the new model Mustang sedan to begin a four-day journey across the American frontier. Waving goodbye through the back window, I can see a grimace of worry on faces of both my parents. Later, I will appreciate the measure of their concern.

We drive by shifts, stopping only to eat and for gas. The sleek 1973 Mustang, with a powerful Boss 302-$v8$ 5-liter engine under the hood, navigates masterfully across every paved terrain. It reminds me of the days I swooped from Camp Lejeune to Greenville in a Super Bee, except this ride tamer. However, what it possesses in power and aerodynamic excellence, it equally lacks in comfort. The backseat too narrow and too short, the front and passenger seat designed like the ejection cockpit of a jet-fighter. Only because of sheer exhaustion are we able to rest at all. Fortunately, Jean has packed us plenty of sandwiches, so we have adequate provisions for the first two days. At crossing the Memphis Arkansas Memorial Bridge Bill develops a taste for beer and potato chips, which Mike motions second. The two of them finish a six-pack in little over an hour and both end up sleeping deeply until the Oklahoma border.

Outside of Oklahoma City, Mike decides we should travel the old Route 66, instead of taking the Interstate, because their *"great grand pappy Hawkings"* traveled that way during the frontier days. It proves to be a long and tedious way posted with many confusing detours. Instead of discovering the nostalgia of the idyllic American culture, we pass through the slow beating hearts of dead and dying communities with giant rusted relics reminiscent of the days when the American automobile king of Route 66. At one time this was the only automobile gateway from east to west before the completion of the Interstate. Once this way a fabled passage advertising objects of fascination; now ghastly fallen effigies, signifying the end of an era, the highway cracked and unkempt, which only further slows our advance. I see in eyes of my two companions the horror of the thing they fear most in life. Dread that they, too, might one day become acronyms to a way of life doomed in the racing river of progress.

"We need to get our asses to California," Mike announces outside of Amarillo. "That's about as much of the old American west I care to see. California here we come!"

Jumping back on the 40, Mike floors the 290 horse power engine, and the Ford 302 propels us smoothly across the barren expanse. I am secretly glad for this renewed dedication of purpose, since my first day of class less than thirty-six hours away. The trip, fun at the start, begins to cut into our tight budget, the little cash I have nearly gone; my new credit card already near limit. Mike and Bill have less than fifty dollars between them, a fiscal reality I had not fully considered in the beginning.

We arrived at my West L. A. apartment late Sunday evening, exhausted and starved. I go down to the corner market and buy a pound of ground beef and package of Hamburger Helper.

"Boys," I announce, sitting down to our first real meal in four days; "the Lord has safely delivered us home. Let us pray and be thankful."

They hang their heads in silent respect. I am not sure that they consider Hamburger Helper a feast, but it is food, and we are all hungry. They prepare beds for themselves on the living room floor, using the couch cushions and scavenging all the available extra linen. Bill is particularly concerned about the open window.

"Aren't you worried about somebody coming in while you sleep?"

"That's so Shadow can come and go. Don't worry Bill. I have faith in the Lord. Not a hair will perish from any of our heads, except he allow it to happen."

The next morning I discover all the windows and doors locked. I suppose that my two friends little share my optimism of divine protection. All the next day I spend on campus preparing for a new academic quarter. At least my job at the bookstore is still available. With three mouths to feed, I need income more than ever. That night we have Hamburger Helper again. They do not say anything, but I can tell my friends are reminiscing about Jean's Christmas left-overs and their absentdose of daily beer.

"Old Bill here is a certified Security Guard," Mike announces during dinner, "and hell, I can do most of anything as long as I can use my golden tongue. We read in the paper that there's a shopping Mall near here that needs someone with our qualifications. Tomorrow we are going down early and applying."

Bill retrieves some official looking certificates from his pocket to show me. Bill is qualified all right, but Mike is another question considering the convictions of his past.

"That sounds really good," I encourage. "Even if you both don't get hired, maybe at least one of you has a chance."

Mike only wrinkles his nose, resembling in that moment the sly old fox I remember from my youth. In truth, I find it difficult to altogether trust Mike. Not that I think he might take anything from me. I have nothing to take; confident a code of honor exists between us as friends, never once doubting this bond of integrity. Rather, I do not trust his calculating nature, a con man always looking for a con. I become apprehensive that hounds of justice might follow him to my lair one day.

To my surprise and relief, they are both hired. Their first paycheck, they treat me to dinner in a restaurant and a night out on the town. It is an enjoyable evening; but I have come to realize that despite the nostalgia of childhood friendship, they must go. Now that they are working, and with money in their pockets, Bill and Mike start hanging out at the biker bar a few blocks down on Washington Boulevard. One night after closing hours, they stagger in drunk inconsiderate to my need for dedicated study time. I have had a particularly long day, am exhausted, and in little mood to be disturbed. When they persist on interrupting my concentration with idle ramblings, I rise up frustrated and go to bed without saying anything. I should insert here that I have the habit of sleeping with my Bowie knife under the mattress, a tradition from my days in Nam, and one I will stop after the events of this night.

As Bill passes my bedroom on the way to the toilet, he hears me mumbling in my sleep. Then I yell something about 'killing them all." Both Bill and Mike come running into my bedroom only to see me leap pass them, Bowie knife in hand and begin stabbing a jacket hung in the closet. I awaken in a tangle of garments, seeing my two friends hovering over me with terror in their eyes. I feel embarrassed, upon hearing then relate the witnessed event.

"What were you dreaming about?" Mike wants to know, his jugular racing up and down his long neck.

"I don't remember, only that it was dark. I guess that I scared you boys. I'm pretty sure that doesn't happen very often."

The doubt in both their faces speaks louder than the words they say. I think the source of this trauma triggered by stress accumulation of the past several weeks. The presence of Mike and Bill is like having two harbingers living here. They consume much more than they give back. Their idea of contribution is to keep cold beer in the refrigerator, stock the cupboards with chips and pretzels, while allowing me to buy and prepare all the real food. However, the final real show down between us comes that same weekend.

Saturday afternoon we all go down to Venice Beach for a picnic and a day in the surf. However, we never make it to the water's edge. Like a trained bird dog, Mike finds the only beachside bar in the area, and he and his brother instantly blend into the fray of drunken patrons. After an hour, I unceremoniously announce it is time to go home.

"You are worse than a nagging woman," Mike slurs back. "If I wanted to be nagged I would've stayed married-- and Bill, too! Since finding Jesus, you just don't know how to have fun. If that's what it means to get saved, then Bill and me want no part of it. Don't worry about us, we'll find our way back."

I depart without further intervention. They are big boys, and as Mike predicts, they will unfortunately 'find their own way back home'. The next two weeks, we see less of each other. Nor do they join me anymore for dinner, preferring to eat out.

Nevertheless, they liberally consume my milk and cereal every morning, without any thought of replenishing what they use. I make a decision to inform them that either they will need to start paying rent or else find their own place. As though in anticipation to my thoughts, Mike and Bill arrive one evening, each riding backs of slightly used Honda 450 Sport motorcycles.

"What happened to your Mustang?" I ask, looking over the machines.

They are without question things of engineering beauty.

"Traded it in for these, plus some traveling cash," Bill brags.

"I thought you said you still owed over $2500.00 on the Ford."

"Mike is as slick a businessman than you will ever know," Bill continues, winking at his brother. "He gave the bartender a sob story about him and me wanting to get back home to Mississippi, only we didn't have the money. Some guy who owns a motorcycle shop and a friend of the owner of the biker bar, said he would take it off our hands in a trade. I think they bought it to chop. Once we get back, we'll report the car stolen, and no one will be the wiser. And don't worry, we never gave your name or address to anyone."

"So what are your plans now," I inquire, absorbing the duplicity of this new revelation.

"We decided to go back to Carolina," Mike confides in his matter-of- a-fact way. "California just isn't a place where we want to live. Maybe you ought to come back home once you finish your schooling."

"Maybe I will do that. Why don't you come up and let's have a last meal together, then you can light out early tomorrow morning."

"We best be getting on the road tonight." Mike says, shifting his eyes toward Bill, as a partner in crime. "I figure we can be in Arizona before it gets too late."

"Yeah, it's better we get going," Bill shyly agrees. "Besides, Mike and me ate already, and there's no point tempting fate."

I cannot say that I am sorry to see them ride away. It has been sometimes fun to share a few last adventures with these friends of my early years, but they are also trouble to the core. I do not wish to know the details of their transaction. I only hope to avoid any collateral damage.

As though in fulfillment of my worse dread, I awaken the following night to the sound of frantic voices and the clamor of a person, or persons running up the front staircase leading to the top balcony. Instantly awake, I grab the Bowie knife under my bed and twelve-gauge shotgunhanging over the television. Clawing at the door are two well-dressed people of Mexican descent: a man in his thirties, and a lovely young woman no more than twenty years old.

"Please let us in," pleads the man. "They are right behind us."

At this moment, three low-rider vehicles pull up in front of my building, and out pour several Chicano gang members carrying knifes and chains. There is no time to think. I go instantly into combat mode, step boldly at the top of the landing, allowing the couple to pass into my apartment.

"Stop right there!" I shout in my most commanding Marine Corps Sergeant's voice.

"This is not your business, man," says one of the men, halting his ascent.

"It is my business now. These people have sanctuary here. This is my home, and you will have to go through me to get to them."

"You think you can take us all?"

"I will take you first, and then the one behind you, and I might take a few more down with me."

I feel in a Billy Jack movie, only this is not Hollywood. I am committed now, certain in my ability to take down a few of them. Strangers have entered my home requesting sanctuary. In my mind, this makes me their protector. A real Mexican standoff ensues as I remain resolute, blocking the top of the staircase shotgun and Bowie knife in hand. Several gang members armed with assorted weapons congregate near the bottom, uncertain of what to do next. The young man, nearest the top, glares into my eyes, considering carefully his next move. He then whistles shrilly, waves his arm, and they all pile into their low-rider vehicles, screeching away into the night along Washington Boulevard.

It is common knowledge the Chicano gang territory begins several blocks south of here, extending all the way west to Venice Beach. It is rare to see them this far north and east, unless on a crime spree, and even more rare for them to stalk members of their own community.

"Thank you-thank you," the young lady says sobbing, as I enter my apartment. "Fernando and me just want to marry and be happy. My brother does not agree. He swore to kill Fernando first. You have done a brave thing for us."

"I will call the police," I volunteer moving toward the phone.

"No police," Fernando insists. "We will be leaving soon."

A taxi pulls up in front, horn blasting. Fernando grabs the hand of his young love, and together they race down the stairs. The young woman looks longingly up at me before vanishing inside the vehicle. Seconds later the taxi speeds away, followed by three low-rider cars racing in hot pursuit. I heave a sigh and hang-up my shotgun, making certain this night that my door locked. A habit I will practice from now own. It takes more than an hour for the adrenaline to subside. I often wonder what happened to that couple. Did the leader of the low-riders catch up with them; or did Fernando escape with the jewel of his love? This will also be the last night I sleep with the Bowie knife beneath my bed.

Glenda calls me one evening sounding somehow different. At long last she wants to come to my place for a change, so I give her the address. Half an hour later she arrives dressed in jeans and a sweat shirt, looking uncommonly common. Tonight, Glenda is wearing little makeup, only sparse jewelry, and has a duck-tailed hair style making her almost look boyish. I am accustomed to see an elegant lady, a touched-up billboard model glittering expensively. This night Glenda is real-- an observation more disturbing than I wish to acknowledge.

"I wanted that we spend one more evening together," she croons, embracing me.

"Why-- are you going to stop seeing me?"

"My husband has been called to Mexico City for six months and wants me to go with him. I cannot refuse to go."

"The bird in her gilded cage," I say sarcastically.

Glenda does not respond. She knows I am right. In a way, I guess that we both accept this will be our last night together. Taking Glenda into my bed, I peel away the husk of her unappealing clothing and discover for the first time the exquisiteness of her naked body. This night we are truly intimate, flesh touching flesh. For the first time, I feel Glenda within my soul; feel her pain, as she whimpers release into my ear. Then I succumb to euphoria of the moment, descending into a pleasant slumber.

The next morning, I awaken to find Glenda gone. On my dresser a hand-written note that reads simply: *'You will always be inside me'*, along with a single earring from a pair she wore the first night we met. Surprisingly, I begin deeply missing Glenda. I cannot say why, exactly, only that final evening we had shared something real, something to last beyond life's mortal restraints.

The end of fall quarter, I receive a letter from the campus director for a rendezvous Friday morning concerning my academic performance. I think the meeting about my grade point average, which has again fallen below 2.8. Entering the office of Mrs. Fine is reminiscent of when I attended grade school and sent to the school counselor after receiving a failing mark in a particular subject.

"Upon review of your records, it has come to my attention that you have not yet declared a Major."

"I always assumed that English my subject."

"Yes, you have taken many of the primary English courses, including French as a second language. But you have also taken Sociology, Psychology, Physics, a class on the Holocaust, and even a series on the plight of the North American Indian. Unfortunately, most of these do not provide you with the credits you need to complete an educational curriculum."

"I am under the impression that a university is a place of learning. I thought this my criterion. I am here to learn what the world knows, and understand the foundation elements of knowledge."

"It is, of course that too, but you also have a certain obligation to the terms of your grant. Let us see if we can make any of these credits work for you."

She is a nice lady, whose job to ensure the proper processing of a future alumnus. This is a disappointing example of education reduced to a formula. I suppose this why the more specialized an academic becomes, the less versatile in terms of common sense. It is the metaphorical destruction of knowledge in the attempt to justify doctrinal instruction. UCLA has recently authorized an experimental project allowing students to design their own academic program with the approval of the student councilor. An hour later, I leave the office of Mrs. Fine with a custom newly declared major. I am officially an American Studies Major with a primary in English literature. Now I am able to apply some of the Psychology, Sociology, and American Indian classes as credits toward my new degree. It seems all very political to me, but now I will be able to graduate in six more Quarters, providing I take an array of specified courses, mostly in the English department.

Upon preparation to return home, I meet a woman in the motorcycle parking area, whose Yamaha has inadvertently fallen against my Honda, locking her handlebars into my back spokes. Together, we manage to free them without damage.

"You are very strong," she purrs charmingly. "Thank you. You come by bike every day?"

"I am taking a design class once a week."

She is wearing a tight-fitting black leather-riding suit, which truly suits her small body well. Her motorcycle is twice the CC's of mine, and new. She introduces herself as Dorothy. She lives in Beverly Hills, specifically making it clear that she is married and with two children. To my surprise, she proposes I join her and her kids and those of a neighbor for a desert camp-out this very weekend.

"I'll be taking two Suzuki trail bikes, and you are welcome to ride one. We go out every year at this time; it would be nice to have a man come along for protection."

The idea of doing some real trail riding in the California desert enthusiastically appeals to me. I thank Dorothy, making arrangements to meet at her house early the next morning. I call in sick at the bookstore. By now, I no longer care if they keep me on, since the pay poor, as are the hours. Besides, I have already applied for another job at the V.A. Mental Hygiene Clinic through the Jobs for Veterans Post, and feel that the subsequent interview went well.

We hit the road before sunrise, Dorothy's Rover overflowing with giggling, screaming pre-teenaged girls, a sleek silver camper trailer in tow, and two Suzuki Trail bikes strapped on the back. The early light splashes over the distant horizon creating a collage of red and golden hues unmatched by any artist stroke. Today I am a passenger, able to appreciate the view from the perspective of an observer. I hate to say it, but I find myself wishing that Dorothy's children and their friends not present, so I might better appreciate fully the magnificent solitude of this moment. By latemorning, we turn off onto a well-used trail, little more than a narrow path between boulders and dry sage-covered gullies. Dorothy skillfully navigates the treacherous terrain with experienced familiarity.

Upon arriving on a flat knoll, I detach the two small motorcycles, easily lowering the light plastic and alloy 250 cc machines to the ground. First on the agenda after setting up camp, we roast some hotdogs over a cowboy fire and wash them down with soft drinks. The four girls want to hike to a known cave at top of a nearby ridge. Dorothy instructs them to check for wild animals and rattlesnakes before going inside.

"Rattlesnakes," I whisper apprehensively.

Dorothy assures me thather two daughters know how to take care of themselves. She and her husband have been coming here as a family from the time their children born. She also has a stock of prepared antivenom kits just in case.

This day I learn the power and precision design of a real trail bike. The extra suspension, the immediate acceleration, the low gearing composes a symphony of control. I become master over this hostile landscape, leaping over rocks and small gullies, stepping down steep embankments and gunning the throttle to gain access up the shear opposite face. Dorothy is even more agile, exhibiting skill and experience far exceeding my own. Once she sees I am comfortable handling my bike, she instructs me to follow her. I think the request odd, but I comply anyhow. After all, if not for Dorothy, I would not even be here. Besides, she is more expert of this desert region, so I assume she is acting for my well-being. This, however, proves not to be the case.

Dorothy is fully clad in protective riding gear; whereas, I am not. She leads me through narrow briar patches that rip holes in my jeans and flesh, down into rocky craters mined with waiting obstacles. She tricks my pride to take jumps disastrously too high; luring me into valleys of imminent danger. Being the macho Marine, I leap back onto the bike after each spill and continue without acknowledging intensity of the pain. I can see a glint of excitement in Dorothy's expression each time; as though she takes personal pleasure seeing me suffer through the obstinate will of my male ego. I cannot say these experiences lack a certain amount of anticipated exhilaration, or that danger not intricately exciting when doing desert trail biking. In retrospect, I am lucky not to have broken a limb, or suffer serious injury. By end of the day, I am left with an uncomfortable feeling that Dorothy is testing my durability and pain threshold. Nothing she says, but something about her impish smile and the hypocritical inquiry of my physical state after recovery from each spill.

As the sun crests the desert horizon, we return to the camping trailer, where Dorothy's two girls and their friends are waiting around a blazing campfire. We consume an open range dinner consisting of burgers and foil-wrapped baked potatoes cooked in embers of mesquite wood. I must admit I am completely exhausted by this day of trying to keep up, looking forward to curl up in my sleeping bag. I thought I would be sleeping outside under the stars, but the girls have made plans to spend the night in their cave. Dorothy insists I take one of three bunks inside the camper. I have just crawled into bed, when Dorothy brings me a cup of cowboy coffee: a recipe of fresh coffee grounds thrown into a pot of boiling water, and then allowed to settle to the bottom. It smells good, so I slip on some jeans in acceptance of the offer.

"Don't bother to put on a t-shirt." Dorothy instructs, snatching the garment out of my hand. "You have a nice sculpted build. My husband and I are always looking for new models."

"I didn't know you were in that kind of business," I reply, feeling a little self-conscious.

"Mostly men's and women's underwear and you have a perfect body for our bikini line."

"Thank you," I say, after a long uncomfortable pause. "Well, I guess I had better get back in the sack."

"Not... just yet," Dorothy moves close to me. "The girls won't be coming back until morning, and it is just you and me out here all alone."

I find myself in a situation of compromise. I like Dorothy, but I never considered the possibility of a romantic encounter. First, she is married, and with a family. Second, she is at least fifteen years older, still attractive, but older and with a husband.

"You're not afraid, are you?" She challenges, running her hand along my bruised arms and chest, then down to my crotch.

Reluctant is a more accurate description. Nevertheless, my young hormones are always ready, conspicuously betraying my resolve. Contrary to the sweetness of her name, Dorothy turns out to be a real lioness, digging her nails into the back of my neck, and biting my lips in a way less than romantic. Then, in the middle of the act, she begins panting, and her eyes narrow wickedly.

"Slap me," she commands, her voice trembling.

"No, I protest."

"Yes, slap me... I need you to slap me in the face."

Not knowing what else to do, I slap Dorothy lightly in the face.

"Harder-- hit me harder!"

When I do not comply, she slaps me across the mouth as hard as she can.

"Slap me like that!" She cries.

With the taste of blood in my mouth, I slap Dorothy hard-- not as hard as I could have, but hard enough that I hope she does not ask for more. She then scratches me across the chest having an orgasm lasting for several minutes.

So horrible the experience, I do not even remember if Ihad a physical release. Perhaps I did; however, this basic act of sadism I wish never again to repeat. I feel ashamed, somehow compromised, andalso angry. I am not angry with Dorthy— exactly. I am angrier at myself for not anticipating possibility of this event.

The next morning, the girls come down from their cave and eat a cowboy breakfast. I try to act as if nothing happened, nor do Dorothy and I talk about it. I am not very hungry and decide to take a last ride through the desert. It is less exciting, and less lovely than I remember just yesterday. Something different, something inside of me changed. Something lost, a dream shattered into a nightmare, a pleasant imagining I will not imagine again. By the time I return, the camper, packed and ready, needing only that I remount the trail bikes on the back.

During the drive home, I try not to dwell on the previous night's experience, with part of me wishing it all just a bad dream that never really happened. Dorothy remains also silent, except for the occasional chat with her daughters, who seem suspicious of something. Or maybe it is just my conscience. Nevertheless, I am glad when the three-hour drive ends and we pull into Dorothy's Beverly Hills driveway.

"You won't mind to help us unload everything," Dorothy demands without shyness.

"Of course not," I reply.

In reality, I do mind. I want nothing more than to get as far away as possible from this shadowy web of events. As I push the second motorcycle into the garage, an overweight man wearing a soiled t-shirt appears. His receding hair disheveled, and his eyes red from consuming too much alcohol.

"So, you are the young man that took care of my wife and kids this weekend."

"Yes sir," I say respectfully, and extend my hand.

"We don't need to be as formal as that. Come in and have a drink."

Reluctantly, I accept the invitation, not wishing to arouse the husband's suspicion. This situation is like none I have ever been in before. It is not that I am afraid of consequence; rather, I feel guilty of betraying a position of trust by sleeping with this man's wife.

"Was she good?" He nonchalantly asks, passing me a glass of Scotch and water.

"Excellent bike and made for the trail," I report uncomfortably.

"I mean my wife. Was Dorothy good to fuck?"

"Sir— Dorothy is a wonderful woman. I don't know what you think happened, but I assure you—"

"I know exactly what happened. You fucked my wife. That's okay. It's not the first time something like this has happened."

Moving to a large Mahogany desk, he retrieves a business checkbook from inside one of the drawers.

"I want you to fuck her again, only this time I want to watch. Dorothy tells me you are a good candidate to model a line of our underwear. Maybe you would be interested in a down payment."

"No-- I don't want any money. Believe me, I am sorry it ever happened, but I am not a prostitute."

Without touching the offered drink, I run out quickly, coasting my Honda down the driveway kick starting it into gear. My sin found out, I wish only to escape. Instead of going home, I drive up the coast highway to Leo Carrillo beach. I walk along the point until midnight, asking God to forgive me in Jesus' name for my weakness. It will be many months before the uncleanness dissipates.

The following week I receive confirmation that the *V.A. Mental Hygiene Clinic* has accepted to hire me starting in two weeks. I give official notice to the bookstore and say farewell to my fellow employees. The last weekend I work both Friday and Saturday because of a special book signing at Beaver Hall. Saturday morning I arrive as usual at the front door wearing sunglasses to pick up several boxes of books staged near the entrance for a scheduled delivery to the author. This particular morning a construction scaffold partially bars the entrance; and positioned outside the door, a hefty looking young man redirecting pedestrian traffic.

"Hi," I say, "I'm here for some boxes of books."

"You'll have to go around."

I point out that the books are stacked in labeled boxes to his right, and that going around to the back means nearly a mile detour to the other side of campus.

"I'm an employee. Those books are for a reading that begins in less than an hour. Please, it will take only a minute."

"I said you will need to go around."

"That is not reasonable. I want to speak to the floor manager just over there."

I step to one side and knock on the window to gain attention of another employee inside. This young gladiator abruptly swings open the door, roughly grips my shoulder, spinning me around. He then reaches out, grabs my sunglasses, crushing them in his hand. My reaction instantaneous: two jabs to the lower stomach, with an uppercut to the chin. In a fit of rage, he rushes forward as a linebacker tackling me to the ground and falling on top like a ton of bricks. Just beside my head is a hammer; and for a reflex instant, I consider grabbing the weapon. I manage to roll him off instead, twisting his right arm behind his back. The store manager and two workmen break-up what is left of the fight. I suppose there could have been legal charges being that I am an ex-Marine and considered a lethal weapon in the eyes of the law; but fortunately, there are none. I do, however, receive a letter instructing me to report the following Tuesday to the Dean's office.

Here is a man born not into privilege, but who has worked himself up through the ranks of the elite. In an unspoken way, we bond immediately, understanding one another without having to say it.

"You decommissioned the campus star quarterback," states the Dean matter-of-factly. "The head coach wants blood-- your blood. Witnesses support your account of self-defense and that you did not initiate the altercation. But you must remember this is not the Marine Corps, and the boy you hurt comes from a very wealthy family. I have saved your ass this time, but being right is not always a guarantee of justice. If anyone asks, you are on suspension for three days. I recommend you stay clear of any Bruins from now own."

I take the Dean's well-meaning advice. I receive a lot of evil looks from the UCLA Bruins after this incident. They never actually confront me, so I just ignore them. I guess they figure I am oneof those crazy Vietnam vets capable of most anything. I guess they areright. The following week I start my new job at the V.A. Mental HygieneClinic as an assistant to outpatient therapy. In the months to follow, Iwill learn a great deal about the fragile threads separating the sane fromthe insane. I will learn even more about the masks of hypocrisy worn over twisted faces bound in brotherhood of the social elite.

Part Eight
Venus Ascending

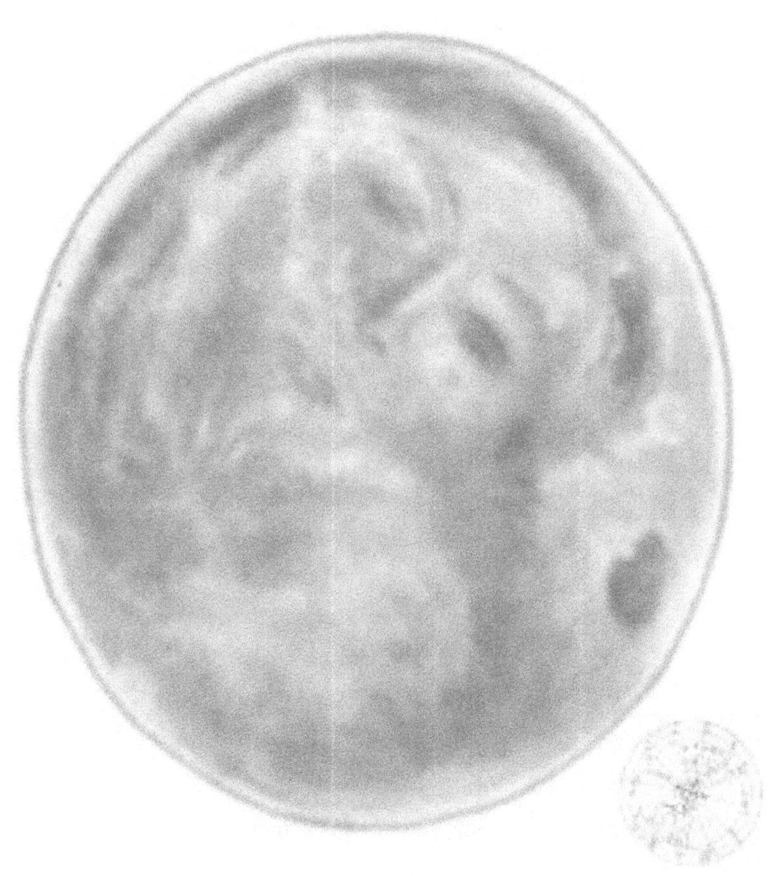

The Glimmering

To glimpse a moment in her eyes
A dark exotic wood in forgotten deeps
All that is truth all the lies
Satin nights warm with her sighs
Reflections deep where she sleeps
Dreams of youth that she keeps
Between her thighs his dream dreaming
Through her pure and forever being

And all the world seeming dreaming
Of things pure and forever gleaming
Forever fleeting in her eyes
Where nothing lives nothing dies
Broken angels cloaked in summer flies
Church doors open to the last
All stand veiled before the mast
And she a shadow on the wall
To those present and those past

All things fallen and all things to fall
All creation gathered at the last call
She a spirit in church bells ringing
In her heart lost souls singing
She the past of all remembering
A guiding star in distant glimmering

*F*irst day of Creative Writing Class I arrive late. This new academic quarter has begun with the usual panic scrambling between lines on a map of walkways leading to new instructors with new agendas. Professor Kessler, a cool, well-groomed man in his fifties, wears faded corduroy pants and a tweed jacket over a turtleneck. He only glances at me inconsequentially and pretends to ignore my bumbling to take an empty chair beside a distinguished young man. During the usual introductions, I learn this to be the youngest son of Hollywood actor *Charlton Heston*. Seated on the opposite side of the table is an interesting looking older woman named Barbara, dripping with gold and prestige.

Our first assignment is to write a three-page short story on any subject. The next week I arrive once again late, muttering weak excuse about having difficulty starting my bike. Professor Kessler grunts unimpressed, making comment that if I am late again, I should skip his class and stick to auto mechanics. This will be the last time I am tardy.

"Okay, Barbara, please continue to read your story." Professor Kessler says to the affluently dressed lady.

Although, Professor Kessler insists we address him by his title, everyone else is first name bases only-- no Misters or Misses. Barbara continues reading her piece by starting back at the beginning. It is well written, grammatically correct in every way, except that it is the most boring, uninteresting collection of sentences describing a day of shopping in an expensive fashion store by two women. After two pages of tedious dialogue, they finally agree on the purchase of some trivia item symbolic to their friendship. At the end of this reading, Professor Kessler looks straight at me, demanding I make a critique of the story in terms of interest and style. I reply honestly that I think the piece architecturally flawless and rich in character development, but lacking identifiable interest or cathartic elevation.

"An insightful observation," the Professor agrees, and then continues in order, soliciting additional comments.

Barbara just sits and glares across the table at me; her eyes daggers. I perceive I have made an enemy today, making point to avoid this woman's scorn.

"Next week will be your turn to impress us with a jewel of imagination." Professor Kessler announces to me at end of class session.

The following week, I arrive early with my first short story in hand. As with composing a poem, it comes to me only the night before by inspiration of images felt in an unconscious stream, as though raw elements mixed with imagination form into substance through contours of light and shadow. It is difficult to explain exactly, only that I feel the characters within context, analogist to the creative process experienced by a sculpture artist upon seeing and releasing an anthropomorphic entity trapped in a piece of raw stone. It is as though these characters attempting escape into the real world through the conduit of my thoughts. The experience exhilarating, as voices within a living tale take on life and measured meaning, pooling into a collage of vivid imagery. I spend nearly all night, first writing on paper, and then laboriously typing three finished pages.

I walk into class the next day proudly clutching my first ever truly qualified short fiction titled, *The Frogs*. Even Professor Kessler is impressed, contemplative of my creation. He then turns to my nemesis, the lady in gold, granting her first stab with the sharp blade of criticism. I brace myself in anticipation. However, to my surprise, Barbara relinquishes her right to attack with staves of revenge. In light of a public reading, even I can see the several grammatical errors waiting for the hatchet.

"I really wanted to find fault with this piece," Barbara articulates reflectively. "However, it is one of the most interesting short stories I have ever heard read. I prefer to leave my comments at that."

In the end, the young actor's son makes the honorable kill. Professor Kessler confers that the story well presented, but agrees with the criticism that the piece needs a lot of polishing. At end of class, the Professor intercepts me at the door to deliver a special footnote.

"I believe you have a lot of talent; but many writing obstacles you must overcome. Your use of language is rich in metaphor and content, yet lacking in mechanical precision. I suggest you purchase a copy of Elements of Style. It will greatly improve your skills as a writer. Who knows, you may even one day write the next Winesburg Ohio, or even the next great American novel."

I bump into Barbara in the hall upon leaving the classroom. Shyly, I say hello, and thank her for the kindness to my ego, also apologizing for my apparent insensitivity to her own work.

"For the entire week, I thought about nothing, but to rip your story to shreds. I never expected such powerful imagery. You were unkind in your criticism of my story. Yet, I forgive you only because you have a true gift as a writer. They say that even Ernest Hemingway was a social bull."

I must admit I appreciate the adoration shown by this beautiful woman and her comparison to one of my favorite authors, feeling even more miserable about my rude character that first day of class. What had gotten into me? In the moment, I thought to be honest as a critic. In retrospect, there harbored perhaps an element of latent jealousy. Everything about this woman represents a material world I do not altogether understand. A part of me irresistibly attracted to that world, a distant glimmering to tempt my faith and depth of character.

Barbara and I become acquaintances over the course of the Quarter. We often sit at one of the cafeteria terraces talking and sipping coffee. Recently divorced from a powerful man, who is presently vice president of Capital Records, Barbara is determined to reconstruct her lost identity.

I think we share a lot in common, as we are both in process of trying to piece back together our lives damaged at a critical junction in youth. It fascinates me the way she resurrects humor from even the most serious trauma. For example, when she was in her late twenties, she and her husband, Barry, involved in a terrible automobile accident while driving home from a party. Barry had fallen asleep at the wheel of their Mercedes because of too much alcohol, crashing into an oncoming truck. Miraculously, there are no fatalities. However, Barbara suffers severe facial injuries: a crushed jaw and all of her front teeth shattered.

"Thank God for German ingenuity and modern medicine! Had we been in any other car, we both would have been history. Now I have all new porcelain caps even better than my old teeth. Can you appreciate the irony? The Germans tried to exterminate all the Jews, and today many of those that survived and their children drive German cars because they are the safest on the planet."

Over the next several weeks, Barbara and I confide more and more, sharing our deepest hurts, past disappointments, and present frustrations. She is presently seeing a man named John, an accountant, to whom she feels a debt of gratitude for helping her through the worse of the divorce; only he is superficial, lacking the strength she needs from a man. I share with her the secret of my poetry, which she thinks particularly fascinating, although sometimes a little dark.

"It surprises me that someone with your recent war experience can see things so beautifully. You have Barry's strength and John's sensitivity. Those are rare qualities to find in one man."

Honestly, I do not feel very strong in the presence of this fabulous woman. She is a thing unobtainable in my mind, worldly, far removed from my reality of thinking. I am as an unkempt motorcycle jockey groomed by wind and Freeway grit. Barbara is a queen of the Palisades, born of high fashion and with Mercedes taste. What could we possibly share in common?

Professor Kessler assigns a final class project, teaming us together two by two to co-op a piece of literature. Barbara and I become logical partners. Once a week, I ride my motorcycle or drive my MG to her Pacific Palisades home for a two-hour exchange of ideas. This is when I meet Barbara's lovely three daughters. Ellen, the oldest, is a depressed teen, whose boyfriend recently committed suicide; Dale, a cheerful middle teen, reminding me of an always smiling chipmunk; and the youngest, Amie, who possesses an intimidating intelligence far exceeding that of a ten-year-old. And of course there is Issie, an annoying parrot that squawks endlessly during daylight hours the names of everyone in the family, including the name of Barry-Barry-

Barry! I like the three girls from the beginning and form a bond of immediate kinship, as with those dispossessed, lives changed forever by the disparagement of a divorce.

I take these sessions of collaboration seriously, devoting all my creative energy to realize the perfect story. Perhaps, my zeal overly zealous, ignoring the cautions of instinct. One evening I arrive in the middle of a chaos. A week earlier, Barbara purchased a new couch and two armchairs from a local upscale Asian import furniture shop. Unknown to anyone, a colony of Carpenter Ants nest within one of the chairs. It seems Carpenter Ants hatch with wings and swarm from their nest in search of a suitable location with goal of establishing a new colony.

Early that morning, they do just this. Barbara and her three daughters awaken to a nightmare of large black ants covering the walls and ceilings. The exterminator has already departed, gone only minutes prior to my arrival, leaving behind a massacre of dead or dying insects.

"My God— you should have seen it!" Barbara exclaims good-naturedly. "Like Armageddon—I never saw so many ants in my life—and in my house! You would have been crazy."

"Even in fiction, I never imagined something like this could happen," I remark, sincerely awed by magnitude of this domestic invasion.

Insisting on helping with the clean-up operation, I remove my jacket and go to work. It takes three vacuum cleaner bags to remove the carnage, some still writhing; some disoriented trying to fly-- all victims of a misconceived hatchery. The remains of the dead queen– or at least she is presumed dead— remain interred along with countless drones somewhere within the frame of the expensive piece of furniture. No way will Barbara exhume these at the cost of bringing harm to her new chair.

"I'm sorry that we missed our session tonight," Barbara apologizes later as we walk along a meandering path of a Japanese-style garden created in her backyard. "I promise sweetie, I'll make it up to you."

Our hands touch briefly, electrifying, sensual. The way she calls me 'sweetie' makes me feel good. Barbara has a seductive quality that tugs secretly at my immature senses like the lure of exotic bait to an expectant hungry fish. I find myself willfully resisting her charms, as Odysseys the Sirens. That evening powering along the Pacific Coast Highway toward my West Los Angeles apartment, I ponder the brightness of the night sky. I see the planet Venus hovering over the ocean horizon, seductively near, reminding me of the distance between our two worlds. Yet our emotions somehow more near.

The following Tuesday, we must cancel again because of a problem with my MG. Just prior to jumping on the coast highway, the engine starts to overheat, smoke billowing from under the hood. It turns out to be one of the radiator hoses. An hour of diagnosis, another hour to get the car home, equals another scrapped evening with only three weeks remaining until the end of the quarter.

Friday night I receive an unexpected call from Glenda.

"I'm in the area, and would like to drop by and see you," she whispers sheepishly at the other end of the phone.

"I thought you would be gone by now. Sure, come over."

Glenda's voice sounds strange, which makes me wonder what she wants really, considering our last goodbye encounter. I decide not to dwell on it. She is here, and frankly, I feel a little lonely. Maybe Glenda not my dream girl; nor is she unpleasant to spend an evening. She arrives deckedout, as I had never seen her before, wearing a beautiful designer dress, sexy high heels, adorned with gold and turquoise jewelry as one mightimagine an Inca Princess. I invite Glenda inside, swoop her familiar body into my arms and attempt to kiss the perfect contour of ruby lips madetoo perfect. She backs impulsively away and smiles teasingly.

"I'm sorry, but I am meeting someone later. I just came by to thank you for everything… and to give you this."

She hands me a small black box with the word Bullock Wilshire etched into the leatherette case. Inside is a handsome man's gold bracelet. Shocked by this act of unexpected charity, I hand the gift back to her.

"I can't accept this," I choke. "It is very kind of you Glenda, but this is too extravagant. You don't owe me anything. Please, take it back and get a refund."

She looks at me incredulously, her eyes glassy with hurt and scorn.

"It is your loss," she says taking back the gift, "remember that I loved you!"

"I thought you were going to Mexico with your husband-- so who are you meeting tonight?"

"It doesn't matter-- even if you think it does! I am a woman used to certain things. I was once poor like you, and I could never go back to that life. I really do love you. I hope one day you will understand."

As Glenda flees down the stairs and into a waiting Cab, a profound sense of emptiness, mixed with guilt overshadows the moment, making me feel as though I have committed some wrong. Upon deeper reflection, I suppose I could have accepted Glenda's gift. Only to do so would make me feel a gigolo. In my heart I know I do not love Glenda; yet thethings we shared pure and spiritual. Yes, it was an act of flesh; however, something also we both needed at the time to unlock future passage. Deep downI hope what she says true, and that Glenda really does have a date this night. Later, I pray for myself and for Glenda, pray that my last gift to this woman might be a release to us both. Little do I know this not the last time I will see this woman of worldly affection.

Following the next Monday's class, Barbara invites me to come over early that evening and join her and the three daughters for a family dinnerbefore working on our project.

"Come around Seven. You were such a dear to help us with the clean-up. This is the least I can offer." Barbara proposes sincerely.

I arrive precisely at seven o'clock. This time I come by motor cycle, dressed in my traditional combat camouflage jacket, worn, but clean, and bell-bottom blue jeans. I do not know if I look tuff, or just unstylish. Barbara's daughters are impressed and want to know if I killed anyone during my tour in Vietnam.

"Don't be so nosy," scolds Barbara. "We do not ask our guest such things. Just be thankful that men like him are willing to defend the freedom of others."

Barbara embodies the eloquence of a regal queen. It is not so much what she says, but how she says it, which makes me feel important, as if I belong. I think she instinctively senses my fleshly need to belong; senses the true depth of emptiness and lack of connection in my life.

After an excellent dinner of poached salmon fillet-- which I always thought came only in cans-- Barbara and I settle into the den to exchange ideas on the new couch that has accompanied the ant-infested chair. At half past ten, we decide to conclude for the night. Once again, our hands brush together. It is electrifying and altogether primitive. I gaze deeply into her captivating hazel eyes. Suddenly, they change to bottomless wells sucking my soul into depths unknown. I grow dizzy, a feeling of falling-- out of control.

We spontaneously embrace each other and kiss as never two people kissed before. Sweeping her up in my arms, I carry Barbara into the adjoining bedroom and make love to this golden woman with such worldly passion, frightening, threatening the solidity of my self-resolve. I awaken in the night startled, feeling an irrational need to escape. Escape what-- I do not know-- only driven by an imperative desire to get far away. Barbara lies sleeping in beautiful repose, as one might imagine an enchanted fairytale princess. Part of me wants to stay, but something deeper, more venerable needs desperately to get far away. Dressing quickly and quietly, I slip out the back patio door and coast my motorcycle several blocks down the hill of Barbara's street before engaging the engine.

Upon arriving home, I try again to sleep, but cannot. Something disturbs my rest, something I am unable to put my finger on. I go into the living room and continue studying for upcoming exams. It seems always I am catching up on one subject or another. Shadow jumps up on the chair, wraps her body familiarly around my neck, and begins purring warmly. After several minutes of fruitless concentration, I close the boring text. Again, I try to sleep. Finally, I break down and call Barbara even late as it is.

"Hello," her familiar voice answers, sending chills over my entire body. "Is that you, Sweetie?"

"Yes, I reply after a long uncomfortable silence.

"Why did you leave like that?" She inquires. "Are you angry about something?"

I discern the hurt in her voice, a hint of familiar rejection she has experienced before in her life.

"No— it was perfect…maybe too perfect. I left because… I don't know why. But I would very much like to see you again."

"I understand. I would like to see you again, too. Goodnight Sweetie, and have good dreams about us."

My peace restored. I am admired by a woman who I admire. I stand at the threshold of something new; beginning of a passage into uncharted depths of emotion and spirituality. I will sleep this night and have an unusual dream, a dream neither pleasant, nor unpleasant. In this dream I arrive home on a visit. Rudy and Jean receive me as always they do, only this time they are unceremoniously gay. Rudy asks if I plan to join the monkey train. At first, I am confused and replied that I have not made up my mind yet. Then I am outside and see a train car filled with gibbering monkeys. I am just about to climb on board, when I see Barbara standing at the top of a steep incline. As the train prepares to pull away, I hear the voice of my mother.

"Sunny get on the monkey train before it is too late!" She says frantically.

I choose to go toward Barbara instead, who I think for some reason is waiting for me. Upon nearing top of the hill where she stands, a host of gibbering monkeys carrying briefcases whiz past me on roller skates. They begin mocking me with taunting gestures because I have chosen not to pursue the easier way.

"You should have boarded the monkey train and learned first how to skate."

This leaves me with some regret, but I have made my choice. Then it is morning. The rising California sun fades my dream away, leaving behind only a skeleton of cryptic meaning.

I share my unusual dream with Ron. His expression looks perplexed as he considers the possible meaning conveyed by the images. Ron, the first-born of a full-blooded Cherokee mother, at times like this is a wise Indian Shaman in my mind. He has a simple gift of discernment to unravel the shadows of life, sorting through the mundane, and coming straight to the point. I do not always easily accept his insights; nevertheless, his unique sightedness deserves my respect.

"Well… Little Brother, sounds like you met a siren. I'd be careful that she doesn't pull you away from the path God has prepared for you."

"There is nothing about Barbara that is right. I just never felt this way with any woman before. Just to think about her I feel on fire."

"I would do a heap of praying before leaping too fast into lust. Have you forgotten about your experience with that little thing, Debbie?"

"This is different, Ron. I doubt Barbara and I are meant to be together in that way. There are so many differences between us, age, economics— everything! I just feel something special when I am with her. Something I never felt before." I sigh, feeling an overwhelming sense of despair. "What do you think about the monkeys in my dream?"

"Darn if I know, brother. I remember as a kid seeing a cartoon about a circus train hauling a caboose filled with squabbling monkeys. They were all wearing business suits and pulling at each other. Your dream makes me think about that. A monkey on roller skates is just plume funny, but I don't know what it means. Besides, I can't imagine you ever with a briefcase. All I can say is that the world and the spirit are contrary one to the other."

In many ways, Ron is like Rudy in that he stands in solidarity with the working class. Yet, beneath this veneer of distrust, seethes envy and self-loathing, a jealousy of the ruled against their taskmasters. Those denied, for one reason or another, the reins of power. Barbara represents the social extreme, an exalted presence, far removed from what the poet William Wordsworth calls the state of the 'common man'. Indeed, there is nothing common about Barbara. She represents in my mind a celestial golden girl descended from a pedestal, worldly and wonderful, essence of the femme fatal of my creativity, consuming my reason in desperate passion without me being aware.

The weeks that follow are every day exciting. Barbara teaches me new ways of experiencing sex by using Jungian techniques of Yen and Yang, allowing the bodily senses to meld into one. We spend many wistful nights just embracing closely, allowing the shadow-self of our beings to mingle into one shared organism of extraordinary potential. This combining of the senses is indescribable and altogether mystical, another migration of spirit new to my experience. I consider that perhaps this the true meaning embodied in the mystery of two becoming one. Really I do not know, only that I will never again allow myself to feel what I feel now in this mix of tangled emotion: a mortal hook into the flesh of my flesh and the bone of my bone snared in unsearchable depths of our two souls touching.

We try to keep our relationship secret. After all, Barbara is officially seeing John, and we know that people will gossip because of the age difference between us. I finish my Quarter, which also means suspension of my grant at the V.A. Mental Hygiene Clinic. Thanks to the eager recommendation by my friend Ron to the hiring department, I land a summer job working for Farmer Brothers Coffee Company filling order requisitions in the transport division. Maybe Ron had been too insistent.

Apparently, the transport supervisor ear-marked the position for his son. However, company politics prevents him from doing much about it because of a first in-line, first-served clause. Rumors begin to circulate that I have stolen his son's job. I assume an attitude that I will show them all what I can do. My assignment is to load pallets with orders of coffees, spices, along with a whole array of condiments, and place them in different staging areas dependent on destination. Those first few days, I work tirelessly without even taking a break, determined to prove to all I am the better man for this job. I check and then double check each order, before wrapping the pallets in plastic labeled with the appropriate POD tag. At the end, I stage the tagged pallets on the loading platform labeled: Fresno, San Francisco, San Diego, Detroit, and so on. None of this is new to me. I was after all a Supply Sergeant in the United State Marine Corps responsible for the state-side deployment of an entire battalion. This job is simple in comparison. An hour before my third day on the job ends, the intercom blasts for me to report to the supervisor's office.

"I'm letting you go," informs the supervisor unceremoniously.

"For what," I protest.

"You have made too many errors labeling your orders. Orders to San Francisco staged for Fresno and Fresno to Chicago— lucky I had someone go behind you, or else you would have cost the company a lot of money."

"Sir, that is impossible. I double-checked every order, and sometimes more than twice. I was a Supply Sergeant in the military. I know how to read requisition orders."

"This is not the military, and I am in charge here. You are fired."

I can see a shrewd satisfaction in his eyes, as one who has achieved victory. I should have remembered better the reading of Machiavelli. I refuse to go easily and make a complaint to the head office for wrongful discharge. Yet, it is my word against his; and he has made sure to have a witness. In reality I never had a chance, only too naive to realize it. Ron tells me that he later heard jokes circulated about how they got rid of the college boy.

"I'm sorry you were wronged, but I have to work with those guys. I guess, they just didn't like your attitude. Maybe this is God's way of making you more humble."

"I don't like being betrayed, Ron. If I were not a Christian, I would go back there and kick ass! I needed that job, and it angers me that I lost it because of petty politics and deception. I don't blame you, but I do blame them."

Nevertheless, Ron is right about one thing. I do feel more humble after this. It is just one of many lessons to come. There is a lot of truth in the adage that God knows what we need more than what we think we want. And at this point in my life I want only to be with Barbara when I can afford it and when she is not with John.

A week later, I take a position in Ventura as Rep for Jewel Tea Home Shopping Company. My employment is to drive from house to house along a designated route and fill orders of an existing clientele, as well as following up on new referral leads. Basically, it is a job servicing the emotional needs of unhappy-- often over-weight housewives-- whose greaterinterest is just to have someone familiar to talk to, even if only for few minutes. In retrospect, I suppose I was a pusher to bored home junkies, who fed their frustrations by eating unhealthy snacks while watching the Price is Right.

Daily I would drive my familiar pale green junk food wagon loaded with a cache of processed foods into these suburban neighborhoods: tubs of greasy homemade potato chips, bags of sugar enriched pastries and cookies, sodas by the gallons, and anything else that might block the arteries or guarantee an onset of diabetes. At the time, it represents just another job, provided with a truck, travel and living allowance, including a salaried commission. Jewel Tea Company even helps me secure a rented room in someone's home for four days a week. The potential harm of these comfort food products will not occur to me until many years later.

Over the course of several weeks, I gain a familiarity with the Ventura area and my customers. There is one very attractive blonde named Christine on my route, who seems to like me more than is comfortable. She makes it clear from the beginning that she is unhappily married and looking to have an affair. She spends as much time as I allow, sharing the intimate disaster of a marriage vow she regrets; her espousal more a prison than marriage. Although I do not consider her unattractive, my primary instincts tell me to keep it professional. For a month, I resist Christine's overtures for numerous personal reasons. But one of those reasons not Barbara. She often qualifies that she and John are friends since many years and has no interest to hurt him. I accept the situation, even though it does not entirely agree with my values. This past weekend I speak to Barbara by phone and she informs me that she and John are going to spend a few days together at Palm Springs.

"Palm Springs…" I mutter stiffly. "That sounds nice."

"Don't be jealous, Sweetie. John and I share nothing like what we experience together. Besides, you would be bored stiff there. Nothing to do except lay around all day in the sun. John and I are both sun worshippers— at least we have that most in common. So I'll come back witha tan. Nothing else will change— I promise."

John and Barbara are roughly the same age and share the same economic strata. Nothing I can say or do that might change the realities of our relationship. Relationship— no— how can I call it a relationship? We are friends— maybe very close friends-- but friends all the same! Or so I tell myself. How can we ever be anything more?

The following week, I accept Christine's indecent proposal to meet at local bar for a drink. After downing more than prudent for either one of us, we end-up going out to my Jewel Home Shopping truck and making out. It is raw and animal for both of us, a violent expression of internalized frustrations we share pent-up inside. During this session, she confides that her husband a local cop, who has a history of physical abuse. We next drive to my rented room and have sex.

This proves to be poor judgment. Christine is a screamer. By the time I drop her off in the bar parking lot it is past 2:00 A.M., her solitary carthe only one there. The next morning, I get the riot act from the owner of the house where I am staying. A few heated words later, we agree toa refund for the balance of the month. I now find myself homeless— at least during the week. My first thought is to find another place to stay. Then greed sets in. In less than three weeks, my next quarter will begin,which also means the end of my contract on this job. Why not savethat extra money? For the rest of my summer occupation, I sleep in my distinctively pale green home shopping truck. Monday through Thursday I park behind business buildings or in uncensored parking lots. Ventura is a small town, so I exercise caution not to call too much attention to my gypsy lifestyle in the short time I have left.

I will see Christine one more time. She sits alone at the same bar of our first rendezvous. I ask to buy her a drink, which she eagerly accepts. Suddenly, she stiffens, her gaze fixed somewhere behind me.

"Don't look around," she whispers. "My husband and his partner just walked in. He thinks I am having an affair, and swore to kill whoever it is. I know him. You should leave before he sees you."

I am not afraid of a confrontation, even if the odds stacked against me. Nor am I stupid. I consider Christine attractive, but not worth killing or dying for. I follow her directions and move to the far end of the bar. As I have already indicated, Ventura is a small town. People who know each other since a lifetime; and they talk. First time here, Christine and I were all over each other. Surely, someone saw us leave together. The man is a brute, his partner even more so. In uniform, they look intimidating, like unleashed pit bulls sniffing for a kill. They see Christine, and move toward her. Someone in the bar intercepts the husband and begins giving him a description of someone that fits my height and build. He instantly bolts toward his wife, grabs her violently, and begins screaming loudly. Christine snarls something back, which causes him to release his grip. After an unpleasant exchange between husband and wife, it becomes obvious that this more a final showdown.

"Who is he" growls this distempered man in uniform, realizing his tactics of intimidation ineffective.

Ordinarily, I might have rushed to her defense. Only this is no ordinary situation. I suddenly find myself in middle of a domestic war that existed long before I arrived. I know this manwants to kill something— anything just to vent his jealous rage. Also, I know that will change nothing. Before tonight, this man and his emotions remained faceless. Now I feel some of the intensity of his pain. But more I feel guilt that I am the one to open the cage door. I see in Christine's stance that this the point of no return and her shackles loose. She needed someone— anyone to break the chains of a vow made when she was too young. No one else in the small town would have dared an affair with this feathered beauty restrained in a guarded cage.

It took a stranger, someone ignorant of the dangers, someone like me. I manage to slip out the back door near the lady's room and jump into my Jewel Tea Home Shopping truck. From here I make a bee-line up to Ojai Valley for the night. I will avoid servicingChristine again, deciding it better this way. In another three weeks, someone else will inherit my route; and maybe by then Christine will be truly liberated. As for me, I have learned other important life lessons: avoid personal politics and the dangerous snares laid by unhappily married women.

*P*assion between Barbara and I continues to escalate, taking on a dimension of proportion bordering on obsession. I feel very much like the main character in George Bernard Shaw's drama play *Man and Superman*, when Tanner's natural reason becomes clouded by an irresistible passion characterized as the *"life-force*. My indiscretion in Ventura only heightens my desire for the woman I really love, without admitting I do love her. Try as I might, I cannot get Barbara out of my dreams or waking thoughts. What power does she possess? What consumes me every time I see her? As with Shakespeare's Cleopatra *"She makes hungry where most she feeds!"* I keep telling myself that I am strong, the one in control, and that John does not matter. Literature and analogy aside, Barbara has unknowingly burrowed into some unconscious part of my soul triggering animal passions altogether unrecognizable. And in each dark corner of my mind is John, a nemesis I have never met and know nothing about.

The week beginning my new quarter, Barbara and I have our first real argument one evening at my apartment. It has to do with my personal experience in Christ.

"Before this supernatural experience, I knew nothing about being a *Jew* or what the word *Christian* really means. By power of the Holy Spirit, I am born again into the knowledge of both. Jesus, a man born a Jew, is God's chosen Messiah. I share this testimony with you Barbara because I love you—but know that God loves you even more!"

"That is ridiculous," she scoffs; "maybe Jesus was a prophet, but no Jew in their right mind would believe him to be the Messiah! If that were true then why would he allow so many to die in the concentration camps? I think God fell asleep a long time ago and has never awakened."

"It is a fact that Jews are sown into every tapestry of history. Even the significance of Israel restored today an earthly principality a sign irrefutable that God is not asleep and the words of his many prophets true."

"Woody Allen once said: *'If only God would give me some clear sign-- like making a large deposit in my name at a Swiss bank.'* Sweetie, if Jesus is your Messiah, then I am happy for you. Tell him to make me successful, and maybe one day I'll believe in him, too."

"There are many signs, Barbara, only you don't see them. God did not lift up the Jew to be better businessmen; but as an example to the rest of mankind that his judgments are true and his promises sure. He made man in his own image. Surely, he can decide the paths of his creation. Just as the Jew is made a standard of righteousness to the world by the Law of Moses, Jesus Christ is made the standard of salvation for all, Jew and non-Jew. Jesus came into this world a Jew made after the genetics of flesh and earthly heritage; but now risen from the physical grave as Christ, the Messiah. This is the fulfilled covenant made by God to Abraham!"

"I don't like when you talk like this. You sound like a fanatic. Rabbis read the Torah in temple— not your New testament! We Jews have nothing to do with your Christ!"

Angry, I leap up, take my Bible, and open it to the end of the last book of Malachi of the Old Testament. I rip the book apart, dividing it at the first chapter of Mathew, separating the New Testament from the Old Testament.

"Here, this is your Torah with books of the prophets. If you look within these pages you will find the witness of Jesus Christ."

Tears well up in Barbara's eyes; she gathers her things to leave.

"You are too much like Barry!" She wails. "I do greatly admire you, but I won't support this."

I listen to the sound of her new model Audi start and screech into the night. What has just happened? Inexplicably a spiritual force has stirred within me, opening a dimension deeper than flesh and blood. Barbara is right, I do sound fanatical. Yet, this is who I am. Nothing to do-- nothing more I can say. Unable to sleep, I lie in bed tossing and turning, I worry about an important lecture early next morning. At half past ten, I call Barbara and leave a message with one of her daughters. I know she is with John! Abandoning the idea of sleep, I jump on my motorcycle and go for a ride.

For some self-destructive reason, I go to a bar of poor reputation in Venice and start drinking more heavily than I should. It is a glimmer of my old self wanting to emerge. Unconsciously, I am looking for trouble, and in the right place to find it. I challenge one of two men wearing colors to a contest of Eight Ball. During the game a third walks in and demands whose Honda outside. I say it is mine, causing the three men to snicker. The one I am beating on the table enquires sarcastically why I am riding a pussy bike. I am in no mood for conversation, so ignore the question. He then hits my stick in the middle of a shot, and shouts loudly so everyone can hear.

"I'm talking to you!"

I instantly snap the stick across the table, breaking it in half. In one motion, I fling the surprised brute on his back across the table my hand squeezed on his throat, the splintered end only inches from his eye.

"Yeah, it's my Honda. You and your friends don't like Hondas?"

There is a tense silence, followed by mumbling threats. I do not think that they really wanted trouble, because they let me walk out without further confrontation. There are a lot of crazy vets during these days. Probably they decide it not worth taking a chance. I will make conscious effort to avoid this bar in future. In my zeal to find a bad guy to vent my anger upon, I have become the bad guy. Looking back on it I suppose I am just lucky they did not resort to an escalation of weapons. I leave this place feeling now even worse than before and ride down to the beach to watch the low tide. It is past 1:00 AM, by the time I return home. The phone rings just as I walk in the door.

"Sweetie, are you all right? Ellen told me you called hours ago, and that you sounded terrible. I've been worried sick."

"I'm sorry, Barbara. I was wrong to preach the way I did. Your soul is your own. It's just that I feel so…"

My voice trails into a dilemma. I know what I have spoken to Barbara the truth; and that it not just me speaking to her. Yet, I have hurt this woman I care about, which in turn hurts me. For her sake, I have separated the word of God, and now pray no dispensation of separation might befall either of us because of my momentary weakness in the flesh.

"Why don't we both just forget what happened tonight. Barry was my Savior, and I don't want to be saved again. Even Moses could not save everyone. I really do respect the conviction of your beliefs, and who knows what life might bring."

"I miss you, Barbara."

"I miss you, too. Go rest for now. We will try to see each other this weekend."

I am not use to having someone care about me. I can tell in her voice that Barbara really cares. She has a way to soothe my savage beast, to make me feel better even when there is no evidence that I should. This begins one of the busiest periods I can remember: new classes, new Professors, filling out forms, and buying new books. First on the list is to renew my grant with the V.A. Mental Hygiene Clinic. Fortunately, they waste no time putting me back to work. Had Barbara's schedule been a little more flexible, we might have stolen at least one evening together. But Ellen is in need of a psychiatrist to come to terms with the suicide death of her boyfriend. Dale needs braces; and little Amie too smart not to need something. Therefore, we decide to see each other on a Saturday afternoon three weeks later at my apartment.

It is a day of California dreaming, neither too hot, nor too cool, but just right. I stretch out on the couch, anticipating Barbara's arrival. I have fallen into a light slumber, when suddenly she appears, stepping energetically through the front door. She looks dazzling, as an angel of light. A small white dog with shaggy fur sits in the middle of the room and begins barking excitedly. Callously, she kicks the animal, sending it crashing against the wall.

I awaken just as Barbara enters the open front door. She is even more radiant than in my vision. Immediately, she snuggles up beside me. For some inexplicable reason, I remain strangely disturbed by my daydream. I suppose I should have shared the unsettling experience with her, except it seems ridiculous within context. Instead, I attempt to push the abrasive images out of my mind and begin the act of making love to her. I snuggle against her neck, caress her body; can feel the throbbing anticipation of her heart. I next affectionately begin kissing her thighs. Then another presence appears, wedged between us. It is John-- at least it is an image of what I imagine John to be. My vision blurs, a sickening convulsion felt in my stomach, and I go numb from the waist down.

In all my young life, I have never experienced anything so debilitating. To have an erection as normal as eating or breathing-- and just like that— it is gone, replaced by anxiety from a source unidentifiable. Barbara tries to make light of it, saying that it is a normal experience for most men and that it will go away if I don't dwell on it.

"It is not normal for me!" I snap back defiantly.

We move into the bedroom, talk for a while, thinking that a diversion from sex will make me relax. However, as soon as we become intimate, the numbness returns, my penis shriveling into my gut. I sense that Barbara's ego is not taking this well-- but I am taking it even worse! After hours of failed attempts, Barbara gets up, dresses, and says something consoling before leaving.

I feel for the first time in my life divorced from earthly affection, abandoned-- no, I am betrayed by this horrible joke ofnature. What did it mean? I cannot even masturbate with Barbara gone. It is as though something alien curled up inside of me, consuming the very essence of my fleshly desire. I remain home in bed the rest of the day and into the night. I pray the next morning everything might be back to normal; but as soon as I so much as look at my penis, it begins to shrivel away.

That Sunday, I meet up with an acquaintance named Bernie to help repair a closed-in porch for Jane Fonda's Santa Monica dance studio recently damaged by a storm. Yes, the infamous Hanoi Jane, who became the embodiment of betrayal in the minds of many Vets! Bernie is a likable burned-out alcoholic with sandy hair, dried parched skin from years of unprotected exposure, possessed with a demur of one beaten. The best thing about Bernie is his skill of carpentry. I appreciate opportunity to make a few dollars with him when work permits. This particular day he is badly hung-over from a previous night of over indulgence. We start early in the morning, taking a break at noon for a beer (two beers and a shot of Old Crow in Bernie's case) and a bite to eat at a local café. As we eat, I casually mention my disturbing recent experience.

"You too," he shakes his head dubiously. "The same thing happened to me."

"When," I ask hopeful.

"Well… it's been more than ten years now."

"And how did you get over it?"

"I never did. In all this time, I never was able to get it up with a woman. That's the reason I drink the way I do. You'll learn to live with it… or rather without it."

I am altogether devastated and wish I had never broached the subject. So, this is what happens to men— robbed of vitality, robbed without warning of their power of erection in the prime of life? This moment I see myself in Bernie, a futureless shell of a man, whose life ended before turning twenty-five. No wonder Bernie became an alcoholic! Is this vision of my future self? I avoid the subject after that, preferring to finish my day and depart quickly from this shadowy reminder of things to come.

Monday I am assigned my official weekly work schedule at the V.A. Mental Hygiene Clinic. Dr. Laving, one of two resident Psychiatrists, summons me in his office to review the prescriptions for his patients to be distributed during my next interactive therapy session. No one in the clinic really likes Dr. Laving. There ebbs an aura of dispatch about him, cold and aloof, an air of professional arrogance, which makes one apprehensive that he is probing into their psyche without permission. Not that there anything precisely unpleasant about the man, except that Dr. Laving's 'blue-blood' snobbery inaccessible of any meaningful acquaintance. Nevertheless, as I prepare to leave, I decide it might not hurt to get a little professional advice.

"Dr. Laving," I venture cautiously, "have you ever been impotent with a woman?" His eyes narrow, as he slithers from behind his desk and into a chair beside my own.

"Of course," he coos in a seductive tone. "Why-- are you experiencing something… unusual in your sex life?"

I share with him in as much detail the events of the past Saturday and the peculiar numbness since. He seems particularly interested in my disturbing dream of the small white dog so brutally kicked aside. Dr. Laving calmly looks down, places his hand on my thigh, and exhales deeply.

"Have you considered that perhaps you are Gay?" His eyes gaze longingly into my eyes. "The small white dog may represent desire of a repressed nature trying to emerge."

I do not know what I expected, but certainly not this! A sense of revulsion hits hard and unexpectedly that I might be a homosexual without consensus. Dark images invade my mind of a short story written by D. H. Lawrence titled The Prussian Officer about a man haunted by his irreconcilable desires for his young orderly. I see in Dr. Laving that same bitter longing, his eyes filled with dark craving. Most of all, I fear that he might be right.

"But I don't feel Gay!" I blurt out near tears.

Dr. Laving quickly removes his hand and recoils back to his own chair behind his desk. He mutters something about a patient waiting to see him. I thank him for his time and promise to give his advice some thought.

That night Barbara and I speak over the phone. I miss to see her, but fear the consequence if I do. Even the thought of having sex makes my penis shrivel away, as though my body determined to betray all desire, condemning me to solitude-- or something even worse than solitude! I can only imagine what Barbara feeling.

Barbara's birthday is in six days and I want to do something special for her. I book dinner reservations at a restaurant in Marina Del Rey called the *Black Whale*. It is not cheap, but neither is the golden girl. I even arrange to have a cake presented to our table at the end of the meal. By now, we both reconciled to the reality that our passions fizzled into a friendship only.

On day before Barbara's birthday, I have a meeting with Dr. Goldstein, the other resident Psychiatrist. An ex-Army Major, he dresses more like a lumberjack than a doctor, preferring jeans and a plaid shirt to a suit, completely opposite to the refined tailored look of Dr. Laving. He is a short stocky man, with receding hairline, wears thick coke-bottle wire-rimmed glasses, and has an abrasive personality to the uninitiated. Presently, Dr. Goldstein working on a research paper related to the psychological ill-effects of what he terms '*caffeine poisoning*' soon to be published in a medical journal. He believes that there to be many misdiagnoses of Schizophrenia attributed to acute caffeine overdose, triggering secondary attributes mimicking a psychotic episode. His preliminary research infers application of revised guidelines for new admittance, requiring a more lengthy observation period before administering dangerous psychotropic drugs, such as Thorazine and Stelazine. Since these laboratory agents designed to alter the delicate chemical balance of brain function, they can cause as much harm as good, potentially condemning an otherwise mentally healthy individual to a lifetime of drug induced psychosis. The conclusion of this respected Doctor is that drug therapy should never be a first-line offensive.

Since all this very technical in my mind, I accept assignment to sort through volumes of journals and references supportive of this caffeine overdose theory. As a personality, Dr. Goldstein is one of a kind. Either you like him, or you do not. I like him.

"Dr. Goldstein…if you wouldn't mind, I have a question to ask you." I hedge hesitatingly.

"Shoot," he sounds off in military fashion, his eyes large and bulging, a hungry frog waiting for a fly.

"Do you think a guy could be gay and not know it?"

"Why— do you think you are gay?"

"I don't know. I don't feel gay… but then… I don't know."

"What do you mean you don't know? I think I would know if I were gay. What makes you think you might be gay?"

I proceed to tell him about the inexplicably horrible reaction I am having since that afternoon with Barbara, where it all began. I tell him about the white dog and how in my dream she kicks it against the wall. I leave out the part about John.

"Dr. Laving suggest the reason of my impotency is because I am gay and that the small white dog is my suppressed sexuality."

"Laving is as queer as they come-- and because he's gay he thinks everyone else is. I don't think I would give much stock in what Doctor Laving has to say on the subject of being gay, unless you are gay. There's nothing wrong if you are, but I think you would know by this time in your life."

"Then why since the past few weeks do I have this paralyzing feeling of numbness below the waste every time I think about sex?"

"I once had the same thing happen to me a year after marrying my first wife. For nearly a month, I wallowed in my self-pity until I realized the problem. I was angry with my wife because of decorating differences we had after buying our new house. I didn't mind her choosing the color and style of our bedroom; then she decides that my private office should be painted a pastel purple. I said I didn't like purple and wanted beige-brown. She has it painted purple anyway. After that, my teeter went dead as a door nail."

"So, what did you do?"

"Once I figured out the problem, I fucked the hell out of her, and told her to repaint my office beige. Even a man needs his own space."

"But Barbara never painted anything, or made any changes at all to my place. I just don't see how that can have any relevance to what is happening."

"Anger— don't you understand that the problem with me was internalized anger. And that's your problem, too. For some reason, you have a rage against this woman, and that rage is eating you up. Find the source of your anger, and you will find your teeter."

"No— Dr. Goldstein, you are wrong! I feel something special for Barbara— something I have never felt for anyone before!"

"Then maybe that's the problem. You know what they say about love and hate: both stem from the same emotion. Maybe because you love her too much, you are betraying your own nature. I think the small white dog is you. Have you ever told this woman how you really feel?"

"Not in so many words. It is a complicated situation. All I know is that I would never do anything to harm her."

"Okay— it's your teeter. But I still say it's all about anger."

Upon leaving Dr. Goldstein's office, I am even more confused than before. I am either gay or a latent psychopath. Even if the doctor right, what could be the source of my anger? No— I prefer to think I might be gay, rather than driven by some unidentifiable rage against the most wonderfulperson I have ever known.

The night of Barbara's birthday, everything proceeds nearly perfect. Barbara as always radiant, wearing an exquisite new leopard dress with matching scarf and shoes; her hair a shiny Hanna red and eyes as flashing tiger stones. I observe in detail her every movement, her every expression-- her every word-- sadly aware that this will most probably be our last night together. After a steak dinner, our hostess presents the cake dropped-off earlier with one sparkle candle in the middle. Barbara's eyes change glassy with emotion and she makes excuse to go to the bathroom. Upon her return, we enjoy our desert of cake served with coffee. I want this evening to last as long as possible, but finally it is time to take Barbara home.

I cannot describe the heaviness I feel as I escort this golden girl to the front door of her Pacific Palisades home. A stiff September breeze slices into the Palisades hills rising from the coast, the distinct chirping of crickets from within crevices hidden along the walkway leading to the landing.

"I just want you to know that I appreciate every minute we have spent together," I choke, trying not to sound apologetic. "I think you are very desirable— in fact I never met anyone more desirable! I just don't know what happened."

"It's okay Sweetie. You will meet someone else, and it will all come back. Trust me—I know about these things. I had a lovely evening, and will never forget the many wonderful things that we've shared."

Embracing each other for the last time, my eyes wander to the counter separating the kitchen from the living room adjacent to the entry. A bottle of wine poised prominently on the edge and a note propped against it with the name John scribbled boldly on the face. It is a stake in my heart, that terrible numbness clawing its way through my chest and up into my throat. I feel a sense of becoming petrified, stiffly turn, and leave. I am nearly at the end of the walkway when I freeze, altogether changed into stone, destined to remain here for all eternity.

I am minutely aware of the singularity of this moment in time and of everything around me. Sounds of crickets cease in mid-song, the wind stilled; the moon paused in an arena of distant constellations— all electrifying, silent. This silence split by a defiant roar— a battle cry from the most primitive depth of my being."

"It is John!"

Now I know the name of my anger-- know what I must do! Denied ability of reason, I turn back and knock vigorously on the door. Barbara looks at me perplexed, even annoyed. I push my way inside; grab Barbara affectionately, boldlyentering into the swirling shadows of her enchanting eyes.

"I love you, Barbara! I have loved you since the first day we met. I will not share you with John-- or anyone else!"

I am a man and Barbara my woman. With brutal force, I rip open the front of her expensive dress, feeding her exposed flesh to my reawakened passion. Sweeping her bodily into my arms, I carry her to the living room couch and make love to her as never I made love before. It is savage and altogether primitive! Altogether I am free, the power of my being unleashed truly for the first time.

An hour later, someone calls and hangs up after several rings. Just before midnight, John arrives, the headlights of his car shining through the front bay window. I suppose that he saw my car, wisely deciding it better not to knock at this hour.

The next morning, Barbara proclaims to her three daughters that she and I are seeing each other. I do not think the news a grand surprise to anyone, especially to Amie, who misses very little. I believe they are glad for their mother, glad that she has chosen me over John.

"I will break it off with John, Sweetie," Barbara promises, gazing adoringly into my face, her eyes shards of a smoldering comet.

Now anything possible! I know through every fiber of my being I have over shadowed the golden girl of my dreams with raw purchase of earthly desire.

I also learn an important life lesson from these unsettling events in my youth. Never attempt to label someone, unless you are able to see life through their experience. And never allow someone else to label you without bearing of true reference. Everything made conventional in the moment: all things designed to run course immutable in season of the animal kingdom.

$\mathcal{I}$ feel in a real relationship for the first time since a long time, a sense of belonging and of purpose. This new beginning passage in my life represents mature comprehension on what it means to be head of a family unit. Barbara and her daughters were in need of a strong center, and my feeling is that God has placed me here for that reason. I begin to study up on Jewish customs and search diligently the scriptures, comparing writings of the Torah with the Old Testament Bible to better understand the historical patriarchal linage so important to Jewish tradition. However, we do not attend temple, which is probably a good thing.

First, Barbara and her daughters are not very religious, and second, I will not deny Christ for the sake of a rabbinical definition interpreted by Talmud philosophy limited to prescribed doctrine. To me personally, there is no Old and New Testament. No separation of Torah based on earthly tradition changed within historical context. I know there is only one testament from the moment God calls Abraham in a dream, while an earthly resident in theMesopotamian city of Err, to become a nomad without a place or land to call home.

But what I begin to embrace more is historical significance of the Jewish history beginning with Issac, who Abraham loved, but whose faith in God greater. Issac will sire Jacob, whose name changed to Israel. From Israel are born twelve sheepherders that enter into Egypt and sojourn there for 400 years. In fullness of time Moses is born and raised secretly in the house of a King that fears the nation that has flourished in the midst of his kingdom. This Moses will be educated according to Egyptian customs, only to reject tradition by commandment of a greater voice. Through this man God gives to mankind Ten Commandments written in stone tablets on Mount Sinai. This same Moses will lead the twelve tribes for forty years through a wilderness to the boundary of a promised land, only to die without ever entering.

The unknown God rejected by mankind through deception will instruct a people in preparation for a Messiah to come. Judges and Prophets will raise-up in times of correction, as a reminder that the God of Israel is the same God that created earth, and man in his own image. In darkest time God renews his covenant that none might forget.

This is the messianic message found in pages of the Torah, beginning with fall of the first Adam made sin to resurrection of the second Adam made perfect. The Jesus Christ I now know is template of new heaven and earth predestined to run course to fulfillment. This is Messiah that will surely come again.

These are not just stories in my mind, but words of spirit and truth, bearing record of this world history, of things present, and of things still to come. I find within my heart a Jew reborn by revelation of

God's inalienable promise to fulfill in me the abiding presence of the Holy Spirit. This I cannot deny for the sake of any congregational acceptance. Therefore, when Barbara invites me to share Passover Seder with her and her three daughters, I am over joyed to embrace this culture always denied.

Unfortunately, the affair is not without sacrifice. Afternoon of the dinner, as I am driving along the Coast Highway toward Barbara's Pacific Palisades home, a dog bolts across the road causing the car in front of me to break hard. I remember hitting the pedal, but it is already too late. Instantly, the front of my car crumples, shattering the windshield. This no small accident I can easily repair; and a miracle that I am not hurt. My car-- my wonderful MGA with a crumpled frontend no longer recognizable! It is a tragic loss, representing the end of another era. Nevertheless, I am determined to keep my engagement. Within minutes, a toll truck comes and I leap into the cab, providing directions to my back alley. I will later sell the remains to a collector for $450.00, this personal page in history turned and forever archived.

I arrive at Barbara's Palisade's home on my motorcycle more than half an hour late, briefly providing a history of events as they happened. I think Barbara correctly perceives I am still in shock, and a little more shaken than I let on.

"Sure that you are alright?"

"Better than my car," I reminisce, now feeling more relaxed, and more accepting of my loss in context of being with Barbara and her daughters. "We'll discuss it later. I'm late, and the girls look hungry. We should not keep the Lord's Seder waiting."

I push my long hair into the cap of my yarmulke and take a place prepared at head of the table. To look into the eyes of Barbara and her children, is like looking into the soul of a nation. I give thanks to the Lord, raising my hands in humble supplication. I imagine this duty of supplication passed-down from generation to generation of patriarchal linage bearing witness of God's irrefutable covenant with his chosen people. This covenant going back to Abraham, a man living in ancient metropolis of Err, to whom God spoke in a dream, making promise that from his loins would issue a nation, and that from this nation will come Messiah. These stories recorded in the Torah not a history of fairy tales, but are in my mind evidence of prophecy fulfilled and prophecies still to come.

"This we do in memory of the Passover lamb to cover the sins of the people in day that the angel of the Lord passed through the land of Egypt. Those who obeyed the voice of Moses and consecrated their homes with blood of a lamb, the angel of death and judgment passed over. Through shadow of those things the promise of deliverance provided to all mankind by the Lamb of God. Amen."

They sit there silent, bewildered. These are not the traditional words of *'Magid'* recited at Passover Seder, nor do they altogether understand the significance outside of context. For them Seder is a family day, commemorated byreenactment of a story with good ending, followed by a joyful holiday dinner. Barbara is not so traditional, as to have the six symbolic food items with bitter herbs representative of the Seder Plate. Nor am I expected to say *Kiddush,* since the girls too young to drink wine. However, we do have matzos and the customary roasted lamb, which is Barbara's specialty. This will be my first and last Seder, a special appointment that I will always remember with profound reverence.

I need another car, and Barbara kindly loans me $300.00 to buy an old Rambler. It is beat up from more than a few fender benders, but runs like a top with a durable flat-top six-cylinder engine. It will serve me well for the next twenty months. Upon receiving cash a few weeks later for my wrecked MGA, I pay Barbara back with a hundred to spare. Although my self-image suffers more than a little when driving this old work horse around the affluent Palisades hills, I am impressed by difference between package and reliable performance. The engine and transmission prove indestructible, requiring little to no maintenance. This particular generation of Rambler proves to be an urban tank, able to plow through any obstacle or idle all day under the heat of a California sun.

I am now down to my last academic quarter, and I need completion of one more Creative Writing class to fulfill the three-course requirement for my major. However, this is not to be. The first day of class, I check the posting, discovering that my name the only one missing from a roster of the previous session. Certain of an error, I knock on Professor Gullen's door.

"Excuse me, sir, my name is not on the list for your class this Quarter."

"And why do you think it should be?" He replies snidely.

"I successfully completed Creative Writing one and two, and everyone else from previous classes is on the list except me. I believe there has been a mistake."

"I do not make mistakes. I personally reviewed each name. If your name is not there, then consider it a misfortune. You can sign up again next Quarter."

"But sir, this is my last Quarter, and I need your class to complete my major."

"Then I guess this will not be your last Quarter after all. Now if you will please leave, I have preparations to make."

"Professor Gullen, I don't think you understand--"

"Must I repeat myself? The class is officially closed."

He sits smugly back in his chair like an arrogant Cesar casting the final decree of execution.

"You pompous demigod," I growl, looming across his desk, my hands grasping the arms of his chair, pulling him toward me. "I deserve enrollment in your class. You would make me take another Quarter just because you refuse to be reasonable and admit that you have made a mistake? You are as a blind Pharisee divining your own interpretation of the law with no consideration of the circumstance or the consequence!"

This limp bean of a man withers as a mouse in the face of an angry lion. He dares not say another word, his eyes glazed over with terror. I take a deep breath, considering carefully the consequence of my next action.

"I intend to appeal your decision to the Dean." I threaten, withdrawing toward the door. "You are not a just man, and you know it. I will not be the one to judge you."

Upon leaving the Professor's office, I bump into Bruce. By now, he has completed his Masters and presently working as a Teacher's Assistant while preparing for his Doctorate. T. A.'s are paid well, good job security, and easy hours. The only problem is that you can only be a T. A. while working on your Thesis. For the next few years, Bruce will remain in this academic limbo. I never knew if he actually completed his Thesis. Nevertheless, a good T. A. hard to find and Bruce is one of the best.

"What happened in there," Bruce demands. "The whole wall shook, and I could hear your voice down the hall."

"I was trying to be persuasive," I say, relaying to him the preceding events.

"Diplomacy is not your strongest trait," he snickers. "I bet you gave that peacock something to think about. He is the viper of the English Department, so watch your back. I doubt anyone likes him; and I doubt he likes anyone. I would've given anything to see the look on Gullen's face."

Gullen strikes first in fulfillment of Bruce's warning. At the end of the day, I go to the Dean's office to file a formal complaint of discrimination. The secretary frowns when I tell her my name and asks me to have a seat. She then disappears into the Dean's office, taking a file sitting on her desk.

"The Dean will see you now," she says very officiously, returning several minutes later.

I can detect a certain disdain in her attitude, as though I am an already condemned prisoner awaiting execution. I doubt any defense of explanation enough to sway the verdict of this elite alumni department administrator.

"Have a seat," the Dean grunts, as I walk into his office. "This is very serious."

"What is serious?"

"You assaulted and threatened a Professor at our University."

"Assaulted--I never touched that man, nor did I threaten him!"

I then proceed to explain what happened, leaving out the part that I did consider squashing the arrogant dictator like a bug. The Dean listens intently; his large blue eagle eyes piercing, as though searching for some flaw in my account of the events.

"So, you are saying that you never physically touched Professor Gullen? He claims you grabbed his shirt and threatened to do him harm."

"I swear upon my honor as a Marine I never touched that man. If I had, you can be sure I would have done more than ruffle his pride."

"Were there any witnesses?"

"No sir. We were alone. He refuses without any reason to let me take his class, and I need that credit to graduate the end of this Quarter."

"I believe you, son," the Dean concludes after a moment of deliberation. "There is no point in forcing Professor Gullen to let you into his class after what has happened. Go see Mrs. Fine tomorrow morning. I will instruct her to find you a class with substitute credit."

I thank him and prepare to leave.

"One other thing," he adds before I exit. "Try to stay out of trouble, and please avoid doing anything that will bring you to my office again."

"I will most certainly try."

I thank him again for his fairness of mind. It is not ideal. Nevertheless, I have narrowly escaped the vicious revenge of a most subtle creature. I have also learned that not all battles fought able to claim victory on the battlefield. Through a Machiavellian tactic, Gullen has bested me despite my righteous indignation or physical prowess, providing me with a political lesson that will continue to serve me in life. In future I make a point to avoid meeting this dangerous Medusa that slithers through shrouded catacombs of the English Department.

Mrs. Fine finds me a class pertaining to poetry of the Renaissance to satisfy my needed credit. It turns out to be one of the more provocative courses, embellished with academic importance. The instructing Professor, a kind, gentle soul, takes pleasure in reading texts of often obscure originals collected in a translated book taken from his personal library. He judiciously photocopies specific pages and passes them to the class as sample texts to study. I discover these works inspiring, no less enlightened than the more commonly referenced Dante's Inferno. In retrospect, I suppose that I am even indebted to Professor Gullen's arrogant nature, forcing me to take a class I otherwise never would have considered.

Ron now romantically involved with a fellow employee named Patty, who works in the shipping office of Farmer Brothers. Both now more sedate and mature since knowing each other. Patty also divorce has worked for Farmer Brothers as long as Ron, and is rather pretty in a way complementary to my friend. Both have children from previous marriages and appreciate the meaning of responsible commitment. Ron no longer has desire to go cruising on the town, nor does he drink anymore, saying only that God has provided a rudder to his life, setting him on a truer course.

He and Patty will eventually marry a few years after I leave California and remain together to this day. My experience with Barbara proves less predictable. Barbara is highly intelligent and ambitious to a fault. She hates routine almost as much as I do; determines never again to be a stay-at-home wife and mom. This makes Barbara dynamic and exciting in my mind, but this will also become a future source of contention.

My graduation from UCLA anticlimactic, little more than a by-line, as I prepare to enter a Master's Program in Psychology with an acceptable grade point average. I have begun conducting group therapy sessions at the clinic, and even assigned a few individual patients to follow weekly, providing log updates in collaboration with the department's resident psychologist. Now I am convinced the field of psychology to be a promising career. However, something happens that changes this conviction.

One of my assigned patients named Robert, diagnosed with a psychotic disorder ever since having an episode in Nam, comes into my office every Tuesday after Group Therapy for a one on one. He is roughly my age and had served in the north near the Laos border as a field Grunt. His memory of what happened that day vague. He was point man on routine patrol, when suddenly he feels a wire snag his leg. Time and his heart stop, then nothing. Nothing happens! He wonders if he is in shock, and that maybe he is on the ground surrounded by smoldering limbs-- his limbs! The sound deafening, followed by a peculiar snap in the back of his neck, and the next thing he remembers with any clarity is being transported to a field hospital. According to the official dossier, this man experienced a complete nervous breakdown after triggering a trip-wire attached to a dud claymore. Had it not been a dud, the powerful mine would have been enough to kill everyone in the unit. But it was a dud making only a pop. Yet, in Robert's mind, it happened with intensity, triggering a drug induced psychosis and disconnecting his fragile psyche from reality. Since discharge from the military, he remains on psychotropic drugs, unable to hold a job or to have an intimate relationship, his life dead and without hope. Because of some special unidentifiable connection, I feel compelled I try and help him.

After weeks of counseling, I determine that his original episode resulted from an opium-laced marijuana overdose, something I am well aware of through experience. I ask if he still smokes marijuana, and he confirms he does in small quantities. I advise him to stop taking illicit drugs, particularly the associated drug that might have contributed to his original episode. After speaking to Dr. Goldstein, I further suggest he gradually reduce his medication of Thorazine and Librium. I instructhim to call me any time of the day, either at home or at the clinic. Within six weeks, Robert shows remarkable improvement. He secures a regular job as a stock clerk at a local *Seven-Eleven Convenience Store,* andmeets a girl. It seems he is on his way to a new life paved with great expectations.

One weekend, I spend both Saturday and Sunday with Barbara at her home. We go to the beach, drive for hours up the coast, relishing in the spring of our romance. Upon arriving home late Sunday night, I know something terribly wrong. My answering service is full of frantic messages from Robert. Apparently, he and his new girlfriend had a lover's spat. For anyone else, this might be traumatic; but for Robert, it is altogether earth shattering. I try returning his calls, but there is no answer. Finally I decide to ride my motorcycle to his Brentwood apartment. It is dark inside and no response to my much knocking on the front door. Next day I discover the shocking reason. Unable to reach me, Robert calls the Duty Nurse at the clinic. Instead of referring to the patient's chart containing my notes, she opens a summary roster showing the last prescription doses issued by the doctor. Not knowing that Robert has reduced his intake, she recommends that he increase his dosage by double until the clinic opens Monday morning. This must have sent the poor man into a psychotropic tail-spin, as his blood levels radically alter, his mind unable to cope.

They find Robert's lifeless body at the foot of his three-story balcony early Sunday morning. In a fit of blind delirium, this man of confused reason had dived-off into oblivion.

I feel tremendous guilt-- guilt that I was not there when he needed me most. What I feel most guilty for is not providing Robert sufficient information on how dangerous his medications when radically changing the dosage. I had planned to sit down with Doctor Goldstein this very week to discuss Robert's progress and recommend that he be reevaluated for his prescription intake. This poor fellow let down by everyone: the system because of prevailing policy that mind altering drugs the primary solution for all mental disorder, and the local administration because of overburdened demand creating a callous bureaucracy of procedure. But I betrayed him most by not being there when most he needed my council. I only pray that I said enough during our brief exchange concerning his soul in Christ, now this opportunity forever silenced.

I realize now that I am unable with clear conscience to pursue a career in a profession that amounts to sorcery. I do not agree with the premise that mankind a balanced formula of prescribed behavior. There also exists a dimension of spirit, which feeds and energizes the soul, a mystery of existence surpassing flesh and blood. Knowing this, I can no longer allow myself indoctrinated into a system that defines being in terms of a normative model.

"It's not your fault, Sweetie," Barbara consoles. "He just wasn't strong like you. Some people just can't find their way. I'm certain you did all you could."

"No, Barbara, I did not. Christ drew me to salvation through testimony of those who knew him and by power of faith. I allowed myself seduced by pride and self-importance, my testimony diluted by worldly clinical ideas. I should have told Robert plainly that Christ could heal him of his infirmity, instead of beating around the bush. Now it is too late to say anything more, too late to cast out his demons through prayer."

I see in Barbara's eyes that she thinks me also in need of medication. Nevertheless, this tragic event has brought me to a major crossroad in my life. Still more change on the horizon before deciding which road to take. I am sitting as usual in my study chair when Shadow pounces through the open window whining in pain. She jumps into my lap, a trail of blood streaked across the pages of my open book. There is an injury on her tail resembling two fang marks. I doctor the wound with alcohol and Merthiolate. After a week, the wound begins to fester and exude a foul odor. I take her to a vet, who lances the wound and prescribes a regiment of antibiotics to administer with her meal. This seems to work for a while, but as soon as the antibiotic regime finished, the infection erupts worse than before.

Barbara owns a rare breed of dog called Lhasa Apso, which she says is a Tibetan temple dog. I think this fitting for a *Temple Prostitute*, as she always teasingly refers to herself. The poor animal is partially blind with age, arthritic, and with stomach disorders. Nevertheless, Barbara spares no expense keeping this animal alive and healthy for as long as possible. She insists I take my cat to her Malibu Veterinarian for a proper diagnosis and treatment. I drop off Shadow Wednesday morning. The next day I receive a call back from the Vet at the clinic.

"I am sorry, but your cat has Feline Leukemia," the voice on the other end of the phone reports gravely. "I could place her on a treatment to prolong her life by perhaps several weeks, but it is expensive and will be painful for the animal."

"What other option is there?"

Weakness in my stomach knows already the answer.

"I could euthanize her now before she begins to suffer. It is only a matter of weeks, maybe days before the real pain of the disease sets in."

"I prefer that she not suffer. I will come straight after work. Wait until I after I get there. I want to see her one last time."

I arrive just past sunset. Shadow knows as soon as I walk in the door and begins meowing loudly. After a brief conversation, I open the cage allowing Shadow to spring into my arms. Immediately, she begins purring loudly, looking steadfastly into my eyes.

"Now," I whisper to the Vet, standing by with a prepared syringe. "Do it now while she is at peace in my arms."

Almost immediately, Shadow's eyes glaze over, as her small body stiffens. After holding her for several minutes, I kiss her and hand the small still corpse to this compassionate animal doctor. Paying him $25.00 for the necessary dispatch, I leave behind the shell of my friend and companion for anonymous cremation. After all, her soul gone, returned to the essence of all creation. She is part of me—will always remain part of me. I weep as I drive along the coast night highway to my home. I want to be alone tonight. Profound darkness enshrouds the ocean horizon. Somewhere in that darkness, Shadow rising from a smoking chimney dispersed to the elements.

The following Monday I submit my resignation at the V. A. Mental Hygiene Clinic and officially withdraw from my Master's program. I am now in need of a real job; this passage of my life ended.

*L*os Angeles is an austere environment when you have little money and no income. The law of the land is the have and the haves not. And I have very little at this particular time in life. I owe the Grant Department almost a thousand dollars and another four hundred dollars to an overdue Bank of America credit card by not understanding properly the credit interest system. By checking daily the UCLA job placement bulletin board, I find a position of interest with a starting salary of $700.00 a month, plus commission for a forms printing company named Moore Business Forms. The interview goes well and I get the job starting on the first of the month two weeks away.

That same evening a police cruiser pulls me over for a burnt-out tail light while returning home. I am summarily arrested on the spot for a number of unpaid parking tickets accumulated before wrecking my

MGA. It seemed at the time a benign solution during the time my motorcycle out of commission. Believing I have found a way to secure free parking by slipping under the gate with my low-profile vehicle. I do this trick three days a week, and continue this practice until the loss of my sports car. The deception works for a while, but then I begin accumulating tickets. Thinking these infractions limited to university jurisdiction, I never bother to pay them. Tonight, I learn the infractions extend to legal prosecution by the California Vehicle Code.

I spend Thursday night in the Santa Monica jailhouse, a pleasant spacious area, the food not so bad, and the environment tranquil. Therefore, the next morning when I pass before the judge and am given a choice between paying a fine of almost three hundred dollars or to spend an equivalent of 9 days in jail served on weekends, I choose the latter, thinking I can use the time to catch up on my reading.

"Okay, bailiff, take this man into custody," the Judge concludes and bangs his gravel.

"Excuse me, your Honor," I politely interject; "I would prefer to start my time next weekend, since I have nothing to read and this weekend being a holiday."

"Bailiff, arrest this man immediately," demands the judge, little amused by my brashness to think incarceration a tailored weekend retreat optional to my schedule.

Returned to a cell, I decide to make the best of a bad situation. If nothing else, I can at least get some rest. At noon two armed officers enter the cubical, lock shackles on my arms and legs, and lead me to a waiting County Prison bus. Wedged beside a huge, not so pleasant black man, reminding me of Mr. T of the A Team, I begin to consider my situation differently. This is no weekend excursion; and the people on this bus no traffic violators. A guard with mirror sunglasses holds a loaded rapid-fire shotgun, standing behind a mesh gate near the front door. In his bright lens reflect the angry glare of many criminal eyes, me among them. I am now counted as an offender of society, a target   in the eyes of the law mixed with the reprobates.

Upon arrival at L. A. County, a processing procedure commences not unlike Boot Camp. Herded from one cell to another, we receive instruction to remove our shirts, shoes and socks; and then told to lean prostrate against the wall, placing our hands palm down. Two officers walk along the inside parameter ordering us to lift first the left leg, and then the right, so they might examine the bottoms of our feet.

"Raise your right leg higher," screams one of the officers in my ear.

"I have a war injury in that knee," I apologize, lifting it as high as I can manage.

He brutally grabs my foot, jerking it toward the ceiling. The pain excruciating, I reflexively whip around and jab my fist into his chest, and another on the chin that knocks the shocked fellow to the ground. A swarm of police officers pour into the chamber, overwhelming me in a barrage of nightsticks. The next thing I know I am tossed into a room no larger than a broom closet. Here I remain for several hours, until someone opens the shutter of a small window, demanding why I am there. I reply simply that I do not know. As they begin searching for the paperwork, I ask if I can make a phone call.

"You didn't make one, yet?" A lady clerk inquires.

"No, but I think I would like to ask a friend to come bail me out."

"What were you arrested for?"

"Parking tickets-- I volunteered for weekend arrest, only I didn't know it would be here."

She frowns, and tells one of the attending offices to escort me to the phone room.

"Hello Ron... I made a big mistake and need you to bail me out of County."

"What in Tarnation are you doing in County lockup?"

I commence to tell him about the slew of unpaid parking ticket and that I considered a weekend in the Santa Monica jailhouse not a bad idea.

"But I never thought they would send me to County. It is as bad as any place I can imagine. I'll pay you back somehow, I promise."

"Don't you fret Little Brother. I'll come quick as I can."

After the phone call, my escort, a short over-weight man resembling the character of Porky the Pig, asks if that my girlfriend.

"Just a good friend who lives down in Torrance," I reply. "He'll be here soon."

The man smirks, as he examined my naked chest, and nonchalantly asks if I am queer.

"No, are you?"

The smirk changes to an enraged squint. He grabs my arm and ushers me roughly into another cell. Here I remain until a new shift comes on duty. Caught in a system without democratic say, and where my pride subject to keeping my mouth shut, I accept the only thing I can do is just grin and bear it.

In every way, it is like Boot Camp allover again, except the goal not discipline, but designed to crush the collective will of society thugs. I constantly remind myself that Jesus, a man without any guilt at all, submitted willingly to brute will leading him ultimately to the cross. I am one less innocent. By letter of the law I am guilty as charged for a crime knowingly committed. This is submission to my judgment prepared, my pound of flesh for a pound of flesh. Finally, after more than twenty hours, my processing continues. I pass through one shower of disinfectant soap, a second stall of cold water, and then some kind of blow dryer system that makes me think of a car wash. Afterwards instructed to raise my arms, I am sprayed front and back and from head to toe with insecticide, followed by a series of inoculations.

At end of the processing, I am issued a blue prison uniform and escorted by two guards along a brightly lighted promenade surrounded by hundreds of cell chambers stacked many stories high, above and below the level I am on. This modern prison, originally built in 1963, and later expanded in 1976, has a housing capacity of more than 5000 inmates. Thirty years later I will read where as many as three times that number packed into this facility like nonproducing livestock. This says little about the effectiveness of society's correctional programs, futile to address the root cause of escalating crime in America. But this particular day I am here counting among them, witness to the sound of gnashing teeth and hysterical cries of souls lost in the shadows of outer darkness. The echo of men screaming and cursing deafening, a bedlam of inconsolable torment, men driven mad with boredom and anger. Once inside my own cell and the heavy bars rolled shut, I am just another prisoner alone.

By now, my head splitting with a migraine, I am lost in time, not even knowing the hour or the day, or if it is day or if it is night. Nor have I eaten since Friday morning breakfast at the Santa Monica jailhouse. I lie in my bunk   staring up at the peeling cracked ceiling thinking that here is a place of purgatory, a place between heaven and hell. Outside my cell a rain of paper, discarded cigarette packages and other garbage, fills the lighted theater. I fall asleep finally, feeling abandoned and altogether forgotten, wondering with profound disappointment why Ron never came.

It is dark, strangely quiet for this place of anguish. My cell door stands open, the shadow of a figure looming at the entrance like dark Charon to ferry me across the river Styx.

"Follow me," the guard instructs glumly.

I follow his instruction, wondering where I am being taken, and why. I am reminded of a Wiesel Holocaust novel of when the Jews in Europe rounded-up and led sheepishly into extermination chambers, unaware of the next step in the process. This is truest example of what it means to be an unsuspecting victim. All still; and except for the dim glimmer of small pale lights shining along the floor, altogether bleak. This is, indeed, *Hotel*

California, a depository for a host of unwilling guest with no future and no past. We pass through a maze of electronic gates, moving from cell block to cell block. Then handed a paper bag with further instructions to change back into my street clothes, I find myself moments later standing in a parking lot somewhere near Alameda Street beneath the belly of an overpass, liberated at last.

I am uncertain of the time-served calculation used by the court system; only that for some reason my release occurs at three on a Monday morning. Perhaps it is a way the institution uses to save on food. I am starving, but at least free.

I managed to hitch a ride with a trucker as far as the Olympic Boulevard exit; and from here a walk of another half hour south to my apartment. The sun is just rising as I step through the front door and collapse on the couch. I will later learn that Ron had come and spent over three hours in an attempt to locate me, which implies new dimension to the term *'lost in the system'*. Strangely I am never contacted to serve more time. Maybe that also lost in the system. This is one weekend in purgatory I will always remember.

There is sadness to leaving university routine after so many years. I have grown accustomed to the routine and to the many challenges. As a young bird on a ledge, I know the time come to spread my wings. Nevertheless, it is difficult to say goodbye forever. Then something happens, adding an aspect of revival to my decision. My car still in Impound because of a lack of money to pay the fees, I go by motorcycle Tuesday morning to the Campus Director's office to finalize some paperwork. Upon leaving the parking lot, I take Charles E Young Drive toward Westwood Plaza, negotiating a steep hill near the intersection. I should have been going slower, except that the visibility excellent and very little traffic. A Van in the on-coming lane makes a left turn immediately in front of me. There is no time to break, no time to do anything. I plow into the right rear fender; fly like Evil Carnival over the vehicle making a somersault, and land feet-first on the opposite side, sitting down sharply upon impact unharmed.

The female driver is hysterical, apologizing incessantly for not seeing me. As for my bike, it remains upright, the front wheel tightly wedged into the passenger side wheel cavity of the other vehicle. A tow truck transports my mangled machine home after several torturous minutes of jacking up the van and unraveling the crumpled twisted spokes. The other driver's insurance company wastes no time contacting me. They ask if I will settle for $500.00, and so I do. A certified check arrives by special courier within the hour. I probably could have gotten much more. However, I consider the bike unreliable and well past its prime. Since I am unhurt by a miracle, what advantage is there looking a gift horse inthe mouth? The next day I cash the check, remembering to this day how crisp the money felt in my hand. Not wishing to get Barbara involve, I take a bus to the West Los Angeles Police Impound and pay for the release of my old Rambler. I consider these fortuitous events signs thatthe Spirit leading my life into another direction. Old things passed away; all things made new.

The first two weeks at Moore Business Forms proves fascinating, as I learn about the instruments used to transact business all over the world. I receive instruction on how to create new forms for specific use and how to edit and customize existing ones. I become familiar with printing presses, about different types of inks. For example, some contain magnetic properties, such as those used to print bank checks. I become educated in every aspect of a business, from the creation and purpose of multi-part invoices, purchase orders, and all those little things that make business operations, even packing slips. There is a gold mine in paperwork! It is an interesting knowledge base, with as much precision execution, as anything else I have engaged to study over the past five years. Each morning, I prepare my own lunch; travel the Santa Monica Freeway going east into the core of Los Angeles during rush-traffic to sit through early hours of indoctrination training. At noon, I stroll a few blocks over to the Evergreen Cemetery, renown to be the oldest in L. A., where I eat my sandwich beneath the rich shade of old California Oaks. Four hours later I fight the L. A. rush traffic jams to get back home. The only thing I find disturbing in the beginning is the more than two-hour drive to and from work; nevertheless, the pay adequate and the career promising.

I will discover the prospect of actually selling this product disappointing and stressful, upon realizing the competitive nature of vending business forms to bottom-line businesses. The base prices of Moore's forms are between thirty to forty percent higher than the competition. For every ten dollars of reduction, the salesman loses one percent loss in his or her commission. The base commission is only six and a half percent. Therefore, a good sell might net three percent or less. The $700.00 a month salary not a real salary, but considered a draw against commission, meaning that before I even get into the field, I am already more than $350.00 in the hole. Nor is this the only aspect of the company I dislike. Every few weeks the Moore local office sponsors a company picnic and encourages all employees to attend with their wives or girlfriends. Barbara expresses discomfort to attend, saying she has already participated in company sponsored picnic events in the past when married to Barry. I think the actual reason is that Barbara self-conscious of our difference in age, more evident when reflected in open society. And if Barbara will not go, then I will not go alone. Perhaps things would have been different if I had.

"We missed you at last weekend's employee gathering," my office supervisor queries after one such event.

"I didn't know they were mandatory?"

"Of course they're not. But we encourage our people to get together, share ideas, become like a family. The next one will be in one month. I hope to see you there."

"I'll try," I respond dubiously.

I think that even had I been alone, I would not have liked to be pressured into sacrificing part of my weekend to commute downtown and talk shop with people I barely know. What bothers me most are the continuous pep talks about what kind of car we should drive, the kind of mortgage we should look for, and that the nuclear values of the company ought to become our values; an indoctrination that sounds all so familiar. Nevertheless, I submit to doing my job, finding the experience tasteless after a while. In less than eight months, I tender my resignation. Invited the next morning to a company breakfast, I find myself seated beside Mr. Engle, the regional Vice President. Afterchatting for a while, he inquires why I wish to leave the company aftersuch a short period of time.

"It is mostly the long commute every day. I rarely get home before seven, and usually too tired to make a decent meal."

"Then how would you like to work from our Beverly Hills office? I have reviewed your record, and I think it would be a loss to the company if you were to leave us. I think you have the potential one day to be sitting in my seat."

Beverly Hills is only fifteen minutes from where I live along surface streets, which means two extra hours in my day. I must also admit that the idea of one day becoming a regional Vice President appealing. Therefore, I accept the challenge.

All seems to go well in the beginning. My territorial limits extend between Rodeo Drive and Sunset Boulevard to West Pico and Beverly Drive. This stretch of city, considered the most affluent commercial area in the L. A. basin, catering to the extravagant appetites of the wealthy and the prestigious. One would think this Mecca of prosperity an instant guarantee of success to any business person fortunate enough to grace the doors of these reputed worldly institutions. In fact, the opposite is true. These merchants of fame and affluence count every penny as though it the last. In a short while, I realize how little profit to be made here. Nevertheless, there remains a certain self-importance associated with being a rep to this international hot spot.

The first thing I must do is invest in some new digs. Barbara knows an exclusive men's clothing store in Century City that provides free tailoring and insists upon going with me. She is, after all, used to grooming men of success. Upon her knowledgeable advice, I purchase two silk shirts, one black and one tan, two pair of slacks made to measure, a Camel Haired sport coat, and a second made of fine tweed.

"Don't worry Angel, you will pay me back," she says at the checkout counter. "You must look successful in order to be successful. You think for one minute Barry could have made it to Vice President of Capital Records without me. Trust me, investment in new clothes never wasted and is worth every penny."

I am not so certain; nevertheless, I feel already successful, even though I am more than a hundred dollars in the hole. We next go to a leather shop where Barbara willing to pay sixty dollars for a pair of Italian handcrafted boots reduced in price. Even though I like the comfort and the look, I tell the store clerk that I will think about it and maybe come back another time.

"No, we will take them," Barbara commands. "This is my gift to you, Angel. I know it seems like a lot of money, but money makes money. This is just how the world works."

"Then I will pay you back, Barbara. It is enough that you are buying me these things today. It is the least I can do."

She sees the resoluteness in my eyes and agrees, rather than make a scene in front of the salesperson. At the check stand, we take two leather ties at a price of two for one, although I could have bought four at Sears for the price of that one. However, where else can one find dyed leather ties? By the end of our shopping spree, I owe Barbara over two hundred dollars. I am poor as a pauper, in debt to the one I love, but look like a million dollars and change.

Barbara will also make some dramatic changes that will prove detrimental to our already fragile union. She sells her house in the Palisades and purchases a fixer-upper in Brentwood. If this not enough, she opens a high-fashion women's clothing boutique branded *Made in California* on the new Brentwood outdoor shopping center. I perceive both of these changes further threat to my youthful dreams of us one day becoming a real family. I commission Bruce and Ed to help landscape the yard of her new home and install a lawn sprinkler system. In this way, I am able to pay back the money I owe Barbara by not charging for my own labor. It is again like military all over. I must remain constantly on the backs of my friends to ensure an hour's work for an hour's wage. By the end of the second day, we run into an obstacle of a termite-infested tree in the backyard that refuses to go down. Ed and Bruce have successfully dug around the roots, yet their combined efforts of two hours unable to bulge the stubborn monarch.

"You're not trying hard enough. Move aside-- it will come down!"

I detect doubt in both their eyes.

With concentrated force, I slam both palms against the center. There is a resounding painful crack, the Goliath sways back and forth, and then pounds into the earth.

"How did you do that?" Ed demands in total amazement. "I've done some lumber-jacking up in Oregon, but I never saw anything like that!"

"It's all in the will," I reply seriously. "Come on guys, we still have a lot of work to do before sunset."

Bruce only snickers, reminding me of another cartoon character from the past. Very little about me surprises him anymore. In retrospect, I believe this tree just hanging on by a thread, needing a final thrust of sympathetic vibration to give up the ghost, reminding me that life all about timing, coupled with force delivered at a precise quantum. A grain of sand can cause or prevent a landslide; a clump of fallen ice can precipitate an avalanche. Because of my present gift of faith, I believe all things accordingly. Therefore, coincidence little amazes me when it happens. It is not my resolve that brought this tree down, but coincidence as sure as splitting of the Red Sea, or Jonah being timely swallowed by a great fish, or defeat of a giant with a simple pebble. We successfully complete the project in a record time of two weekends. My debt to Barbara now paid in full, extra cash for my two best friends, and a job well done. It seems my new life taking shape and direction of its own. But upon each new horizon looms always the prospect of change; often shadowed by possibility of future disappointments. And there is also always that thing about paying the Piper.

Barbara's new business goes well in the beginning,

with promising potential that the *Made In California* logo destined to become a new label style in an industry my girlfriend knows so well. Barbara is a perfect Anne Kline petite, as astute in women's fashion wear as she is in real estate. However, I suppose her ability to balance cash flow and adjusted business expenses against sales projections somewhat lacking. Within the first few months, she needs more money than expected for inventory and advertising. At this time, I am unaware that John has presented her with a flawed business plan to incorporate, offering her friends and family inflated shares to buy into the company. I never knew the number of certificates or their value. I probably might have bought some shares myself had I any money. *Made In California* quickly circulates as a locally branded Brentwood name. Barbara is on course to establish another Anne

Kline logo on future fashion runways.

I still do not like working for Moore Business Forms, even though the Beverly Hills territory has far greater potential, and the local office near to where I live. Moore has fulfilled its challenge to me, the rest now up to me. I might have remained with Moore were it not for the irascible nature of the office manager, a German fellow named Steiner Twitten. Steiner is a radicalized company man from the stiff suit he wears daily to the car he drives. He surveys the clock incessantly, keeping a close tab on who early and who is late. Who stays after hours; and who does not. I feel he has his prying eyes on me from the beginning.

One very hot day in July, I have lunch at a local Beverly Hills restaurant. The cool air-conditioned facility offers welcome relief from the heat. I remove my tie to allow my neck to breathe. I always did hate the noose of a neck-tie, so conservative, so proper, an anchor of conformity to traditional values reining in individual expression. I wear it only because of the job, but deep down resent this symbolic bondage to my truer nature. Therefore, I suppose my unconscious mind masters my better judgment, because after lunch I forget to put it back on. My first call is the nearby office of a well- established Jeweler and longtime client of Moore Business Forms. As I sit across a massive polished desk looking into the withered face of the business owner, I sense something wrong, only I do not know what. He only glares at me with contempt, reminding me of an undernourished ghoul hanging onto the present by wispy threads spun through a lifetime of structured existence; little more than an abandoned web in a dark corner of this elegant chamber soon to vanish in time. He makes renewal of the usual things and dryly tells me to leave. Upon returning to the office later in the day, I discover the reason for this oddly cold reception.

"In my office-- immediately--" sounds-off Gestapo voice of Steiner Twitten, even before I have chance to sit down. "Where is your tie?"

Only then do I realize the neck piece still in my pocket. I attempt to explain the events of the afternoon and that not wearing my tie just an unfortunate oversight. Instead of accepting my explanation, Steiner begins berating me, emphasizing that I have made insult to a customer of more than twenty-six years.

"It is clearly written in the handbook, that every employee will wear a tie at all times as proper business attire."

"May I see that in writing?" I demand not too pleasantly.

He hands me a handbook containing a section on dress code while continuing a monologue speech about client satisfaction, and then dismisses me. I am back in the military all over again, but do not recognize this toad- stomper's authority to attack me personally. That night I read through official Moore Business Forms Handbook and find a loophole of exploitation I am unable to resist. So Steiner is a man of the rules, then the rules I will interpret to the letter.

Next morning I arrive to work with my necktie tied to my wrist. Steiner sees the discrepancy immediately, unceremoniously demanding that I report to his office.

"Are you stupid?" He attacks. "Why is your necktie on your wrist?"

"The official handbook states clearly that a tie must be worn by all employees. But it does not specify where said tie must be worn. I have noticed that a couple of women in the office wear bowties below the fringe of an open collar blouse. No one instructs them on proper business attire. I elect to wear mine on my wrist. Until which time the manual states differently, this is where I will display my tie from now own."

"You think you are smart. Look out this window. Do you see your car? Look at mine-- a Mercedes Benz! That is the reward of being with the company for thirty years."

Peering out the window, I respond that after being with a company for thirty years I might hope to conduct myself in a vehicle more recent than his 10-year-old Mercedes.

"I don't like you Mr. Twitten," I further add; "I think you are a bully and a zealot. I have met your kind before, and if you had any real balls you would fire me on the spot. In the meantime, I am not breaking any company rules. The manual clearly states that all employees must wear a tie. It does not state where it must be worn. Until I see differently. I will wear my tie where I feel. If you will excuse me, I have business appointments."

In the moment I thought the man choking to death or ready to explode on the spot. My fellow employees only hang their heads as I pass. They know it only a matter of time now. This goes on for nearly two weeks. Steiner actually contacts the home office in Michigan and demands priority revision of the handbook. In the meantime, I add another element of rebellion.

Gucci products are considered status symbols in the richer hills of California at this time in history. Everyone, who is anyone in Beverly Hills, owns at least one article with the Gucci logo printed across it. Particularly popular are Gucci handbags and men's briefcases trimmed in rich brown leather, which frames a tan weaved canvas resembling embroidered Sampler's candy boxes. On the face a stylized monogrammed *G* facing an upside-down *G* linked in series to form a crisscross of design. This status emblem of the elite, undeniable proof of wealth and success, I will desecrate with unashamed antithesis. By coincidence I find at a weekend garage sale a briefcase that is a perfect knock-off, except instead of the Gucci logo, it reads *BULLSHIT— BULLSHIT* repeatedly across the front. I arrive in the office the following Monday carrying this rebellious icon and display it prominently on my desk along with my leather wrist tie. Steiner says nothing, and only glares at me like a restrained German Sheppard biding his time.

Wednesday morning my office manager gleefully intercepts me as I walk into the front door, summoning me to his office. Slamming a freshly printed manual on his desk he turns to a page that reads 'all employees are required to wear a necktie around the neck as proper dress code'. I nonchalantly place my briefcase on Steiner's desk, remove my tie from my wrist, and tie it around my neck.

"Is there anything else, Mr. Twitten?" I enquire, looking him squarely in the eyes.

"And get rid of that obscene briefcase!"

"I work in a status society where logos and trademarks are important. Even you have stated the defining quality in the kind of car one drives or how one dresses. I am just being part of the status quo. I see nothing in the handbook that dictates the definition of fashion collections."

"The writing on that briefcase is profanity!"

"Bulls do shit, just like I am sure Gucci shits, as do you, as do we all. Who's to say whose shit is more obscene than another?"

Steiner turns red with rage. He stammers, then coughs, saying something about firing me. I have come prepared. I slam a termination form in front of him all filled out, needing only his signature.

"You are resigning?" He demands suspiciously. "Does this mean your work ethics incompatible with our company politics?"

"Either that, or you are firing me. But being you are a good company man, I am sure you are willing to give me another chance to conform. Besides, I'm starting to like it here. I think in time we might even become friends."

His hands shaking with rage, Steiner places his signature on the appropriate line. I quickly snatch away the paper and place it into my *BULLSHIT* briefcase.

"Thank you, Mr. Twitten." Adding, "it has not always been a pleasure working with you. I wish many successful years with your Mercedes Benz."

I travel immediately to the West Los Angeles Unemployment Center. Steiner was right to be suspicious. Over the course of the last two weeks, I have reasoned this to be a dead-end job. Checking the requirements to collect California Unemployment Insurance, I realize that all I need to do is make Steiner fire me in an emotional frenzy having nothing to do with my work performance. Much the same as provoking an unruly hound, I cunningly maneuvered my office head into a personal vendetta irresistible to the arrogance of his German pride. Steiner has taken the bait.

"He tricked me!" I hear Steiner scream over the receiver.

"Is this your signature, or not?" The female unemployment agent demands crossly.

After several moments of listening to some lengthy explanation, she calmly hangs up the receiver and processes the form in accordance with California law by placing a dated stamp approving my claim for Unemployment Insurance. At least for the next twelve weeks, I will continue to receive two thirds of my base salary with no draw against commission or travel expenses. This means three months of work-free income, time to relax, time to think, and time to launch a new career.

"Don't worry Sweetie, you will find another job much better than the one you are leaving." Barbara encourages. "Your former boss sounds like a Nazi. You should be glad to leave that behind."

Barbara is right, I am glad not to have to fight my way to the office and face the junkyard dog again. Maybe Steiner not as bad as I remember; nor do I really think him a Nazi; but certainly not a pleasant individual. I do not consider myself an Alpha Male; nevertheless, this man of ill temper brought my warrior to the surface. I never did like bullies.

Tragedy invades Barbara's business twice in a month. First, a masked armed robber enters her store and demands all the cash in her register. A week later, someone breaks in at night stealing nearly all of her inventory. I console the best I can, but know what she needs most is money. And this I have very little of.

I interview for several jobs: insurance companies, banks, brokerage companies, anything that has high-rolling salaries. Foolishly, I feel a competitive need to secure a job making a lot of money if I want to keep this woman of my dreams. All these bleak opportunities have the same thing in common: all entry sales positions with modest salaries. All bear the same yoke of oppression. I realize that these institutions of success represent that *monkey train* in my dream. Then I find an ad in the paper for a job promising freedom, creativity, as well as economic reward. The ad reads simply 'Writer wanted' and a phone number. I book an appointment to go to a mansion on Sunset Strip near the old location of Hugh Hefner's famous Playboy Club on the corner of Alta Loma.

"It is the large house on the right just one block from the Playboy Club," the man on the telephone instructs with a hint of victory in his voice.

Mention of this particular landmark reference and emphasis placed on it by the person at the other end of the line should have been a tip-off. The premise is a grand gated mansion with a security guard posted at the entrance. I drive along a circular drive lined with columns and colorful rosebushes planted on one side. Opposite to these stands a grand mansion with a large byzantine style porch surrounded by a tended lawn. This is true wealth rooted in a tradition of slow acquisition and patiently nurtured for future posterity. Unlike the *Noveau-Riche,* who flock the avenues of Beverly Hills, these are the true barons of worldly dominion, unpretentious, harboring in the shadows and possessors of real earthly power. It is not so much, how these people dress, or the kind of cars they drive, or even just where they live. Theirs is a presence of affluent excess, bright fortresses embodied by every dark force since the earliest landmarks of civilization.

A butler opens the door and ushers me to an office located in an adjacent wing that could have been a museum room of historical art. Entering first, he formally announces my presence. The man seated behind an enormous oak desk bears little resemblance to this lavish interior, somehow out of place, belonging to a less savory decor.

"Do you live here?" I venture.

"No, I am only the publishing editor. So you are interested in writing for our magazine?"

"Yes sir. I have a major in creative writing with some journalism--"

"Have you ever read our publication?" He interrupts, shoving a copy of *Hustler* across the desk in my direction.

"I don't believe I ever have."

"We want raunchy material. Can you write really raunchy?"

"I'm sure I can write most anything if that's what is required."

"Can you get inside a cunt's head while at the same time fucking her brains out? There is no need wasting your time or ours if you can't. We are explicit in our material designed to cater the expectations of a specific clientele. We are looking for seasoned writers able to produce what our audience likes to read. Take a copy of the magazine and my business card. Read it through, and get back to me."

I agree that perhaps this presently the best idea. Without further ceremony I am ushered back to the front door feeling a little nauseous. Not because of the interview, but because of its content. I will discover that of all the pornographic magazines on the market at this time, Hustler the most graphic, making Playboy look like a fashion magazine. I find it degrading to my concept of women, altogether degenerate, making bestial the sexual act between two people. After much soul wrestling, I chuck the disgusting material into the nearest trash can along with temptation of thebusiness card. I will find another way of expression.

Barbara and I have our second major argument at the end of summer. It begins with a second-hand Swedish car she buys for her daughter Dale by recommendation of a friend. I always suspect this friend John. Being mechanically inclined, I am able to make a few minor repairs, change the front brake pads and grease the rear wheel bearings. After owning the car for only two months there is now a problem with the hydraulic clutch assembly. *Svenska Aeroplan Aktie Bolaget,* better known as the Swedish Airplane Company, exclusively designs and produces airplanes, until after the end of World War 2. This is when the company turns to making cars and the rest automobile history. I discover the *Saab V-4 96* an impressive Swedish design, solidly made and with impressive specifications. But best of all it is made with superior Swedish steel and easy to work on for someone like me, who does not mind to tinker from time to time. Dale thinks the car lovely in the beginning, falling in love with the unusual aerodynamic body design, but quickly becomes disenchanted by its several mechanical issues. I try to convince her and her mother it is an engineering marvel, considering that all it really needs is a little routine maintenance. I purchase a Chilton Work Manual for the vehicle, determined to restore confidence in this nine-year-old machine. Barbara grows to hate the car, deciding to sell it and buy Dale a second hand Audi instead. In trying to convince Barbara to reconsider, I find myself in opposition to her strong will. Once Barbara makes up her mind, there is little chance of changing it.

Rashly, I agreed to buy the car from her for the original purchase price of $600.00, adding that she has little faith and less imagination. Words I will regret. I give Barbara a $300.00 down payment, with a promise to give her the balance as soon as I get a paying job. In retrospect, I appreciate the trust she had in me concerning money transactions.

After a long and heated discussion, we decide to take a break from each other. My suspicions concerning John are beginning to take root again. Barbara has placed herself in financial jeopardy; and the kind of debt she has far out of my league. John, on the other hand, is an accountant, understands money, and is always somewhere in the shadows of my mind. In one way I am glad she knows someone able to provide her with fiscal advice. But why does it have to be John? The part that bothers me most is she will neither deny, nor confirm it is John, insisting only that I need to trust her on what is best for the future. A week after buying the Saab, the indestructible flat-six engine on the Rambler blows a head gasket. I sell the car as-is for a hundred and fifty dollars. Half I use to live on, and half I give to Barbara. My search for the perfect job grows ever more fruitless. Less than three weeks before my unemployment insurance expires, I awaken in the middle of the night with a profound epiphany. *"Econ-o- Money Business Forms"* is born.

Once, while working for Moore, we had a very large web-job delayed because of a downed press. Steiner had me locate a local printer to produce a 250 minimum order of invoices. This quick maneuvering saved an important account, as well as giving me some outside experience. I decide that since I did it once, I can do it again.

Next morning I go to City Hall and register a business license for an annual fee of twenty-five dollars, and then locate a thermograph business card printer and place a batch order for five hundred cards with raise-printing bearing logo of *Econ-o-Money Business Forms*. It is a simple black and white card with my name, address, and a phone number. Next, I put on my professional attire and begin pounding the pavement in my local area. By end of the second day, I have four jobs. The only problem; I have no printing sources. I spend an entire day checking the phonebook, until I find an offset printer capable of doing the work. I produce the text copy and layout myself by cutting and pasting, using a straight razor with the aid of my trusted metal Moore ruler. I make only a little profit from these first jobs, losing most of that because the printer fails to inspect the plate before producing a thousand sheets of Letterhead containing an obvious smudge. My education at Moore has instilled within me the paramount importance of client satisfaction. Therefore, I negotiate an acceptable price below cost, and learn a vital lesson about the importance of quality control. This experience with serve me well in the future.

The second week, I stumble into an established business needing twenty thousand four-part continuous form invoices with carbon sheets and another twenty thousand purchase orders. This is beyond scopeof a small off-set shop without the equipment to collate the carbon sheets. My local printer could have produced a few thousand forms using carbonless paper, but far too expensive for a job of this quantity. I take the order anyway, basing my price on the Moore model, less twenty percent, without fully considering the technical obstacle. Within hours, Irealize the magnitude of my error. I need a web-house.

In this early beginning I never considered competing with the industry giants of form sales as a viable business, hoping only to make a little extra money until a real job came along. Now it looks like I have hit the proverbial brick wall, unless I can find an independent web-printer able to do large galley jobs at a competitive price. None of the small print shops will give me any information at all, and by the third day, I am desperate, thinking I have secured orders I am unable to fulfill at any price. Then I get my break. I have started doing business with a quality reliable letter press shop located in *Olevra District* of downtown Los Angeles. The shop owner of this modest facility is a robust hard-working man originally from Mexico City. After only the first meeting, I realize within minutes this man a professional and as much conscious of quality control as Iam. Today I am here to pick up a Letter Press job. I ask if he knows any web-houses.

"No, my friend, web printers are very hard to find, and very expensive. You should call the Printers Association."

"Do you have a phone number for this association?"

After several minutes fumbling through a stack of cards on his desk, he finds the one he is searching for, freely giving me the cherished information.

"If they should ask, just say you have been doing business since many years, and say you are a registered community member. I think they might be able to help you."

I thank this kind man for the tip, return home, and immediately call the number. In the beginning, there is some reluctance to provide me with any referrals. Therefore, I assume my most professional persona, stating factually that I am the president of *Econ-o-Money Business Forms* and that we have immediate need of a reference for a new web source.

"Our main competitor Moore Business Forms has purchased a major mid-west division leaving our company without a competitive resource."

This may be a well-crafted lie of inspiration, but could just as easily have been true, since Moore Corporation is continuously gobbling-up web facilities across the nation.

"Yes, I know. These large companies like Moore and Standard Register are out to assimilate the entire form industry. You are the second business this week that has made a complaint like this. We try to safeguard brokers like you against these kinds of draconian maneuvers, but you understand it is beyond our control. Please give me your name and address, and I will send you out a current list of industry providers."

I thank her; and she in turn wishes me and my company good luck. Two days later, I receive a six-page document with names, phone numbers, and addresses of every kind of specialty house in Southern California and western U.S. It is a broker's treasure chest. To my overwhelming delight, I find a web house located in Fresno capable of producing my order and at a stunning low price, including shipping direct to the client. This is more than I could have hoped for, as well as leaving me with a comfortable profit of twenty-five dollars per thousand. There is only one problem; I need to give forty percent down on the first order with a term payment of 30 days on the remaining balance. Coolly, I return to my new client and explain that our company requires a security of fifty percent down on the first order and COD on the balance. Without hesitation, the purchasing clerk writes me out a check for $1280.00. I pay the printer; the job produced and delivered in record time.

Now I am on fire, seeing the real potential in being an independent printing broker. This first big job provides me with the security buffer I need. It is only the beginning. I am officially doing business in one of the largest commercial cities in the world. Just a matter of getting the jobs, which as it turns out something I am good at.

This is a good excuse to contact Barbara and ask she join me on a Saturday afternoon stroll along the Venice Boardwalk. I hand her over a wad of cash, counted exactly to the amount I owe her. Even though the debt paid, I still see in her eyes something wrong, something I am unable to penetrate or make balance.

"Thank you, Angel. Know always you are my Angel," she says, gazing into the western horizon where sky and ocean meet. "I knew everything would work out. Today you are a born Merchant of Venice."

Part Nine

Zodiac Map

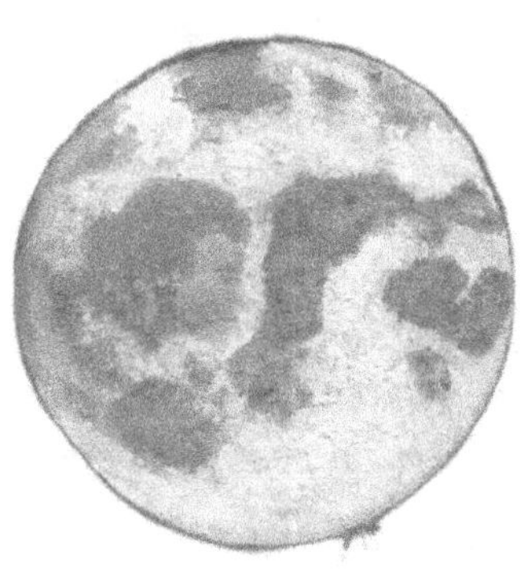

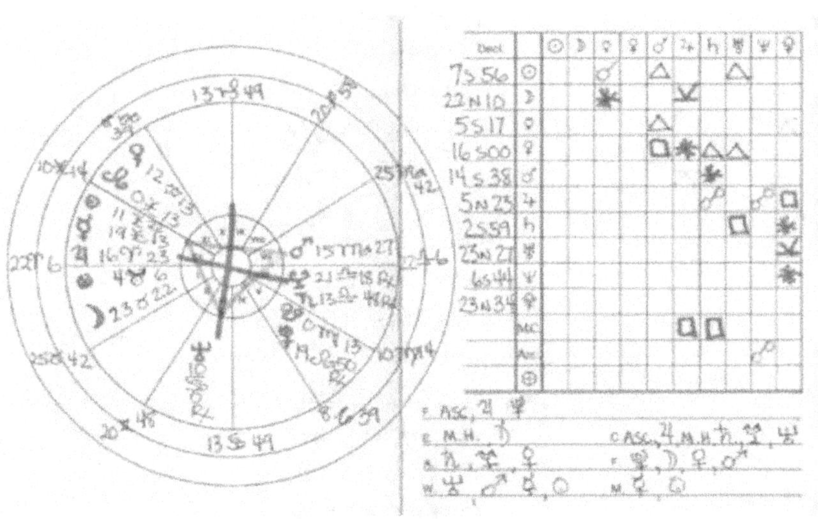

Astrology Chart made by Judi 1979

Book of Parables Ends

*There is the wind
Whispered in desert time
Or is it rhythm of this rhyme
Circles height of sleepy trees
Saying softly Saying sweet
Nothing is yours
Nothing to keep
Close your eyes
To know me*

*There is the ocean
Licked sensual shore
Or is she something more
Slipping translucent in silver sand
Saying softly Saying sweet
Nothing is yours
Nothing to keep
I am me I am me
Close your eyes
To know me*

*There is the moon
Suspended on silver thread
Or is he illusion instead
Guardian over fields of night
Saying softly Saying sweet
Nothing is yours
Nothing to keep
I am me I am me
Close your eyes
To know me*

In one voice sing the stars
I am me I am free
Touch heaven in my hand
Suspended over myriad of sand
Ride wind of the sun
Through course of light all must run
Over peaks of mountains high
Into celestial valleys of sky
Zodiac maps drawn
Where constellations divide
To chase shadow of the moon
Beyond zenith of shadow's noon
I am me I am me
Close your eyes
To know me

*N*ow that Barbara paid back for the clothes she bought, as well as owed balance owing for the Saab, I feel my dignity restored. Of course, this also turns into a good excuse to try and get back together again. I apologize for my jealousy and she apologizes for panicking. She has arranged a bank loan and it seems *Made in California* might make it after all. In some ways, we become closer than ever before, believing in one another, supportive of each other's dreams. However, this complicity will come to an end in September when Barbara celebrates her fortieth birthday.

That evening, I give Barbara an exquisite Seth Thomas clock purchased from a Century City antique shop. Later I take her out to our favorite restaurant. She remains quiet through most of the evening, reflective and preoccupied. Always her silence disturbs some part inside me, making me feel helpless.

"Do you like it?" I ask upon our return to her home, placing the clock in the center of the fire mantle of her Brentwood home.

"Yes, Angel, it is very special. What made you think to get a clock of all things?"

"For as long as this clock keeps time here, then our love will continue on. I have something else for you."

Reaching under my coat lapel, I retrieve a small box. Instead of anticipation, a glimpse of dread flushes Barbara's face, as she physically braces herself. In retrospect, I think in that moment she believed I was going to propose to her. Upon opening the box, her body relaxes. It is the gift of a fourteen-carat gold ankle chain.

"It's stunning, darling. I've thought about getting an ankle chain, but always felt I was too old."

"Don't say that Barbara, you are as beautiful and young as any woman to me."

"You are so vital and intelligent. I am sure other women find you attractive. Haven't you ever thought it might be better to fall in love with someone your own age and have a family one day?"

"I am in love with you. Yes, I see other women in the world, but they are not you. You are my family. I will always love you, no matter how old you become."

I kneel down, securing the chain to her delicate left ankle. In my mind Barbara's foot is a thing of uncommon beauty. Her leg a contour of nature travels sensuously to the extremity of her exquisite thigh and into my raw imagination. To paraphrase the meaning in the words of playwright Harold Pinter's in his play *The Homecoming*, the character Ruth says "*The action is simple. It's a leg moving.*" But this is Barbara's leg, which moves me to passion. In my subconscious mind, this chain represents a greater bond between us. I should have realized when Barbara sobbed deeply after making love that night this already the beginning of the end.

Barbara introduces me to the owners of a neighboring new business opening in the Brentwood Shopping Center next to her fashion shop. It is a startup business called *The Footlocker* owned by two pleasant young men fresh out of Business School. They need sales receipts, business cards, and box labels for their exclusive line of men and women sport footwear. I think the success of this enterprise dubious in the beginning, but soon realize sneakers very much in demand. They become one of my best accounts and regular customers on first name bases for over a year. Their business booms and they open two more locations in long beach.

This is when the big sharks move in. Moore and Standard Register have a *'loss profit'* policy, which squashes the competition. They will take jobs and run them at cost, or even below cost through *'gang runs'* for companies they project as having future-potential. *The Footlocker* growing by leaps and bounds now qualifies as prime candidate for a business blitz. I drop by as usual at their new Long Beach warehouse to check their forms inventory. I can tell as soon as I walk in the door change in the air. Neither of the two partners will look me straight in the eye, and even ignore my presence when I ask if they are running low on anything.

"Is there a problem?" I venture.

"Well... you have provided us with good service," begins one of the men I know as Sam. "We really appreciate everything. A competitor of yours has given us a price for an order of a hundred-thousand so low that we think it unfair to ask you to try and bid against."

"A hundred thousand-- that is a big order! Out of respect for our long-standing relationship can I know what I am up against?"

I know I have a twenty-dollar-per-thousand spread, and this represents by far the largest order placed since that first day when these two young shy men ask for a sixty-day credit on a three-hundred-dollar order. Even if I make less than five dollars per thousand, I will still be profiting well.

Upon seeing the quoted price of thirteen dollars per thousand below my cost, I am altogether devastated. I am aware of what is going on, yet helpless to do anything about it. I only look at Sam and nod my head. I know they feel bad about ending our partnership, but I feel even worse. Business is business, and this day Goliath has won the battle. Today *The Footlocker* is an international trade name worth millions. Giants walk with giants.

I believe that Steiner tries to pull a fast one. One day I receive a call from an ex-Moore employee I knew well in the office named Gunter. Like Steiner, Gunter is also German, only more humble and less assuming. He says he is now working for another Business Forms company, but won't say which one. Gunter first congratulates me for striking out on my own, saying only that he needs an emergency rush order for five thousand three-part continuous forms. I think the request suspicious. Gunter assures me this will remain a private transaction between him and me, and that he is willing to write me a personal check up front. He convinces me that because of an internal dissatisfaction with Moore's Press Union, he lost most of his accounts to a competitor.

I accept the order with a negotiated markup of only a few dollars per thousand, allowing Gunter a margin for extra profit. Why be greedy? The transaction easy, and for a pleasant guy whose desk once just across from mine. Gunter insists I deliver the completed order on a nearby street corner. He acts like a little boy stealing hubcaps, looking nervously around as if someone might be watching an elicit exchange.

"I feel guilty doing this," he confesses, as we transfer the boxes from my car trunk to his. "Don't you sometimes miss being in an office and security of a regular salary?"

"No, I like being independent. Maybe it is not as predictable as a steady paycheck and company benefits. But at least I am free."

"It's easy for you because you have no wife or children. I do what I must do because of responsibilities. There is no such thing as freedom after you get married."

"I don't understand why you would feel guilty about making a little extra money. As for Moore, I am surprised they keep any of their employees by the way their commission structure works. I hope at least this order helps you make a little extra profit on the top, Gunter."

He only wags foolishly his head, gets into his car, and speeds away. I consider Gunter's behavior odd; but then, Gunter always was a little strange. A week later, Steiner Twitten calls to inform me that I am responsible for Gunter's dismissal from his job.

"How am I responsible?" I inquire, wondering how Steiner could have known about the transaction.

"You encouraged him to break company policy by servicing a Moore account independently."

"Gunter told me he no longer worked for Moore. Even so, the small quantity he bought could not have damaged Moore's business model or its reputation. I think it shameful that a man fired from his position just for making a little extra on the side."

"There is an industry code that protects against espionage and unfair pricing. If a Moore employee or even an ex-employee knowingly undercuts a service account, then there might be room for some legal recourse. I believe youand Gunter conspired to steal a Moore account. I am certain Gunter will testify at a public hearing."

"I merely sold him some forms upon his request. I have no knowledge of the account he sold them to, other than the print information he supplied. I doubt either one of us got rich on the deal. As for your charge of espionage, I am a licensed Printing Broker. I provide a service. Gunter came to me and placed an order, paying me with a personal check, which I deposited into my business account. My invoice is made to him and noone else. I doubt you can prove there was any conspiracy to undermine Moore Business Forms. I have all my paperwork in order. I suggest you look at all the facts before making liable accusations."

With this I hang up the phone. Steiner never calls me again. In reality, I believe that Steiner and Gunter conspired together this scheme to prove if I am really legal. In retrospect, Gunter never was very imaginative, when it came to making money beyond the protective umbrella of an employer; nor do I think him so brave to risk crossing company policy, especially not by back-stabbing Steiner. I am convinced there to be espionage at all. Gunter was an assigned agent, sent by his boss on a witch-hunt that proves nothing. It did, however, net me an extra fifty dollars. Nevertheless, it disappoints me that these past colleagues would go to such extreme measures. Just another nail hammered into the coffin of trust in my fellow man.

Unrest troubles Camelot daily. Each time Barbara and I make love, she cries at the end; and each time I feel conflicted by my pleasure. We are no longer able to communicate as once we did. The words the same, but the language changed. We begin arguing frequently over the most insignificant things. Barbara's three children become an easy source of dispute. The two older daughters, Ellen and Dale, are now self-conscious to sunbathe with a man around. Amie now wishes to stay up later and does not want to imagine her mother and I having sex at night. All these objections legitimate, but all add up to greater distance between Barbara and me. I perceive a growing pattern of separation, a wedge of conspiracy preventing advancement toward further intimacy. I begin missing Barbara profoundly. I miss what once we had and the dream of what might have been. Most of all I miss the presence of the love once we shared, now replaced by financial practicality. Each time I attempt to breach the subject, Barbara deflects the question with another question or evades it altogether by saying the timing not right. Instead of loving commitment, I see in the dark center of her eyes a retreat from all emotion-- from me!

It becomes agonizing. The demon of my jealousy again claws back to the surface again. If she is not seeing me, then to whom is she giving her affection? I grow increasingly suspicious of everything she does and of everything she says. Yet, I am unable to expose any tangible evidence. Then one afternoon Barbara makes a mistake.

We are sitting in her back yard taking sun and sipping on her specialty ice coffee, when the phone rings. She goes inside through the back patio door to answer the call. Clandestinely, I move at the edge of the door to ease drop. I can hear the almost familiar squawk of what is certainly a male voice vibrating through the receiver. Yes, it is definitely male! I hear Barbara agree to a date on Friday evening after seven thirty. I slip quickly back to my chair. Upon her return, I nonchalantly ask who called.

"That was just my friend Regina. She wants to know if I can join her for dinner on Friday. She has something important to talk to me about concerning the business. She is, after all, an investor."

"So, I guess that means Friday we won't be seeing each other again?"

"Don't look so glum, Sweetie. It's just one Friday night. Why don't you go see your friend Ron? You told me that you and he use to go out a lot."

I agree to consider her suggestion; but know already in my heart what I will do. Nine-thirty Friday night I call to know if Barbara has returned. Amie answers the phone, saying only that her mother gone, and refuses to divulge more information than this. Her daughters have witnessed us arguing lately, probably deciding I am no longer a happy choice for their divorced mom.

I try not to think about who she is with; only that she is not with me! And in my gut, I know acutely it is John! This suspicion as a knife turning inside my gut, a blade sharpened with two edges. I wish to be more mature— to ascend higher than the animal instinct of my nature! So what if it is John? No-- it is the lie that hurts most! I am not sure of my reaction had Barbara told me the truth, but at least it would have been better than the anxiety of knowing that the woman I love feels need to lie to my face.

By ten o'clock, I determine to do something I never imagined myself capable. I drive to Brentwood, parking my distinctive Saab several streets away. Barbara lives at the bottom of a dead-end. Opposite her front lawn grows a large Spruce Pine with heavy limbs hanging to the ground. I setup a bivouac here, determined once and for all to settle my doubts. As time passes, I become less certain of my resolve. Twice I consider leaving, and twice I turn back before reaching half the length of the short block. No-- I must to know if these irrational feelings based on any fact. I pray earnestly I am wrong; and that a car will eventually pull up with Barbara and her girlfriend. If so, I will discretely return home and never again doubt the strength of our union.

Nearly two hours later, just before midnight, a sleek late model auto with tinted windows eases down the narrow street and into Barbara's driveway. They remain in the car for several intolerable minutes. The interior light flashes on. Out steps Barbara on the passenger side and then the driver. My worst fears realized. John is like a strutting peacock stylishly dressed and with an air of casual sophistication developed through years of cultivated practice. Seeing the two of them together causes even greater anxiety. Clearly they make a handsome couple; and I am in comparison an unpolished stone still in the rough, undomesticated and lacking temperament for diplomacy— *especially not tonight!*

Barbara sees me first, her eyes wide with terror, as I tear from my position, marching straight toward them. I think she perceives a potentially deadly side of me never seen before, a presence of resolve never revealed since the beginning of our relationship. Fortunately, John sees it as well, withering to one side.

"Go home, John," I say coldly.

John only looks helplessly up at Barbara, slowly edging down the stair railing toward the open door of his car. I suppose he wisely considers the unpleasant possibilities of this situation, deciding his date not worth blood. I think I would have retained some respect for this man had he at least challenged me. Not that it would have made any difference. After John drives hurriedly away, I follow Barbara into her house. We sit down on the couch facing each other, neither knowing what to say, both sensing we have reached an impasse.

"Why?" I ask at last.

"You wouldn't understand. I've fulfilled my purpose in life, and you have just begun. The years between us are a cruel reminder of all the reasons why we cannot be together always. I have struggled with this, darling, and I do love you. But you must surely see I am right. You have your whole beautiful life to live-- loves to love-- places to visit-- books to write. It is time we must let go of this beautiful dream that happens onlyonce in a lifetime."

"You are no dream to me. I want you-- I need you! Please... don't let go..."

She begins sobbing deeply. I reach out, desiring to console her. She recoils, crying even more bitterly. Deep down I know Barbara is right, but unable to accept it-- at least not in the now! For a moment, I am overwhelmed by compassion and think to leave. Then I remember again this night of betrayal. But most of all I think about John!

"If John is what you want, then that's fine with me! I want back my ankle chain-- and my clock!"

"Here... take it!" She screams, removing the slither of gold from her lovely slight ankle. "Take everything and go..."

As the door closes behind me, I hear the lock snap into position. It is like stepping into an empty void of outer darkness. Part of me wishes I had never braved to come here tonight; but a part satisfied because at least now I know all the ugly truth.

I enter the familiar shadows of my apartment, a dungeon of regret and solitude, a place without penitence and devoid of presence. I know profoundly that I am alone, separated, with even Christ seeming far away. I feel abandoned in mortal depths of purgatory, my soul divided, cleaved in two. Barbara represented flesh and blood embodiment of my muse, that sensual part of myself I could never bring into light. Now stake of reality driven into my heart, some vital part of me dead. Drawing the curtains closed, I sit in the blackened interior and listen to the hollow ticking of the Seth Thomas clock droning to the end of existence. No longer am I among the living of this world. No longer will I dream of love and idyllic future promise.

Time a condition no longer relevant, only twilight of being. I remain in this belly of the deep for a night and a day— then I think it is night again. I do not eat, do not sleep, do not think. Then ticking of the clock abruptly stops. Breaking the silence, I become aware of an incessant distant ringing. After many screams for help the ringing ends. The ringing starts again, only this time more desperate, becoming urgent that I answer.

"Are you all right, little brother?" An anxious disembodied voice asks. "I've been trying to reach you since two days."

I try to reply, but instead of words, I begin sobbing bitterly. I mumble something about Barbara, something about death, something that makes no sense at all. I dissuade my friend from rushing over, insisting this something I need to come to terms with alone. Ron accepts, saying he will continue praying for me.

"Call me when you have finished wrestling the demon. Remember little brother 1 Corinthians Chapter 10 verse 13: *"There hath no temptation taken you but such as is common to man: but God is faithful, who will not suffer you to be tempted above that ye are able; but will with the temptation also make a way to escape, that ye may be able to bear it."*

After this exchange I cry as never I cried before. I weep for Rudy and the absent affection of father and son we could never share. I weep for my mother and for all women like her, whose love remains conditional to selfish whims of men driven by a need to control. I weep for Rocky because of a life cut short, without knowing the mystery of why this must be. But most of all I weep for the death of a dream, and for the happiness that could never have endured for more than a season.

It is as a volcano of emotion erupting from bowels of my being. The man I thought I was, still that frightened little boy of my youth desiring only to be loved. Tender ideal of that love murdered by my own hands; or worse, withered on the vine, blighted by anger and frustration. There was never any hope for Barbara and I: a difference of time and materialism— everything about us different! Because I made her that part of me, the part I was always afraid to be; and now in this reality have become nothing, knowing nothing. Cast out, I am abandoned in this solitary universe, vast and measureless. Then in acceptance of the inevitable, I close my eyes to the dream of wings, as a caterpillar that must die.

I open my eyes to a silhouette of light piercing through a crack where the two curtains join. I am Lazarus revived, altogether empty, yet stronger than I have felt since a long time. Shakily, I stand up, go to the window, and throw back the curtains. The bright light of a California morning floods the chamber, chasing away last shadows of the past. Which day I do not know, only that it is a new day for me, the first day of a new life, former things passed away.

Going to a nearby restaurant, I consume a hearty meal. I no longer consider the loss of yesterday, or what might be tomorrow. I am altogether in the present sitting in a diver's place on Washington Boulevard eating the first meal of my new life. As I prepare to leave, a familiar voice calls out my name.

Beth Newhouse has changed little since I last saw her. She still has that same exotic hippie look, the same long raven-black hair, and still the same sweet sexiness of that last morning. She is on her lunch break from the bank, sharing a table with two colleagues. It is only natural that I ask her out on a date; only natural that she accepts so easily. Saturday evening we dine together at a local Japanese restaurant and then go back to my apartment. This is where the evening begins to turn awkward. Something is different, something about Beth less appealing than I remember. I should have realized then I am not ready so soon for another relationship; should have realized that there never any closure between Beth and me. Beth tries to be romantic; slips readily into my bed. My desire fades even before it begins. It is not a feeling of impotence; rather, a total lack of interest, as one might experience after meeting a childhood sweetheart in adulthood.

"I think this is a bad idea," I say to her before she has a chance to disrobe completely. "I always wondered what happened to you-- why you disappeared that way."

"I'm sorry, but I wasn't thinking clearly then. I was in love with a married man since a year. When he again left his wife and called for me to come be with him... you know the rest. I never meant to hurt you."

"I got hurt, but also got over it. I'm hurting now, but no longer because of you, Beth. No, I think I need to heal first."

Beth is surprisingly understanding about the whole affair. Instead of being angry or feeling rejected, she gathers her things and kisses me on my forehead.

"Thank you for a nice dinner out," she says at the door. "Just for the record, you were good then; and I wish now things had worked out differently."

Then she is gone-- or so I think. Minutes later there is frantic knocking at the front door. It is Beth again unraveled by panic.

"My Bug-- someone stole my Bug!"

I rush down the landing and follow Beth to the empty parking space on Washington Boulevard where her powder-blue Beetle had been. Who would want to take a car more than fifteen years old? The investigating officer informs us this not a rarity. Apparently, the older VW coups solicit a high demand south of the border. The insurance investigator interrogates me thoroughly, thinking it questionable that the car just happens to vanish on the night of our date. I consider it incredulous as well, but know I have nothing to do with the unfortunate event.

After the police leave, I give Beth a lift home. She now lives with her parents in Westwood since her break-up a month earlier from anothermarried man. I will later learn from her mother that Beth again packed her things in the middle of the night, returning to the same estranged relationship somewhere in Bakersville. I suppose Beth cursed with a pattern she cannot break. I consider myself lucky to have avoided anotherfruitless entanglement.

In light of the many changes, I decide it time to move. I find a ground level three and a half in a newly renovated apartment building on a quiet street in Santa Monica located on a hill a few blocks from the beach. The owner of the complex, a short stocky man named Simon, is anxious to close the deal at three hundred and twenty five dollars a month. This is close to three times more than I am presently paying on Washington Street. At least here I will receive a direct ocean breeze, conveniently located between Lincoln Boulevard three blocks to the north, and Venice City two blocks south. Simon and I negotiate the color of a new carpet and curtains for the two front windows. I choose dark brown for the carpet and bamboo colored tweed for the curtains. These are colors Barbara would never approve, but as Dr. Goldstein might say *"It is my choice!"* The day before moving in, I visit my finished future dwelling. The kitchen comes furnished with a stove and refrigerator, a garbage disposal, as well as a built-in dishwasher. In the living room is a gas fireplace, complete with imitation wood logs made of ceramic, and a spacious vanity connects the bathroom to a large bedroom. There is nothing like the pristine aroma of a virgin environment. It is like the pleasant odor of a new car or of new shoes.

Lying down on the plus new shag carpet, I look up at the bright freshly painted ceiling, thinking how perfect everything. How splendid it will be to live here. Just then, a deep rumbling growls beneath the floor. The hanging light fixture in the dining area begins shaking erratically. The solid concrete foundation flexes, causing the floor to buckle, and a definite wave like liquefied concrete rolls along my back and down the length of my body.

The earthquake lasts only a few seconds and is over by the time I jump up to run to the recommended safety of a steel door post. This is the most dramatic, but not the first time I have felt the earth tremble while living in Southern California. The first time during my second year at university, awakened in the middle of the night by pictures banging against the wall and my bed violently shaking. I just roll over and go back to sleep without giving the event another thought. But this time, the earth actually comes monstrously alive. I imagine the apocalyptic prediction that one day the big one will hit, possibly detaching the San Andreas Fault, sending the coast of California sliding into the Pacific. I can only imagine what it might be like to experience the beach changed suddenly to quicksand beneath my feet. To witness the foundations of great cities split agonizingly into rumble-- all lost in fountains of the deep. An elation of the Holy Spirit overwhelms me through vision that nothing here made to last; that one day even beautiful sunny California will vanish through distraction in the course of time.

Bruce, Ed, Charlie-- all sacrifice their time and muscle to help me re-locate. Of course, Ron supplies the truck. These are good friends, always there when I need them. I abandon the refrigerator in the previous apartment for the next occupant to acquire. Besides, it is so tightly wedged-in that I doubt anything short of a wrecking crew able to remove it. Murray can greedily rent the unit to his next tenant with appliances. I also leave the pieces of my Honda motorcycle scattered about in the garage. I had begun to rebuild the motor some months earlier, but never finish after discovering a crack in one of the pistons. I will eventually buy an old chopped Triumph, but let that one go as well after an accident.

In a way, I am sad to leave this part of my life. It represents many challenges, many accomplishments, and much sadness of loss. It has been my study haven: the place where I glimpsed into the complex mind of Shakespeare. Saw into the blind bitterness of Milton's tormented soul. A place where I rediscover the rich imaginings of lost childhood, ascending the accolades of so many literary adventures. It is a place of discovery where the shadow of my father walks still; and a place where I found an unsought companion through unique bond of an outcast black cat. Here I have wept, felt joy, and first love. Here, also, I have plunged into a sea of profound despair. This place of innocence, a graveyard commemorating special pieces of my heart, a place of remission faded into darkness... never more.

Once settled into my new environment, I am assaulted by a suffocating longing for Barbara. I know I cannot go back-- will never go back! The Furies of my uncontrolled passions pursue me still. Not all the change in the world able to completely transmute the poison that courses through my soul. Just the thought of Barbara-- the only woman I have truly ever loved-- in the arms of another man drives my soul to darkness! I become physically ill again, plagued with the most sinister thoughts of the mind. Work becomes a joyless mechanical activity, suppliant only to my needs and to the needs of my client's— a fulfillment of responsibility, no longer even about the money! I sleep only when I can no longer stay awake; eat only to sustain needs of the flesh. Every idle moment plagued by thoughts with regret and the often-overwhelming impulse to humiliate myself further. I gain a renewed appreciation for the estate of mad kings in the annals of the past. Madness, a palpable condition of context, the somber clarity of reason envisioned through a fractured glass of dark reflection. The delight most fed, changed to an essence of poison most deadly. Secretly, I might blame John, but deep down I know Barbara is the one to make the choice. And this time that choice not me.

As that familiar darkness begins to close in again, I receive an unexpected letter from Jenny Kelly in Hawaii. In her own unique fashion, she wishes to inform me that she is officially pregnant with what she considers a perfect genotype. Until just recently she lived in a rented bungalow across from a young unsuspecting Hawaiian, who she describes as the physical and intellectual archetype matching her requirements. During her ovulation period, Jenny entices him with wine and a barbecue and seduces him on the spot. For two days, they make love constantly, Jenny checking herself regularly using a home pregnancy test. As soon as the results come back positive, she kicks him out and relocates the same week to another bungalow in a new track several miles away off Kam Highway. This is the practical analytical Jenny I remember so well, never one for sentimentality. At the end of the letter she provides me coordinates to her new address, along with an invitation to visit. And a vacation is just what I need.

The same afternoon I book a flight for Honolulu, Oahu departing in three days from LAX. The thought of escape revives my spirit, momentarily restraining those tormenting Furies of my mind. Even in the madness of a king harbors a promise of reprieve. How fragile the intellect-- so murky the unfathomed passions of the heart! Barbara is a poison inside of me-- but not her really! The love and desire my own, changed to a demon I must resist! But how can I deny hunger to weakness of my own flesh?

Late that night I walk down Hill Street four blocks to Neilson, pass through a green space, and then cross Bernard Way to the beach. The release of *Santana Wind* near the end is final hot blast of pressure released from the desert that blows steadily from the east and out to sea flatteningthe ocean waves; the tide calm. A phenomenon of nature that happens at this time every year, as the final breath of summer exhales westward, bringing moderately warm days and chilly nights to Southern California.

Climbing on the roof of one of the Life Guard Towers, I shake my fist defiantly at the elements, raging as *King Lear* raged against storm of his own lunacy. Then the rage changes to calm. All the universe pregnant and waiting, time stilled in time divided by time. A full moon suspends in nothingness, surrounded by a host of bright distant stars, the darkness repelled by forceful wind at my back. I am instantly translated into a vision of profound liberty—no longer grounded in time and space, free as when first I knew my *Lord and Savior*.

There is the wind
Whispered in desert time
Or is it rhythm of this rhyme
Circles height of sleepy trees
Saying softly Saying sweet
Nothing is yours
Nothing to keep
Close your eyes
To know me

There is the ocean
Licked sensual shore
Or is she something more
Slipping translucent in silver sand
Saying softly Saying sweet
Nothing is yours
Nothing to keep
I am me I am me
Close your eyes
To know me

There is the moon
Suspended on silver thread
Or is he illusion instead
Guardian over fields of night
Saying softly Saying sweet
Nothing is yours
Nothing to keep
I am me I am me
Close your eyes
To know me

In one voice sing the stars
I am me I am free
Touch heaven in my hand
Suspended over myriad of sand
Ride wind of the sun
Through course of light all must run
Over peaks of mountains high
Into celestial valleys of sky
Zodiac maps drawn
Where constellations divide
To chase shadow of the moon
Beyond zenith of shadow's noon
I am me I am me
Close your eyes
To know me

I begin to weep with joy, this poem released from a well of sorrow, spreading into the night, as a winged Phoenix born from ashes. This is the first inspired poem I have written since many years. It is as though a stone lifted from the forgotten deep of my soul. I have been mute too long. Now my true voice restored. I sing in heavenly praise with the angels to a glory not witnessed in present passage. I see through a vision immortal, knowing the certainty that this life— yes, *my life*-- but a dream fleeting and that nothing made of atoms really real. After this epiphany passes, I rush home and write the elevated verse on paper just as I have heard it. This poem the last in a *Book of Parables* sung by soul of a dying muse released into heavenly stream: *unforgettable, immutable, eternal.*

$\mathcal{E}$vents continue to unfold as they should; only my mind unable to see this at the time. Nevertheless, I am drawn acutely toward a destiny by stirring of the Holy Spirit. In confirmation to this, the last night in Santa Monica I have an unusual rendezvous with a complete stranger. Last minute business arrangements made for an order delivery, the rest put on hold, and my anxiously awaited flight scheduled to depart at 2:00 PM the next afternoon. Unable to relax, I decide to stroll down to Main Street and have a drink.

On the corner of Main and Hill is a Backgammon bar, a local hangout attractive to patrons more casual in nature. I sit near the window peering out at people walking along the avenue. Across the street stands a flamboyant lineup of patrons waiting to get into a Gay Bar named the Pink Elephant Saloon. Some adorned in black leather with silver chains hanging down to exposed butts, some in brightly colored silk, and some dressed like any other man in the 1970's, except with a distinctive flare. I have never been inside this establishment, not even in fantasy. At this time in my life, I am little prepared for new discovery. The Pink Elephant Saloon remains in my mind clandestine, existing on the fringe of nuclear society: the terms Gay and Straight standards of definition to describe a condition of obvious enmity. I cannot help but wonder if this particular evening Dr. Laving might count among them.

"You are a strange one sitting all by yourself," a female patron remarks also sitting alone at a nearby table. "You come here often?"

"First time to actually come inside," I reply with polite detachment. "I just moved into a new apartment on Raymond at the top of the hill and haven't had much time to explore the area."

"We're almost neighbors. My name is Anny. I also live top of the hill on 4th."

Anny, an engaging personality, uninhibited, moves her drink to my table. Not that I mind, but the suddenness of her uninvited presence a little obtuse. Nevertheless, we engage in conversation, which does help to relieve some of my internal tensions. Anny comes here often, representing affirmation of her new freedom. She is recently divorced from an abusive relationship, childless, and admits to over indulgence of cheap wine from time to time. Therefore, I offer to buy her a drink from a bottle better in quality than the House Wine. I share with Anny my plan of intrepid adventure to the Hawaiian Islands, leaving out the reason I am really going there.

"Have you ever been to Buffalo Wings just down the street?"

"No, but I have heard about it."

"A friend of mine is a waitress there. She does Astrology readings on the side. I sense something special about you. For $50.00 she can make a chart for you."

"Thank you, Anny, but I prefer not to walk life in accordance to star positions. I live by faith, knowing the same creator that has fashioned heaven and earth, also with power to order my life according to a prescribed purpose."

"So, you believe in God?"

"Absolutely," I affirm, sharing briefly my Holy Spirit experience.

"I prefer to know where I am headed than just going by faith. My Astrologist has been right about a lot of things."

"Astrology is only the mathematical prediction of patterns that have an end. Why is it that you would accept so completely New Age belief in the Astrological position of stars, and not consider the intelligence that made them?"

"I guess I never thought of it that way. Still, I feel strongly that you should have your chart done."

I thank her again, adding that if it is God's will to have my chart done one day, so it will be. In the 1970's, all California public bars stop serving alcohol at 2:00 AM, making night-life far less interesting than the day. Anny has drunk herself tipsy, so I volunteer to walk her home. She insists I come in for a cup of coffee. Against better judgment I accept. While the coffee preparing, she vanishes into the bathroom, appearing a few moments later changed into an alluring pink Japanese kimono, making me a bit uncomfortable, like prey stalked by a potential predator.

"I really need to go home." I apologize, wishing to be tactful. "I still have many things to prepare before my flight tomorrow. Perhaps I should take a rain check on that cup of coffee."

"Of course," she concedes gracefully. "Here is my phone number for when you return." Then gazing affectionately into my eyes she prophetically adds: "You will meet someone in Hawaii to make your chart. There is more to the stars than just points of light in the night sky, and if your God created them, then maybe he also put a secret message there."

"Yes, I believe this a possibility; believe completely the power of God not limited to my understanding."

"I see something else," Anny persists. "There is a blonde woman with a child standing in the north surrounded by mountains. This is the woman you will marry and the child you will call your own."

In my mind's eye, I can see clearly the vision of a slender woman with long blonde hair holding the hand of a child. In the distance, a ridge of smooth mountains, unlike any I have seen before, rolling toward northern lights. Something about the vision makes me feel good and wholesome, a natural inevitability of a future bred of more than desire. I will not see Anny again. Had I been in another state of mind, who knows what might have happened between us? Not that Anny unattractive to me, nor lacking in interest. There is, indeed, a time and place for everything under heaven.

The weather changes overcast as a state-of-the-art American Airlines *Boeing 727* lifts into the skies bound for Honolulu. Many years since last I flew; the feeling exhilarating. I sleep through the first three hours of this flight across a monotonous Pacific expanse, with only the occasional disturbance associated with fall weather depressions. The last three hours I jot down a few lines of poetry, inspired by this bright kingdom hiddenabove billowing clouds, a celestial dominion created by a massive stormfront blanketing the Pacific and stretching as far as the eye can see. Particularly fascinating are huge columns off in the distance soaring higher than our cruising altitude, then spreading out like the mushroom of a nuclear explosion enhanced by lightening pulses miles below. These images richer than any inscribed with pen and paper, a glimpse intothe imaginings of another principality coexisting above the world inhabited by men.

There is something disturbingly familiar that I am unable to put my finger on, as the plane descends through thick cloud cover during the Honolulu approach. A feeling I had once before when another jetliner pierced through tropical clouds. This only the first of many déjà-vu moments I will experience on my mid-pacific vacation. The *727* swoops past Waikiki, out over the ocean, and then banks sharply for a vector approach to the runway.

The city of Honolulu is nothing like Los Angeles. Absent are the monstrous high-rises obscuring the horizon: no traffic-congested roadways, the skyline clear of pollution that obscures clarity of most densely populated cities. From the air, it looks relatively small, clean, possessing a charm of quaintness unique to island paradises. Only, this day the sky overcast, the trees and buildings slick from rain showers, with patches of low clouds that slither through neat avenues of nearby suburbs, curling into the not-so-distant hills.

Even the balminess of the air familiar upon exiting the carrier; something still remembered from not so long ago. I walk from the airport terminal to a nearby street, catching the first bus that comes along. I ask the driver, a long-haired hippy-looking character, if his route takes him along Kam Highway, showing him the address. He nods yes and promises to let me know when we get there. I sit comfortably in a seat behind him and begin taking in the scenery. Every few minutes, the driver's console radio blasts news bulletin updates about a scientific research vessel that has vanished from radar and radio contact somewhere between Oahu and Kauai earlier that day. Apparently, the vessel lost communication while routinely measuring the effects of a local tropical depression. The strangeness of this present phenomenon compounded by lack of any debris, described as if the sea has just swallowed the modern two-hundred foot ship with an experienced crew of sixty. A scenario of unlikely speculation, since the vessel in question designed for meteorological study on waves of the high seas. This particular storm considered mild in comparison, not unusual to these Iles of paradise. The event destined to remain a topic of unsolved mystery the duration of my visit, spawning theories of espionage, sabotage, and even alien abduction. As with most mysteries, the facts more incredulous than anyone could have imagined.

It becomes pitch black outside after departure from the lights of city limits. The bus disperses passengers returning to their perspective neighborhoods, their numbers thinning fewer and fewer. After nearly two hours, the lights of Honolulu reappear off in the distance, the familiar detail of airplanes landing and taking off from the only commercial airport on the island.

"Have we already passed Kam Highway?" I demand in panic.

"Oh man-- I'm sorry dude. I got so engrossin the news about that ship I completely forgot about you! Tell you what-- I'm heading to the bus yard now. I'll take you there later in my car."

I thank him and consider the offer generous. I should have been more on the ball myself. I know from experience and training not to solely rely on others; because in the end only I am responsible for those things within my power to change.

The bus yard is little more than a partially paved enclosure with a gated entrance. My bus the last to arrive; but instead of everyone going home, all the drivers begin partying, passing out beers and lighting-up sticks of Marijuana. This party goes on until nearly midnight. I keep close tabs on my driver, not wishing to make a double mistake. He is quite stoned at the end, asking if it would be all right for me to crash at his place for the night. He again promises to drive me to my destination first thing next morning. What can I do but accept? He lives somewhere in the Honolulu suburbs, a modern apartment on the fifth floor of a building with a remote view of the ocean within walking distance. As soon as we arrive, he clears a glass coffee table and pours two lines of powder from a bag the size of his fist.

"*Ka hoa* have a line of coke," he offers, passing me a rolled twenty-dollar bill.

I do not know what *ka hoa* means, but I do know something about cocaine, mostly from my friend Ed, who claims the substance helps to keep him awake at night and enhances his creativity. Until this night I always considered this white powder to be more of a stimulant than an actual drug. Here it is offered freely a way to get high. I am tired from a long day and in my present state of mind decide to try it. Following lead,I snort down a thick line. The feeling is neither pleasant, nor unpleasant,and nothing like I expected, subtle and unimpressive, like a slightlybrighter light turned on in an already lit room, making my nose and mouth numb. Declining a second line, I tell my generous host that Iam tired and want to sleep. He shows me to a cot in an adjacent room, where I eventually fall into dreamless slumber lulled by the incessant noise of one snort after another. It perplexes me why anyone would esteem this white substance more highly than a good night of rest.

My new acquaintance looks embarrassed, when finally he rises next morning just before noon. He explains this his day off and that usually he gets up more early. Examining the half-empty bag on the coffee table, he asks if I am certain I do not want another hit. I assure him that I am fine. The truth is I am starving for a cup of coffee and my morning breakfast. It is obvious that this fellow rarely, if ever, eats at home. This conclusion made by the disappointing fact his refrigerator empty and his cupboards bare. Who am I to judge his concept of hospitality, so long as he fulfills his promise to me? After a couple of snorts, he ushers me into a late model sport car parked in the basement and drives me to my destination.

"*Aloha*, man," he salutes, letting me out at the corner of an unpaved road lined with several small bungalows. "Enjoy your stay in Hawaii."

Jennie's bungalow is the third one down on the left. She acts not surprised to see me. I believe there little that ever really surprises Jennie Kelly. In many ways, she is as paradoxical as her computer code profession. On the one hand, Jenny exhibits the soul of a wiseMonk divining the shadows of this world; yet with a mind of a machine crunching existence down to a mathematical equation of possibilities. I admire Jennie in many ways, maintaining to this day a profound respect for our friendship. Now pregnant with her first child, Jenny possesses all the attributes of a glowing mother to be.

"His name is *Kanoakai*," she proudly announces after preparing us both a late lunch with coffee.

"How do you know it is a boy?"

"I knew since the beginning. David-- that's my *OB-GYN*-- took an Ultrasound just last week and confirmed it. But I always knew it was a boy."

"*Kanoakai* is an unusual name. Does it have a meaning?"

"In Hawaiian it is two words put together meaning born free from the sea. *Kanoakai* will be a beautiful child conceived of special genes and destined for something great."

In my heart I hope Jennie is right. She is, after all, a beautiful woman changed into a blossoming mother. I am happy for her pregnancy, considering this is what she has wanted since a long time. I will pray that *Kanoakai* turns out as perfect as Jennie hopes. I will also pray that he discovers more meaning denied to Jennie through the blindness of her rationality. Before the child's birth, she and her OBGYN will marry. I never meet David, but feel certain he is a good man. Sometimes I wonder if Jeannie as coldly calculating in his arms; or if she found a seed of true love at last.

The first evening I insist taking Jennie out to eat at a local cafe. As she prepares herself in the next room, I glimpse something crawl up the wall from behind the chair I am sitting in. It is like nothing I ever saw before, a translucent pink colored reptile, a little more than three inches long, and in my mind poisonous. Leaping up, I grab a magazine from an end table and would most certainly have squashed the creature.

"Don't you dare touch my *Gecko*!" Jennie scolds, gliding into the room, fastening an earring.

"You have a lizard for a pet?"

"More or less-- *Geckos* eat insects. Everyone has at least one or two in each room. Watch and you will see what I mean."

After checking that there is not another of these household reptiles in the vicinity, I sit down with Jennie on the couch placed against the opposite wall. Several minutes pass; and then a large flying cockroach with wings flutters through the air, landing several inches from the Gecko. In quick spasmodic movements, the lizard overtakes the larger insect. Immediately, the mouth extends wide, and somehow begins devouring the cockroach hind-first with a slow pulsating action, until only the outline of the insect appears in the Gecko's soft body. It is as fascinating, as it is macabre, this bug-eater remaining perfectly still, its body continuing to pulse methodically compacting the unfortunate insect: a gruesome wayto go, even for a cockroach.

"I see what you mean," I agree, amazed by what I have just witnessed.

"Are you sure they don't bite humans?"

"Don't be silly! Do you think I would let something live in my house that bites? Besides, why would an ex-Marine like you be afraid of a little lizard? I'm sure you saw worse in Vietnam."

Jennie is right, I have seen worse, but there remains something uncomfortable about knowing that while one sleeping, a venomous looking reptile slithers around in the dark. A few minutes after sunset, we sit beside a large bay window of a restaurant dining room, when several of these tiny reapers appear out of nowhere, sticking to the outer glass, and begin feasting voraciously an abundance of moths andmosquitoes attracted to the light. I particularly dislike mosquitoes and decide then a dozen *Geckos* in the dark preferable to even one of these blood-sucking nemeses. I think to catch one of these agile creatures to take back with me to L. A., but after some convincing from Jenny giveup on the idea. This probably for the best, since I doubt it could have survived a California climate.

Jennie goes away on a date lasting the weekend, leaving me alone in her house. I have secured enough groceries to last several days, plus discovering a pleasant beach just a stone's throw on the ocean side of Kam Highway. Here the seashore not made of the pristine white sand found along *Waikiki*, but tiny bits of tan-colored shells crushed and ground together, made smooth and clean by wave action over countless eons since this island rose out of the sea. After hours of swimming and body-surfing I lay on the soft texture, which easily brushes off my skin likeplastic pellets leaving no film to rinse-off later. All the islands have a dry and wet side. I am presently on the side that receives the most rain, meaning that thunder clouds gather suddenly, releasing a deluge of warmshowers, and then sweep out to sea within minutes, only to circle back again later.

On this particular stretch of coast, the waves break sharply on the shore making body-surfing exciting, as well as dangerous. Several times, I fall off a six to eight foot wave smashing hard on the exposed bottom, and then engulfed by a collapsing wall of turning water. Each time I pick myself up and return immediately in anticipation of the next swell. I feel like a child again, having fun, free from the snare of emotional entanglement. Friday night I collapse in Jennie's empty bed exhausted, and rest in the protective comfort that Jennie's *Geckos* will afford me no torment.

Saturday night I walk three miles down the highway to a small local bar on the beach. It seems most things on the beach, near the beach, or within sight of an ocean view. Being from Santa Monica, this attribute less impressive; but it should be noted there is no ugly beach to be found in all of Hawaii. I meet an attractive woman, indulge a few too many shots of a deceptively strong elixir she calls Peppermint Schnapps, and end up going home with her. Her house, a shanty style bungalow, has a detached screened gazebo porch with a large double-wide sultan hammock bed suspended in the center.

The moment truly special: both our injured souls released in the act of making love. All night we embrace, the hammock swaying lightly to contrary gusts of strong pacific winds. On occasions a balmy mist sprays through the mosquito netting, sending sensual chills along my exposed body. It is as pleasant an evening I have ever spent, unforgettable, a time of healing in the arms of a stranger.

Next morning, I think we are both a little embarrassed. She is much older than I remember; and twice reminds me that she has two married sons my senior.

"Have you ever tasted *Kona* coffee?" She questions, pouring me an aromatic steaming cup.

"No, is it something special?"

"It is grown on the Island of Hawaii near the volcanoes. It is very expensive-- even to the locals-- but has a bouquet like no other coffee in the world."

"It is delicious... thank you."

"Some things should be taken only on rare occasions, or sometimes only once... even something beautiful."

I understand her meaning. Finishing my coffee, I embrace her affectionately and leave. It is better this way, since neither of us retain desire to mire in another complicated relationship. Nevertheless, I feel better, some part of me released. I return early and more relaxed to the dwelling of Jenny Kelly and spend the next two days basking in the weather. Each evening at low tide, I saunter down to the beach to watch the sun melt into the sea, creating a rich blend of red, gold, orange, and cobalt. I am not alone. Mingled in the shadows, or perched on black shelves of lava stone, gather several people, some alone, some with their children, all mostly silent, and many smoking hashes and marijuana. The odor so intoxicating that it spoils the majesty of this moment, conjuring in my mind the dreadful darkness remembered during my days in Vietnam.

Per Capitol, it seems that more Hawaiians get stoned on one drug or another than any other population. Everywhere I will go, someone offers me psychedelic mushrooms harvested locally under cow pies, a free joint, or some other mind-altering substance, which I flatly reject. I find it a bit disconcerting that these people, privileged to live in such a paradise setting, should cloud their awareness through chemical sorcery. It goes to support the old adage: *'the measure of truer battles won are those waged within'*.

Jennie returns home late Tuesday and asks if I have done any sight-seeing. I know only a little about these islands, but less of what there is to see here. She offers me a tourist map with precise instructions on how to take the bus, where to get off for some of the more remarkable sights, and how easy it is to get back if ever I get lost. I arise early the next morning, pack a hefty lunch, and jump on the first bus that passes heading in any direction. This first day I travel north along some of the most famous surfing locations in the world. Unfortunately, I am not a surfer, and there are only a few public places recommended safe for swimming. For the most part, this day proves boring. Lush mountains ascend impressively along the border of the western interior; the Kam Highway following the extraordinary vista of sinuous coastline along the eastern shores. It then circles north to where the real surfing competitions take place. However, this time of year promises little activity; or maybe also because it is the middle of a work week.

The second day I disembark at a place called *Kawela Bay Beach Park* and need to walk over half a mile to the actual beach. Here I find a secluded area, eat my prepared lunch, and go for a swim. The currents prove treacherous, so I exercise caution not to stray too far. After a couple of hours, I catch a bus heading back toward the direction I came.

On this day excursion I am to learn some interesting facts about Kam Highway. Kam is short for *Kamehameha,* a road traveling the forty-mile length of Oahu along the north coast. From Honolulu, the bus routes split into two general directions: one taking the Pali Highway to the *Kamehameha* 83 along the east coast to the North Shore, and then to the more densely populated Ferrington Highway 93 outside of Pearl City to the *Kamehameha* 99 that cuts across the interior until rejoining the 83. On the map, all the names are as confusing as the directions, requiring the discerning knowledge of a local.

Nearly all the populated areas are along the coast, the interior mostly uninhabited and inaccessible, except by helicopter or by hiking. This is true for all the islands comprising the Hawaiian archipelago, ranging over fifteen hundred miles, considered the largest string in the world. In recent geologic history volcanic eruptions formed the Pacific Atolls. After the lava cooled these volcanic landmasses became ideal conditions for coral reefs to grow along the submerged ridges. Volcano basins continue to sink while submerged ridges push up from below sea level and rising out of the waves. Mauna Kea, the tallest mountain in the world, located on the main island, has an elevation of over thirteen thousand feet; and the Kaala Peak on Oahu at four thousand feet, whilst the mean elevation of all the islands just over three thousand feet. Of course, the coastal regions are most vulnerable to storms, only a few meters above sea level. This is also where the majority of the inhabitants live.

The third day I travel south to Diamond Head, an extinct volcano crater jutting to an elevation of over seven hundred and fifty feet outside of Honolulu. In Hawaiians this peak is called *Le'ahi*, also designated a U. S. national monument. The name has something to do with a Tuna's dorsal fin, signified by what appears to be a ridged cone when looking up. According to a tour guide brochure, the English name *Diamond Head* originated from nineteenth century British sailors, who thought the calcite crystals embedded in the rock glittering diamonds.

In the moment I do not see the connection and imagine that

maybe angle of the sun has something to do with it. Less than a mile hike to the top, one must climb a series of steep steps and pass through a dark narrow tunnel. I have no light source, and so tag-along with a young Japanese couple in possession of a flashlight. Suddenly, I comprehend why those early sailors thought they had found diamonds. Here in this dark grotto sparkles the calcite mineral embedded in the black walls ignited by bright beam of my companion's torch.

Traversing another narrow staircase that leads to an artillery observation platform built during the turn of the century we emerge back into the open. From here a short climb to the summit and panorama of a commanding vista. A few miles to the north sprawls the clean commercial district of central Honolulu, the buildings staggering near the white strip of Waikiki Beach. Beyond this stretches the grand wilderness expanse of ocean, encompassing both sides of this island paradise. South of here dominate Pineapple fields stretching for miles owned by Dole plantations and ripe for the picking.

While on the subject of pineapples, I would like to make a few personal observations. Of the many fruits and vegetables sold in Hawaiian supermarkets, pineapples are the most expensive. This seems contradictory, considering that the fruit, although not native to these islands, has been locally grown since the early 1800s. Don Francisco de Paula y Mari, the Spanish advisor to the Polynesian *King Kamehameha*, sent containers of the vitamin c enriched food back on ships once it discovered how easily they grow on the islands. Since scurvy a prevailing disability to sailors on long voyages, it was determined that these easily harvested Pineapples a modest solution to a debilitating problem. Not only is the fruit easy to grow, but flourishes with commercial potential. By the second half of the nineteenth century, James Drummond Dole plants his first field in *Wahiawa* and begins a string of canneries famous to this day.

Even in Hawaii pineapples are cheaper from a can. Someone explains to me the higher ticket price is a result of transport cost. The fresh fruit is grown and harvested locally, shipped to the mainland for price and packaging, and then shipped back to the islands to be sold as an import, making it more costly than many of the locals able to afford. It is even considered criminal for a local to harvest just one pineapple. Sounds a bit unethical and draconian to me, reminiscent of how commercial interest once dominated Cuba before the revolution: clear example of muzzling the ox during plowing, allowing a specter of private enterprise to overshadow fairness and common sense.

The hike up Diamond Head and back, takes less than three hours, a rather tame expedition, which I suppose most anyone with a good heart might accomplish easily. I need something with more challenge, more adventure. It is too bad that I lack at this time in my life interest and proper equipment for snorkeling. Such wonders I must have missed. In retrospect, I took the grander aspects of living near the ocean for granted, not discovering exploration beneath the waves until much later. Nevertheless, I am here for other reasons, only I do not yet know what those reasons are.

There are junctions in all our lives, some major as a divorce, or the death of one close; others as trivial as moving into a new neighborhood or buying a new car. I am at such a junction in my passage. I know there is something here to find. If only I might find it. All I do know with any clarity is that I have come to Hawaii for more than a tourist stroll.

I decide to spend the night at *Punchbowl Crater*, site of a national cemetery. I had considered staying at *Puu Ualakaa State Park* where there are facilities, except it is getting late. Nor is there any easy or quick way to get there by foot. Also, I do not see the point to spend money for a place just to lay my head. I am oblivious of a cemetery here at Punchbowl, thinking it just another crater park. I eat dinner at a small cafe near where the bus drops me and walk for nearly half an hour to reach the entrance. There is a gate with a booth, only no one present, so I just wander in. Then I see neat rows made up of thousands of white crosses. It is no different than V.A. cemeteries everywhere with battalions of dead soldiers memorialized because of their ultimate sacrifice for country and ideals of nationalism. As always in the presence of these solemn reminders-- whether in Los Angeles or overlooking the Golden Gate Bridge of San Francisco-- I feel humble, knowing that a part of me lies with these fallen, waiting for the last trump when all rise for final judgment. Moreover, my soul bears witness that I was spiritually dead when I wore proudly my uniform, prepared to die without ever considering the meaning of life; without knowledge of salvation or eternal potential to the soul. Therefore, I pray for these many names, whose faces I do not know. Pray there might still be a provision of mercy on that notable day of resurrection.

I find a discrete place beneath a tree orchard rooted along the west crater wall, where bleeding pockets of hot magma erupted to the surface through the basalt rock depositing the necessary material to create emergence of these lava and coral reefs formerly called the Sandwich Islands, known today as the eight Hawaiian archipelagos of the central Pacific Atolls.

A flat ledge scooped into a shallow basin several feet covered by a soft thin layer of soil and fresh moss makes a perfect bed for my sleeping poncho. Here I rest comfortably, until awakened by morning light and something crawling across my neck. Throwing back the cover, I discover two black centipedes with orange markings have migrated into my cover. My first instinct is to kill them. Realizing no harm to me, I decide that two more or less centipedes in the world will make little difference. So I allow them to escape.

Centipedes, like most insects and creatures in Hawaii, are not indigenous to the islands. Even mosquitoes, rats, and every creeping crawling thing: all brought from abroad by wind and currents, some transported by the first Polynesians settlers, or stowaways aboard mighty ships of trade from many exotic shores. Jenny claims there are no snakes on any of the islands. This is partially true. There is, however, a variety of sea snake seen by only a few, and some species of small non-poisonous brown snakes. I will personally never see a snake. I therefore exercise careless liberty, stomping through uncharted brush dauntless of harm, unafraid to venture into shallow caves. I never consider there might be other perils just as potentially dangerous as snakes. I wander back to the main highway, stopping to have breakfast at the same cafe I ate dinner. The waitress at the cafe insists I must see at least one of the several botanical gardens. *Wahiawa*, located in the central part of the island, being the most famous in her mind. A nice thing about having no specific itinerary is that one can decide to go anywhere at a moment's notice.

I jump a bus to Pearl City, transfer to another bus heading toward Wheeler Air Force Base along the *Kamehameha Highway*, finally to disembark at the corner of California Avenue.

After a three-mile force march, I arrive at the *Wahiawa Garden*, a jungle of tropical and subtropical plants from all over the world. Myriads of beautiful flowers with intoxicating odors sprout everywhere, some of the blossoms larger than my head. Much of the vegetation here has berries, poisonous even to the touch; and there are many posted signs warning against ingesting anything no matter how inviting. A variety of ferns and Palm trees shade the way, including Hale Kola trees, in the same family as Banyans, with climbing roots that form a kind of lattice. Having seen similar trees in South Florida near the home of my grandmother Lee, I decide to experience first-hand the pleasure of climbing one. A small path off the main trail offers access, so I push through the undergrowth to evade the touristic area, as well as the watchful eyes of the curators. To sneak into an unexplored thicket is something I never would have done in Florida, or any other jungle, for fear of any number of deadly possibilities; but here in this tropical paradise I feel exceptionally bold.

I arrive at the dead-end face of a sheer rock wall over thirty meters high. The most accessible *Hale Kola* grows along the cliff side nearly reaching the summit. I scurry quickly up the tree, leaping from one branch to another with agile carefulness. Nearly at the top hangs a lattice of thick vines, a nature-provided Jungle Jim to climb the remaining distance to the top.

Once over the lip of this upper ledge, I find a well-used dirt trail cutting a lane through fields of tall sugarcane. For some reason I never associated sugarcane with Hawaii, no more than I might think pineapples native of California. But here on top of this plateau a distinctive grove of bamboo- like plants I have seen before. It is like stepping into another time, another place. I follow the trail until it intersects with another, then another. Perhaps an hour, perhaps more, I am lost within this intricate dense maze, my mind wandering even farther away. Once again, I am overshadowed by a sense of *déjà-vu*-- this time stronger than ever before.

I see outline of a rusted wire near the wrapper of a discarded cigarette pack. Is this a booby trap? I examine it thoroughly, checking the area for any disturbance-- any sign that Charlie might be lurkinginvisible in this bamboo jungle! He is near—I can feel it! The sun blistering-- the mosquitoes relentless-- where is he hiding? I search every shadow; scrutinize every place of possible ambush: today just another day in the jungle, just another day to be vigilant... and always the fear.

Then I come to my senses, realizing where I am. Many years since I have felt this familiar anxiety-- Nam many years past! Finally, I find another way down from this place in the heat, a place better left behind. I do not know what triggered that flashback event. Maybe the heat or familiarity of the elements; or maybe it just time for some of the poison to seep out of a forgotten wound; nevertheless, it is good to be back among the living again, good that this part of my past already buried... and that I survived.

Jennie is home by the time I return. Her friend Kip is also here. I met Kip only once in Venice, the same Kip that had broken Jennie's heart. How he came to be in Hawaii, I do not know, nor do I inquire. I share with them my recent experiences, expressing that I need more adventure. Jennie tells me the island of Maui a place many tourists enjoy visiting, considered the Beverly Hills of all the islands.

"What about the Big Island," I query, referring to Hawaii itself.

"It's okay if you like active volcanoes" Kip interjects. "It's not as easy to get around there, nor all that much interesting. I suggest you go to Kauai and hike into *Kalalau Valley*. There are only two ways in: by foot or by helicopter. There you will find what you look for."

"I'm not sure what I am looking for,"

"Who does really," Kip says smiling. "You'll know once you find it. Life is all about beginning and ending; and then there is the part about getting there."

I like soundness of this simple wisdom. Yes, I am at the end and at the beginning, a place without a future or a past. Kip tells me more about Kauai and the *Kalalau Valley*; and by the end of our conversation, I decide this to be the place I will find the meaning and adventure my soul searches.

Kauai Island is part of an underwater elevation that forms the mountain range known as the Hawaiian Emperor Seamount archipelago that travels northeasterly from the main island and runs fifteen hundred miles, consisting of over one hundred and thirty emerging smaller peaks. Kauai is only one of four protruding land masses large enough to be habitable, visited annually by tourist from around the globe. Located sixty-five nautical miles (*as the bird flies*) south from Honolulu, one hundred and seven standard miles from airport to airport, this island's more spectacular beauty remains unattainable, except by perilous hiking trails or by helicopter. This garden paradise is approximately the same size as Oahu, except strictly protected from over-development to insure it remains out of reach of those that would corrupt it in the name of making a buck.

Kip gives me a ride to the airport next morning, with the promise to retrieve me upon my return, provided it lands on a weekend. I find myself seated in the same row as a group of sailors during the short thirty-minute flight. We exchange pleasantries in the beginning about military life and the tentative brotherhood that exists between the Navy and the Corps. The young man seated beside me then begins speaking to me about the Lord and Spiritual Salvation.

"My name is James," he introduces. "Do you know Jesus?"

"I received the Holy Spirit a few years ago, and continue in grace until this day." I affirm.

"What church do you belong to?" He probes.

"I belong to the spiritual church of our Lord, which has no boundaries of architect, or denomination. By faith, I am born, and by faith I walk."

I then share with them all how the Lord called me, emphasizing the dramatic event of my rebirth and salvation. I think they are amazed. Not so much that I am a Christian, but that I am not a Christian by birth or indoctrination. Each of these men born into Christian homes, have attended church regularly from Sunday School to adulthood, for whom religion an important part of their lives. Here I am one with a barbarous history; yet receiving the same grace they have taken for granted. I like these fellows, and the simple sincerity of their fellowship. Being neither tough guys, nor braggarts, they sit quietly listening attentively to my testimony without debate or judgment.

Having already arranged a rental car at the airport, they ask if I might wish to accompany them on a day of sight-seeing. I gladly accept, since I have no particular scheduled agenda, considering this an opportunity to see many of the attractions famous to the island. We begin our journey by traveling north to *Lihue* to see *Wailua Fall,* an eighty foot water cascade dropping into a rainbow pool fed by river of the same name. I am tempted to do some hiking, desiring to see this grand phenomenon from the top, but my companions dissuade me with enticement of other things more interesting to see. It is here that something happens, which will precipitate into a series of extraordinary events.

A portly man wearing a Hawaiian and Bermuda shorts approaches us, sweating profusely. An hour earlier, he and his wife accidentally locked their pet Chihuahua inside their late model tan Cadillac along with the keys. My four companions try unsuccessfully to open the door. I volunteer to make an attempt. Searching the area, I find a thin piece of unrecognizable rusted wire approximately three feet long. Shaping one end into an elbow, I gingerly pass the instrument between the glass and rubber weather seal, searching blindly the hidden lock mechanism. The first attempt fails, the frail wire breaking at the hook.

In desperation, these obvious tourists press their faces against the tinted back window shouting words of comfort to the excited small dog trapped within. Extracting the remaining length of wire, I make another elbow for a second attempt. After several minutes, I hook something that causes the lock button to move slightly. I pull one way and then another, but unable to find the lock release. Again, I remove my homemade tool, further modify the hook angle, and make a third attempt. Once more my fishing latches onto something that causes the lock button to move. Since steady pressure insufficient, I allow the wire to slip up along the linkage as far as it will travel. Positioning myself against the rear glass, I begin rapidly jiggling the homemade tool. After a few sharp yanks, the latch button pops up.

The couple frantically opens the door, embraces their equally excited Chihuahua, all the while babbling undying gratitude. They then jump into their Cadillac and leave.

"That is a neat trick," remarks one of the young sailors. "They teach you that in the Corps?"

"To be a Marine is to improvise," I joke.

We backtrack south along the 50, following directions to *Poipu*

Beach, home of the Spouting Horn, a lava vent hole near the shore that emits a massive jet of water during large swells, hissing like a giant lizard as the waves recede. We are just about to leave, when the tan Cadillac noses into the parking area. The portly man in the Hawaiian comes running toward our position with a wad of cash in his hand.

"I promised myself to find and give you a reward for helping us," he puffs.

We all decline, saying that no reward necessary. Nevertheless, he insists, stuffing the cash into James' shirt pocket.

"I said to my wife if I ever saw you fellows again, then by God, I would give you a little something. You don't know how long we waited, and nothing for miles around. You guys were a god-send to our family. This is the least I can do."

He then jumps back into his car and speeds away. We only stand there looking at each other, a little shocked and embarrassed. We agree to count and equally divide the amount later. Once again, we navigate back along route 50, until coming to a quaint town named *Hanapepe*, which means *'bay crushed by landslides'*, with numerous ancient temple sites located in the surrounding valley. We spend a little time here exploring. Then my companions unanimously decide to reserve further hiking for another day. We next head north-west to visit the ruins of Fort Elizabeth, a Russian fortress built during the reign of Czar Alexander the First in the early nineteenth century, as a symbol of alliance with the last independent monarch of Kauai named *Chief Kaumuali*. Although rich with history depicting the unification power struggle of *Kamehameha the Great* to establish the singular Kingdom of Hawaii, I consider this landmark unimpressive compared to the early Polynesian settlement sites at *Hanapepe Valley*.

From here, we turn around and head back toward the Coconut Coast. With traffic, it takes nearly two hours to reach *Opaekka Falls*, stopping only briefly en route for a quick snack. Instead of gushing over the rim as at *Wailua Falls*, the water here slips smoothly along the eroded high rocks like a veil emptying gently, further feeding the *Wailua River*, which from here continues to flow southward and eventually to the sea as do all rivers on these islands.

At Princeville, my new friends book a motel room near to a beach, and we share a last supper together. They encourage me to remain and sleep the night in their rented facility. I thank them, but decline the offer on grounds that I feel compelled to continue my odyssey by making use of the remaining daylight hours. We, therefore, bow our heads together for a departing prayer. As I hit path of a nearby trail, I sadly think this will be the last time I see my new brothers in the Lord, like so many other shades passed along winding passages of this life.

I cut down to the shoreline, following the beach toward the *Na Pali Coast*. There is only one main road that meanders around this small island like a horseshoe. On the dry side, called Route 50 to Lihue, and then changes to the 56 traveling along the North Shore. Both roads end at the opposite extremes of the *Na Pali Coast*, particularly inaccessible this time of year, except by helicopter or on foot. Unknown by me at this time, there are posted warnings against hiking the *Kalalau Trail* during the rainy season. In retrospect, I doubt it would have made much difference to me, considering my presence of mind.

I make exceptionally good time and arrive before sunset at a dry shoal above the tide line where a large clear tributary empties into the sea. Here is a good place to make camp. The night sky exhibits a majestic array of stars not witnessed since returning from Nam aboard the LPD 10. Now aware that all this wonder not by accident, but is a handiwork design, with an eternity of meaning extraordinary.

At sunrise I bathe in the fresh water stream, and drink heartily from this unknown source. Seeing delicious opportunity for a hearty island breakfast, I shimmy up a coconut tree. After an unsuccessful attempt to break open the leathery thick green encapsulation, I abandon this

Gilligan's Island fantasy, realizing I lack tools and proper technique. I find, instead, a tree ripe with golden papaya and fill my empty stomach with this local free-growing cuisine of fresh fruit. Replenished, I connect with the *Kalalau Trail* and begin the eleven-mile hike into a lost valley of imagination isolated from time and civilization.

The first few miles go easily, the incline gradual, the way clear. Out of nowhere, a dense cloud surrounds the precarious cliff face, releasing the barrage of a tropical deluge. The narrow foot-trail changes dangerously slippery, so I remove my shoes, traversing the slope barefoot and digging my toes into the soft mud. Just before reaching *Hanakoa Valley*, I nearly lose my footing, needing to choose between salvation and my shoulder harnessed knapsack. Lost into the sea hundreds of feet down vanishes all my money, most of my camping provisions, and change of clothing.

Hanakoa is a hanging valley with no direct access to the beach, the outcrop of a giant ledge scooped into the surrounding mountains. Considered the halfway point, it provides fresh water streams and a haven of rest to campers. As far as I can tell, it is absent of any souls this day. So far, I have met no one coming or going on the trail. A strange sense of loneliness overshadows me-- a sense that I am the only one out here! Fortunately, I am spared a few tins of sardines in a second bag containing my poncho liner. At least, I will not starve this day. Taking note of the sun's position, I consume quickly my provisions, washing them down with a swig from my water canteen. I need to get a move-on if I am to reach *Kalalau* before nightfall.

In places the trail hugs the cliff of a rock face barely wide enough for a single person— and someone thin at that! Changing again into a safe trail, I follow a meandering path through dry and wet areas with spectacular vistas of elevated terrain. Mountains that disappear in haze and distant green rich valleys bathed in streams of sunlight. The trail narrows again, skirting along sheer bluffs cascading into the turbulent blue of the Pacific Ocean, traversing around dangerous rocks spilling over the edge and promising certain death if the ground should shift unexpectedly. Finally, I see a crude sign that reads *Kalalau Valley* one mile from this point. Were it not for this sign, I perhaps would not have known until the trail ended and my destination achieved. One loses all comprehension of time and distance when hiking alone. After a while, all places appear the same, the greater concentration focused on careful footing and the feel of solid earth beneath one's feet. And of course there is always the challenge of mental discipline, so that the mind does not wander too distant.

Dusk has begun to settle by the time I reach the dead-end of a gushing river. It measures several feet between banks, cascading down a steep slope, over a ledge, and into the dark mouth of the sea. At other seasons of the year, perhaps this barrier provides better access. However, the incessant torrential rains engorging the upper pools cause them to overflow, transforming modest streams into violent impassable channels. Lower down, I find a fallen tree wedged near the edge of a waterfall and decide to attempt crossing here. Midway, the makeshift bridge lurches suddenly, knocking my legs into the powerful surge. I desperately pull myself to safety and secure a perch on the other side.

By now the terrain changed almost pitch-black obscured by shadows within darker shadows. Somewhere below, I can hear the rising tide crashing against the *Na Pali Shore*. Warned that I should always seek higher ground when exploring an unfamiliar coast, I reach an incline and start climbing quickly. Feeling the ground more level, I stand erect, stepping cautiously with my arms fully extended. Blindly, I grope the darkness for anything solid: a shrub, a tree, a rock— none of these shadows as they seem. Then unexpectedly I step into oblivion.

Were it not for the outstretched appendage of a small dead tree, I suppose I would not be writing this now. Time stops. I hang suspended in nothingness. I can just make out the phosphorus outline of large rocks scores of feet below, a chemical reaction caused by the breaking waves. I remain here--perhaps seconds-- perhaps for all eternity, transfixed by the remarkable coincidence of this moment. Off in the distance, I see patches of stars appear through the thick cloud-cover, the open sea as an oily black skin slithering with a pulsing motion. There is something exhilarating in this moment, as I hover between heaven and earth, suspended by an invisible hand, knowledge that I am saved from death by a miracle. No, I will not let go; this not in my nature. Once again regaining my footing, I begin climbing again in an attempt to place a respectable   distance from this sheer ledge of destruction. Finding a level terrace several yards higher, I curl under my Marine Corps poncho liner and succumb into an exhausted dreamless slumber.

I open my eyes half awake, disturbed by more of a rumble, than actual shaking of the ground. The hard plummet of an invisible wave sends me sliding headfirst down the grade. Desperately, I grab anything solid, managing to cling to a shrub until volume of this deluge subsides. Higher up, the river has overflowed its banks, sending a sheet of water over the edge. Now I am soaking wet, cold and shivering, squatting in a dwindling stream, not daring to move. Once again, I am in the hell of Nam, Charlie watching from the shadows. I can feel his bead on the back of my neck; feel the anticipation of his careful aim.

"No!" I shout. "This is past of another place... another time—another person, too long ago to remember. Fear and dream tangled in shadow of someone too young to understand. All dead now— no more to fear-- no more to hate-- no more that kind of love... I am dead to this world since a long time."

I stare up into the moist ether to see the pale shimmer of a full moon struggle behind veil of clouds. It is my soul trapped in a nightmare that must end. My love for Barbara the last dream buried. It is time to let go.   I begin to weep. These are not the tears of madness or of rage, or even defeat, but of acceptance. For the first time, I sincerely submit to things I cannot change. Some things not meant to change in present hour; other things changed immutable on earth as in heaven.

Accepting powerless ability to alter the fixed course of destiny, I surrender to greater elements of existence. I have become humble meaning in Bernard Shaw's drama *Man and Superman*. The proudly defiant Tanner drawn inexplicably into the consuming flame of the life-force, ordained extinguished as chaff in fuse of greater purpose. Barbara had been my *femme fatal*, the substance of my emptiness, and the dream of my dream. Now time to let go and allow that part of me die… forever.

I am squatting in a void for an eternity, slipping in and out of awareness, neither asleep, nor awake. Then a disturbance beside me, and then another, and another. Reaching out, I touch a creature, cold and alive. Fumbling in my shirt pocket, I find a dry book of matches wrapped in plastic and ignite several. The flare reveals the presence of many large frogs the size of small dogs migrating sluggishly down the slope. I remain motionless, allowing this amphibian herd to pass unchallenged.

Light creeps serendipitous over the valley of *Kaulalau* unlike morning anywhere-- except one other place-- and that place only vaguely remembered. I stand up as one rising from the dead, awake to the unnerving demonic sound of wild cats shrieking from abandoned ancient ruins higher up. Peculiar exodus of the frogs long passed, and somewhere odor of freshly prepared coffee indicates clue that civilization exists even here. Finding a well-defined trail, I follow it a couple of hundred yards to a canvass structure suspended between two trees and source of the brewing coffee.

"Good morning," I shout upon approaching the tree house.

"Don't approach any closer," shouts a gruff warning, as two gun barrels appear, pointed in my direction.

"I smelled your coffee, and thought it would be nice to have a cup."

"Go make your own coffee! We don't want any visitors. You best move on."

"Enjoy your coffee," I say backing away. "And God bless you."

I later learn that marijuana growers rampant on the 'Garden Isle', militantly protective of their illegal estates. A little shaken, even disappointed by this unfortunate encounter, I climb to a place where a small waterfall fills a pool feeding into the same river crossed the previous evening. Here the remains of what had once been a grand terrace. The faint outline of a foundation signifies a home or temple of an early Polynesian settlement that inhabited this region before James Cook arrived on the island bringing soldiers and European civilization. Here, also, a tall Mango Tree heavy with fruit, providing me with needed nourishment.

After gorging myself and drinking deeply from the clear pool, I explore briefly this area. From a respectable vantage point, I survey the emerald-green pass journeying into heart of the *Kaulalau Valley*. To my right gleams the Pacific expanse beneath umbrellas of circulating clouds; and further north of my position climb indistinct mountain ranges common to all the archipelagos, a prehistoric frontier at the end of a lost world. This bird's eye view of paradise satisfies my desire for further exploration. I have passed through principality of another demon, now ready to return among the living.

Hiking down to the beach, I think to take a swim on the *Na Pali Coast* before departing. Immediately upon entering the surf, I become apprehensive of the peril of wandering too far from shore. Extreme weather conditions have made the sea treacherous with strong riptides and suctioning under-tolls.

I once was caught in an under-toll swimming along Santa Monica beach, nearly drowning because of exhaustion. I manage to follow a riptide several hundred yards south almost to the Marina Del Rey Pier before touching bottom again. An hour later, just as the sun setting, I managed to free myself from strong hands of the deep.

The tide here unrestrained, promising to drag me out into open sea and into a wilderness of no return, abandoned among the dead. How easily might my life here be erased, a name only added to a list of unsolved mysteries, as changing of the tide pulls irresistibly, promising arms of peace. Who, once I was and all I might have accomplished lost without witness in this solitude of solitudes. *No--I wish to live! It is not my time to go!*

Next morning I take a last look around and begin the long hike back to the world left behind. A world I must still belong to for a little while longer. I am more seasoned now, the way still dangerous, but my step more certain. By late afternoon, I reach the dead-end circle of *Kuhio Highway.* Immediately, I see a car barreling toward me. Something familiar, something that will happen-- *has happened before.* The car pulls in front of me, stops, and out jumps James.

"We prayed, and the Lord told us to come give this to you," James says, stuffing a wad of money in my shirt pocket.

He then gets back into the vehicle and speeds back down the road in company of his fellow Christian sailors. I remain still for several minutes altogether dumbfounded. In my haste to strike out on my own, I had altogether forgotten about the reward money given by the man in the Hawaiian days earlier. What are the chances that any of our paths might cross again? How did they possibly know my need-- and at this precise intersection in time and space?

These faithful brothers in the Lord had obeyed the urging of the Holy Spirit, traveled down an empty solitary road to meet me just as I am stepping back into the world of the living penniless and exhausted. These messengers of God selflessly sent to relieve my poverty. Two days earlier, I had need of nothing. The loss of my knapsack meant also the loss of all my cash, except for a few dollars stashed in the airport locker along with my ID and airline ticket.

The Holy Spirit has prepared everything in anticipation of this hour. I am reminded of the Biblical record of when Peter and Jesus enter into the city of Capernaum and asked to pay tribute. Jesus instructs Peter go to the sea and cast out a hook, and the first fish you catch will have a piece of money in its mouth for the customs duty. A phenomenal event that somewhere a coin slips into the waters, perhaps from a passing boat, and then inhaled by this passing fish. A miracle that Peter arrives at a precise moment to catch it and finds the coin wedged in its mouth just as Jesus predicts. I break into praise, thankful to the steadfast promise in heavenly power. How easy it to forget magnitude of this miracle in light of a meaning existing beyond logical bearing.

This unexpected blessing renews my faith. These men are angels in my mind sent to minister to my ailing spirit after a wilderness trial. I will never see James or his friends again, and have often wondered what ultimate direction of their lives. In the moment, I might have appreciated a lift to the nearest town with a motel and a shower. I suppose they decided me too filthy to enter their rented car, an observation incontestable. A mile down the road I come to a sign that reads *Haena*, a small village with only a few business establishments, consisting of an all-day breakfast restaurant, a gas station, and a launderette. At the gas station, I wash the dry mud from my legs, arms, and face. As for my muddied attire, I have only the clothes on my back, considering the launderette out of the question. Sitting in the restaurant, I sheepishly place an order for the most meager compliment. Served a cup of coffee, I pull out the wad of money and begin counting the bills. I thought them one-dollar notes, but after the first seven, I find two ten-dollar bills, several twenties, and three fifties. I have more than two hundred dollars! Now rich, I grab attention of my waitress and change my order to the hungry man special!

Afterward, I manage a ride to Princeville in the bed of a pickup, where I purchase a change of clothes and rent a motel room near the beach. Here I spend the next two days relaxing under the sun, swimming, and writing poetry. Each poem flows naturally, as though my soul emptied on the pages. The feeling of inspiration overwhelming, a feeling I am symbiotic to all things, yet separate; and a sense of peace that surpasses understanding. Sunday morning of the third day, I check out of my room and take a bus to the airport. After landing I call Kip to pick me up. It is time to prepare for my Los Angeles return.

"Did you find what you were looking for?" Kip inquires, as I crawl into his Import convertible.

"Yes, I passed into a crack in the universe, and came out the other side. I feel a little naked in time... also new."

"Yeah, Kauai has a way of stripping bare the soul and bringing out all the demons. The locals call Kalalau the spirit of *Aloha Kahunas*, or soul of all the islands. *Aloha* means more than hello or goodbye. It is the essence of universal power and the belief that all things have a time and a purpose."

I comprehend the Ecclesiastical meaning of what Kip is saying. Some places in the world do resonate through a special dimension in the unfolding continuum of a clock-work universe, allowing for the manifestation of other principalities, which coexist in present reality: these Hawaiian Islands physical manifestation of such a place. I feel thepresence of many spirits here. Spirits in the air, near to the shadows of the mind; spirits from the past seeking a way back in, but only one spirit born of true light and redemption.

A spirit in the wind I once heard as a child, swaying high in the branches of a Sweet Gum tree. Just as with the *Great White Spirit*, represented in the cultures of North American Indians, the *Aloha Kahunas* is in fact, the Holy Spirit sent by another name to guidemen's souls through darkness to throne of Messiah. Nor has the *Aloha*

Kahunas of this place finished course just yet.

Kip gives me a choice of returning to Jennie's dwelling by the more direct and quicker route of the main highway, or by the longer scenic coastal suburbs. It is a beautiful evening, an hour or so before sunset, so I choose the scenic route. We have just passed a small intersection, when a red Mercedes convertible speeds behind us horn blasting. Kip stares at me perplexed.

"Must be for you," I say nonchalantly. "Who do I know here?"

Kip pulls over and gets out. The attractive female driver of the Mercedes leaps out of her car, runs past Kip, and surrounds me in an embrace.

"I knew it was you!" Glenda exclaims with tears of joy in her eyes. "I just saw the profile of your face when you passed, but I knew!"

I am stunned to silence. How can Glenda be in Hawaii? And what are the chances of finding each other? I decide there no such thing as chance here. We talk for several minutes, deciding that Glenda will shuttle me the remaining distance. This suits Kip well, since his home in Honolulu, and anxious to get back.

Glenda talks incessantly the whole way. She is no longer shy and introspective, as when I first met her years earlier. Now Glenda vibrant, confident, and is more beautiful than I remember. She divorced her abusive husband just after our last encounter and escaped to Hawaii hoping he would never find her again. But there is more she promises to fill-in over lunch the next day.

I wait for Glenda at the corner on Kam Highway. The distinctive red Mercedes appears only a few minutes late, Glenda wearing a sexy loose beach dress, designer sunglasses, and gold jewelry that blends well with her almond tanned skin. I comment on how lovely she is, climbing into the passenger seat. Glenda lips purse into a smile, her hair tossed elegantly to one side, and presents me with a kiss on the cheek.

We drive to a resort restaurant on the North Shore named the

Kuilima, famous for fresh seafood dishes served with sides of tropical fruit. At this time in my life, I am little accustomed to fish, usually preferring beef and potatoes. Glenda insists I try the *Mai-Mai*, a fish famous to the islands; the flavor delicious, delicate, and not fishy, as usually associated with fish. In gratitude to this day with Glenda, I will gradually begin to integrate a healthier balanced diet.

We talk over lunch, but about nothing specific to the details of her present life. Glenda insists upon paying for both of us. Judging by the menu of this establishment, it is far beyond my usual budget; nevertheless, because of my pennies from heaven the macho self-pride asserts itself.

"God has recently blessed me, Glenda; allow me to at least pay my own lunch."

"Don't be silly," Glenda soothes, reaching across the table and taking my hand. "Besides it's already paid for. Also, it is rare to receive a visitor from the mainland, and you are near the end of your vacation. Please, accept this small offering from me."

It seems more of a plea, than a request. Remembering the last time she offered me a gift, I only grin and kiss her delicate hand.

"This is the best meal I've ever eaten... thank you, Glenda."

Afterward we stroll together out to the beach and spread our towels under a Coconut palm. A delightful balmy breeze blows steadily from the sea. The afternoon sun winks warmly between passing clouds. Glenda removes her dress, revealing a skimpy bikini, emphasizing that her shapely body has changed little over the years.

"My happiness today is largely because of you," she confesses, lying comfortably beside me. "You gave me the strength I needed to end a life time of abuse."

"Now things can be different," I say, moving closer.

"Things are already different. I am divorced and now married again to a good man. We conceived a daughter together last year. I wanted you once, but today I just want you to know that because of you I am finally happy. You gave me tenderness and showed me patience. It is gift from the universe to have opportunity to thank you in this way. Of all the men I have known, you are the most special."

This moment I am speechless and pull physically away, realizing that I have altogether misinterpreted the uniqueness of the situation. This is not a fresh new start, but rather goodbye. Glenda has found her way out of the valley of her purgatory. I am sincerely happy for her, but also a little saddened that our star-crossed paths have reached an end. We talk about other things-- common things that good friends usually share. She describes where and how she lives now in a house near the ocean, about her daughter looking so much like the father, and about how simpler it is to live on an island. I share with her my spiritual experience during my hike into *Kaulalau*, and how the Lord has restored my faith, as well as providing for my material loss.

"I'm certain that God is with you," Glenda affirms touching my face. "I pray that will never change."

"Neither distress, nor even death will ever separate me from the love of Christ. I may break, but I will not remain broken. You will always remain in my prayers... and in my heart."

It is past suppertime by the time Glenda drops me off in front of Jennie's home. She must get back to her daughter before the nanny leaves; and I need to start packing. My flight reservation already booked and scheduled to depart Honolulu next day at 1:30 in the afternoon.

"Let me take you to the airport tomorrow. I will pick you up at eleven," she promises.

I feel okay upon returning to Jennie's bungalow, not great, but okay. Glenda is happy, or at least has potential for true happiness. What can be better than this?

"Your friend is very sophisticated and pretty," Jennie comments as I enter her dwelling. "Kip says she is an old girlfriend from California.

Too bad you are leaving tomorrow.”

“No Jennie, it is better this way. Glenda has a daughter and a husband who loves her. It might have been nice to spend a little more time together, but I think that too much time could be dangerous for us both. Besides, it is not in the past my heart must heal. I know I would only hurt Glenda again, and destroy her chance for true happiness. She is a jewel better left buried... spectacular, but better left in the past.”

“I don’t know, looks to me that she likes you more than a casual friend. Maybe you shouldn’t be so quick to close the door on destiny.”

“I believe to do less would be a sin, Jennie. I have always liked you, too; but deep down I know we are very different in all the ways that count. Sometimes I think I am not made for a lasting relationship.”

“Don’t think like that. One day you will meet the right person, and everything will come together. You just aren’t ready now.”

I hope Jennie is right. That evening I return alone to the *Kuilima Hotel* for one last night of disco. I meet a table of girls, who like dancing as much as me. I take them by turns, non-stop until almost midnight. However, one lady in the group refuses my advances, remaining silent and somewhat aloft.

“You don’t like dancing?” I ask, taking a breather and sitting across from her.

“There is a time for dancing, and a time for observation.” She replies.

“So what at are you observing?”

“One with a destiny; only doesn’t know it.”

“I do believe in destiny. What has happened to me since arriving on the islands convinces me more than ever that there is a time and a place to all things.”

“I would like to do your Astrological Chart.” She asserts looking steadily into the eyes.

“Funny, a woman I know in Santa Monica said I would meet someone here to make me a chart. But I don’t give much credit to

Astrology. I prefer to live by faith."

"How do you know that God didn't send me here tonight just for that reason? I make charts for a living, but I feel compelled to do one for you free. Please, accept this from me."

I consider that maybe the Lord wants me to have this chart after all. Did not the *Magi* study the stellar conjunctions to predict the birth of Christ, the Messiah? And were there not signs in the planetary positions for them to predict? Therefore, I provide this lovely Seer with the information she requires, including my Santa Monica mailing address.

"Once completed, I will send it by mail," she promises in a professional tone.

After leaving the club to go home, I realize I never got her name-- just another curious encounter at the edge of the world, perhaps never to be heard from again. The next morning I rise early to take one last dip in this Atoll of the Pacific, the weather exceptional. I return in time to prepare breakfast for me and Jennie before she gets out of bed. It has been nice to visit this special friend; and I think one day to see her again.

By ten minutes past eleven o'clock and Glenda still has not arrived or called to say she might be late. At a quarter past, someone in a neighboring bungalow is preparing to leave for Honolulu, agreeing to drop me off near the airport. I can wait no longer for Glenda, reluctantly accepting the offer.

Arriving half an hour before my scheduled departure, I call Jennie to tell her goodbye again.

"Glenda arrived five minutes after you left," she reports. "I told her that you thought something had happened and made last minute arrangements. She seemed very disappointed."

"If you should ever speak to her again, tell Glenda that maybe it is better this way. Jennie, I hope your future son, *Kanoakai* will bring happiness and blessing to your soul."

In her usual cold way, Jennie mumbles something about probability statistics and hangs up. Just before boarding my plane, there is a news flash stating that the lost research vessel has been located. By some freak parting of the waves, the ship had the misfortune of falling nose-first into a trough, and then sucked into an enormous underwater lava vent. All hands lost; the circle of mystery complete. I consider the uniqueness of this tragedy, and how remarkably unpredictable the conjunction of time and event. Like everything else here, it is a bizarre phenomenon woven into the spirit of *Kahunas*. As the plane reaches skyward, I stare out the window and say a prayer of *Aloha* for all those perished souls, the islands of Hawaii vanishing in a sea of clouds, as all lost worlds do through measure.

Less than six hours later my flight touches down at LAX airport. It is good to be back on familiar shores. Business picks-up immediately and I truly appreciate for the first time reward in being self-employed. But there is one detail more to attend to. I purchase a pack of 100% cotton paper and spend two days typing twenty nine sheets of poetry in duplicate. I then commission a leather shop to fabricate two identical extra-large book covers engraved with the title *The Book of Parables* to Barbara and with the date, February 14, 1979. I then have the twenty-nine sheets of poetry collated and stitched into each leather book cover.

These verses represent all that I have recently written-- save one. This one I will give into Barbara's hand. Once all accomplished, I attach the gold ankle chain to the separate poem folded inside the volume prepared for Barbara.

"I come in peace," I say, when Barbara opens the door. "I only wish to return what I took from you, and to give you this last gift of my heart. I will keep the clock, since it is symbol of our love. It no longer keeps time. There is no more time to keep."

Barbara does not say anything. She sighs; her eyes filling with tears as she graciously receives the book offering. After reading the separate poem, she delicately detaches the sliver of gold and places the ankle chain into my hand.

"You keep this in memory of our love," she insists, and closes the door.

From within, I can hear her sobbing deeply, a sound I will remember always with mixed emotion. It is over. I accept it is over. The full moon shines brightly, as something permanent in my mind. Of course nothing is ever really permanent. Even the stars must eventually die.

I drive along this familiar street-- the street where my love took root and blossomed; then wilted, and died. I am acutely aware of time and space; aware that I, too, am mortal just passing through. This marks nearly the end of a chronology ascribed through heavenly passage and the beginning of many ends not yet begun. This way I will not pass again.

Several weeks later I receive an unexpected letter postmarked *Laie*, Hawaii from a woman named *Judi,* the lady I met at the bar that last night. At first, I think it has something to do with Jennie; but startled to discover this is the Astrologist I met that last night while dancing at the *Kuilima*. She remembers her promise to me after all. It is my *Astrology Chart* drawn in longhand, accompanied by a personal type-written letter. The cover page reads:

"I realize that more than likely you have given up on ever getting this. Sorry it took so long, but got hung up in a very involved affair almost as soon as you left. I do come thru as I promise always, but my timing isn't always as expected. You have a really good chart and would say that you could do anything you put your mind to... guess you'll be a famous writer one day and I'll say I did his chart before anyone knew him!!! Seriously. Hope this will be of some help to you. Maybe on the West Coast later this year... Sept, and will call to see how it goes. Take care. Signed Judi."

Attached with this letter are three pages of information concerning health, career, finances, and relationships: some of the information vague, and many things surprisingly accurate when viewed in retrospect. She speaks about the importance of Karmic lessons, describing them as cosmic corrections, which makes me think in the moment about Jim's story of the *Splough*. She predicts there will be division in my later yearsthat will make it seem as though I have lived two lives: *an observation remarkable within present context.* At the end, this lovely lady, who I barely remember, and who knows almost nothing about me, makes the following special note:

"You have two of the rarest and strongest aspects in astrology...a Grand Trine and a Grand Cross. I believe the combination of the two is probably the most beneficial thing anyone can have in life, but it also promotes "spoiled brats." People who never have to grow because of the incredible luck they have. Yours is in water, which makes you an emotional virtuoso... very psychic and responsive to all sensations. A Grand Cross indicates a hard life, but is considered by most astrologersas beneficial because it develops strength and character. You have yours in Cardinal elements, which places your challenge on a physical level. Your 'cross to bear' will relate to action... underestimating problems,lacking follow through, thoughtless action. But it will also promote initiating action, accepting challenge and proving the validity of what you think is right. With these two giant aspects, you have the necessarybalance to use both to your advantage. Astrology is just a map, but howyou drive is your choice. You have all the blessings anyone could need to do whatever you want...good luck."

Another mysterious gift from the *Aloha Kahunas*; a gift I keep always in my heart. Just another testament of the *Holy Spirit* bearing witness to my spirit that God is the only supreme potentate; and that no course of destiny by chance. I will never hear from this lady named *Judi* again. Like so many other angels, she has passed into shadow, but ever present in my soul. So here concludes another chronicle recorded by my own hand in another *Year of the Dragon:* a true story near the finish, bearing witness of a continuing passage just begun.

9 798986 783871